THE EVOLVING AMERICAN PRESIDENCY SERIES

Series Foreword:

The American presidency touches virtually every aspect of American and world politics. And the presidency has become, for better or worse, the vital center of the American and global political systems. The framers of the American government would be dismayed at such a result. As invented at the Philadelphia Constitutional Convention in 1787, the presidency was to have been a part of the government with shared and overlapping powers, embedded within a separation-of-powers system. If there was a vital center, it was the Congress; the presidency was to be a part, but by no means, the centerpiece of that system.

Over time, the presidency has evolved and grown in power, expectations, responsibilities, and authority. Wars, crises, depressions, industrialization, all served to add to the power of the presidency. And as the United States grew into a world power, presidential power also grew. As the United States became the world's leading superpower, the presidency rose in prominence and power, not only in the United States, but on the world stage as well.

It is the clash between the presidency as created and the presidency as it has developed that inspired this series. And it is the importance and power of the modern American presidency that makes understanding the office so vital. Like it or not, the American presidency stands at the vortex of power both within the United States and across the globe.

This Palgrave series recognizes that the presidency is and has been an evolving institution, going from the original constitutional design as a chief clerk, to today where the president is the center of the American political constellation. This has caused several key dilemmas in our political system, not the least of which is that presidents face high expectations with limited constitutional resources. This causes presidents to find extraconstitutional means of governing. Thus, presidents must find ways to bridge the expectations/power gap while operating within the confines of a separation-of-powers system designed to limit presidential authority. How presidents resolve these challenges and paradoxes is the central issue in modern governance. It is also the central theme of this book series.

Michael A. Genovese
Loyola Chair of Leadership
Loyola Marymount University
Palgrave's *The Evolving American Presidency*, Series Editor

The Second Term of George W. Bush
    edited by Robert Maranto, Douglas M. Brattebo, and Tom Lansford

The Presidency and the Challenge of Democracy
    edited by Michael A. Genovese and Lori Cox Han

Religion and the American Presidency
    edited by Mark J. Rozell and Gleaves Whitney

Religion and the Bush Presidency
    edited by Mark J. Rozell and Gleaves Whitney

Test by Fire: The War Presidency of George W. Bush
    by Robert Swansbrough

American Royalty: The Bush and Clinton Families and the Danger to the American Presidency
    by Matthew T. Corrigan

Watergate Remembered

The Legacy for American Politics

Edited by
Michael A. Genovese and Iwan W. Morgan

WATERGATE REMEMBERED
Copyright © Michael A. Genovese and Iwan W. Morgan, 2012.

First published in 2012 by
PALGRAVE MACMILLAN®
in the United States—a division of St. Martin's Press LLC,
175 Fifth Avenue, New York, NY 10010.

Where this book is distributed in the UK, Europe and the rest of the world,
this is by Palgrave Macmillan, a division of Macmillan Publishers Limited,
registered in England, company number 785998, of Houndmills,
Basingstoke, Hampshire RG21 6XS.

Palgrave Macmillan is the global academic imprint of the above companies
and has companies and representatives throughout the world.

Palgrave® and Macmillan® are registered trademarks in the United States, the
United Kingdom, Europe and other countries.

ISBN: 978–0–230–11649–8 (hc)
     978–0–230–11650–4 (pbk)

Library of Congress Cataloging-in-Publication Data

    Watergate remembered : the legacy for American politics / edited by
Michael A. Genovese and Iwan W. Morgan.
      p. cm.—(The evolving American presidency series)
      ISBN 978–0–230–11650–4 (alk. paper)—ISBN 978–0–230–11649–8
(alk. paper)
       1. Watergate Affair, 1972–1974. 2. United States—Politics and
government—1969–1974. I. Genovese, Michael A. II. Morgan, Iwan W.

E860.W38 2012
973.924—dc23   2011024984

A catalogue record of the book is available from the British Library.

Design by Newgen Imaging Systems (P) Ltd., Chennai, India.

First edition: January 2012

10 9 8 7 6 5 4 3 2 1

Printed in the United States of America.

To Gabriela, an angel and a saint
Michael

To Theresa—for putting up with me since
the Watergate summer of 1974
Iwan

Contents

Contents

Figures and Tables

Figures

Tables

Preface

This is a book about one of the defining episodes of modern American history and its continuing relevance for the early twenty-first century. Watergate was the political scandal cum constitutional crisis that led to the resignation of a president, vice-president, several cabinet members, numerous top White House staffers, and jail time for more than a dozen top government officials. It rocked the United States in the first half of the 1970s and still affects the nation to this day. Watergate has not been consigned to the history pages. In fact, it continues to infect America's body politic some 40 years on from the misdemeanors of the Nixon administration.

What was Watergate and why (and how) did it have such a profound impact on contemporary politics? These are the two questions we have attempted to answer in this book. To do that, we asked noted scholars in the United States and the United Kingdom to lend their considerable expertise to this project. Why, one might ask, involve scholars in both the United States and the United Kingdom? It is our belief that while "insiders" have a story to tell, "outsiders" can often see others more clearly than we see ourselves. In bringing different lenses to the study of the long-term impact of the Watergate crisis, we can gain fresh perspectives, different intellectual angles, and new understandings of the impact of Watergate on the American polity.

In their introduction Michael Genovese and Iwan Morgan examine what Watergate represented then and now with regard to the danger of presidential power exceeding its constitutional limits. They seek to explain why Watergate was only in part a White House cover-up of a botched burglary, but more significantly resulted from the expansion and ultimately abuse of presidential power. To this end, they link it to the growth of executive power that resulted from America's involvement in the Cold War and culminated in the Vietnam conflict. In the specific case of the Nixon presidency, they review its illegal actions, ranging from political surveillance and harassment of critics to the subversion of a presidential election, in the name of what it considered the national interest and its consequent obstruction of justice as its wrongdoing came under investigation.

In the following chapter Jon Herbert analyses Arthur Schlesinger's examination of the rise of presidential power in *The Imperial Presidency*. One of the most important books ever written on the presidency, its title has remained a part of the political lexicon since publication in 1973. Herbert considers how Schlesinger explained the Nixon presidency's misdemeanors in relation to the inexorable rise of presidential power in the Cold War. He then examines how applicable Schlesinger's thesis is to the emergence of a new imperial presidency under George W. Bush and finds disturbing parallels with the Nixon version.

Nancy Kassop next examines the impact of Nixon's Watergate-related aggrandizement of presidential power on the relations between the presidency and Congress from the 1970s to the present. While not attributing all the blame for the deterioration of the checks and balances system on Watergate, she demonstrates just how powerfully it contributed to the decline of civility and comity among the two branches.

Clodagh Harrington's chapter considers the rise and fall of a Watergate hero, the special prosecutor. The holders of this office had critical significance in the investigation of the Nixon White House's wrongdoings, but the post-Watergate effort to institutionalize it through enactment of ethics legislation had disappointing results. Later special prosecutors lost their heroic allure in part because their investigations were judged through the Watergate metaphor in which evidence of presidential guilt was incontrovertible and in part because presidents learned from Nixon's errors in their dealings with the office.

David Gray Adler and Michael Genovese then consider the impact of the Nixon presidency on the distribution of War Powers between the executive and legislature. The war in Vietnam, which began long before Nixon took office, put deep strains on presidential-congressional relations, leading eventually to the passage of the War Powers Act in 1974, over a Nixon veto. And yet, this effort to curb independent presidential war-making has failed to limit executives who routinely act as if, and claim that, they do not need congressional authority to engage the United States in war.

Iwan Morgan's chapter examines Richard Nixon's campaign to resurrect his reputation in the last 20 years of his life and its continuation by others since his death in 1994. It considers how Nixon became his own historian in his effort to rewrite the past and explains why he could never wholly escape the obloquy of Watergate. It then reviews efforts by Nixon loyalists and others to downplay his role in Watergate, culminating in the dispute over how this was represented in the new Richard Nixon Presidential Library and Birthplace that became part of the National Archives and Records Administration in 2007.

Victoria Farrar-Myers then examines the role of money in American electoral politics. The Nixon White House's massive and often illegal fundraising to pay for the president's 1972 reelection campaign prompted a host of campaign finance reforms. Farrar-Myers assesses the effectiveness of Watergate-era and later measures to regulate electoral contributions in the interests of ethical practice.

In his chapter, Todd Belt examines President Nixon's effort to manipulate public opinion during the Watergate scandal, and his going public strategy during crisis. Belt then examines which lessons Nixon's successors drew from him in their efforts to manage or manipulate public opinion.

Kingsley Marshall reviews the representation of Watergate in movies from *All the President's Men* (1976) to *Frost/Nixon* (2008). While acknowledging the potential significance of film in the remembrance and understanding of it, he finds that the cinema has fallen far short on this score. The need to entertain, the emphasis on individuals rather than institutions, and the imperatives of dramatization have all combined to keep Watergate movies one-dimensional in their exploration of this critical episode.

In the final chapter Michael Genovese looks at the big picture and asks just how much can we, should we, blame Richard M. Nixon for the events that followed his presidency. While there is much blame to go around, Genovese sees Watergate as opening a door to divisiveness and rancorous politics that has had largely a negative impact on U.S. politics to this day.

We wish to thank many people on both sides of the Atlantic. Our editors at Palgrave Macmillan, Samantha Hasey and Robin Curtis, were kind and professional throughout the process. Olga Jimenez organized the events at the University of London's Institute for the Study of the Americas, which were the genesis for this project, with her customary efficiency. Finally Brian Whitaker, Administrative assistant at the Loyola Marymount University, Institute for Leadership Studies helped put the manuscript together and typists Matt Candau, and Rebecca Hartley did a great job on the manuscript. Our deepest thanks to all of you.

Chapter One

Introduction: Remembering Watergate

Michael A. Genovese and Iwan W. Morgan

David Frost: "Can [the president] decide that it's in the best interests of the nation..., and do something illegal?"

Richard Nixon: "Well, when a president does it, that means that it is not illegal."

ange in the Nixon-Frost television interview, 1977

"T' 1st paragraph ays right."

Justice Department attorney Steven Bradbury,
in testimony to the Senate Judiciary Committee, 2006

Watergate destroyed the presidency of Richard M. Nixon. Entailing far more than the cover-up of the botched burglary of the Democratic National Committee (DNC) offices on June 17, 1972, it was the generic name that encompassed all the serious crimes and misdemeanors of the Nixon White House. From early 1973 until Nixon's resignation on August 9, 1974, to avoid almost certain impeachment, the nation was shocked by the steady stream of revelations about the misconduct of the president and his men. *Time* magazine called Watergate "America's most traumatic political experience of this century." Looking to declare an end to this sad episode in the nation's history, Gerald Ford offered this assurance on the day he took office as Nixon's successor: "My fellow Americans, our long national nightmare is over."[1]

The Watergate crisis of the Nixon presidency has already received considerable scholarly coverage.[2] This volume is more concerned to explore its legacy for American politics. Its contention is that Watergate has continued to have an adverse effect on the national polity over the nearly 40 years since Nixon's downfall. The lessons of Watergate have seemingly not been learned. The repetition of some of its key elements culminated in the emergence in the early twenty-first century of a new imperial presidency with Nixonian associations regarding the degradation of the rule of law, the misuse of the war power, the assault on the separation-of-powers, the manipulation of public opinion, and the proliferation of secret money into the political process.

What Watergate Represented—Then and Now

The core issue of Watergate remains relevant for twenty-first-century America: is the nation to have a government of laws or of men who assert their right to be above the law? This question is fundamental to the well-being of constitutional democracy in the United States. In the words of one scholar, "Rulers cannot legitimately impose a rule of law on the ruled unless they themselves will submit to it."[3] As the quotations that introduce this chapter indicate, Richard Nixon's fundamental claims to be above the law have their echo in the pretensions of early twenty-first-century executive branch officials with regard to presidential infallibility.

The fact that Watergate is now one of the best-known words in the English language has done little to enhance understanding of its ongoing significance. The descriptor most commonly attached to it is "scandal," but this is a misleading term. To call Watergate a scandal personalizes its association with the disgrace of Richard Nixon and implies its historical delimitation to the period when he was president. Watergate should more accurately be termed a crisis because it embodied the systemic threat to the Constitution that emanated from the 40-year growth of presidential power since the 1930s. The dangers that Watergate signaled remain ongoing because the institutional factors that fundamentally produced it still exist. The modern presidency's drive to enhance its power was neither stopped nor stymied by Richard Nixon's downfall.

As political scientist Andrew Rudalevige observed, the presidential office "as strictly defined by the Constitution, is obstructed rather than omnipotent." This echoed the view of Richard Neustadt in his seminal study some 50 years earlier that "presidential weakness" was "the underlying theme of *Presidential Power*." As the latter acknowledged, however, presidents had long sought creative ways to overcome the limits to their authority, whether through capitalizing on historical circumstance, popular support, or their commander-in-chief role. Accordingly, constitutional scholar Edward Corwin had concluded many years before Watergate that "the history of the presidency has been a history of aggrandizement."[4] From his mid-twentieth-century vantage, this had been an inconsistent and incremental process for the first century-and-a-half of the office. However, later scholars perceived a consistent pattern of presidential ambition for greater power with the emergence of the modern presidency in the crisis of the 1930s Great Depression. Far from being stilled by Watergate, the presidency's drive to enhance its authority has remained a potential threat and sometimes an actual one to constitutional democracy from 1974 to the present. As former Clinton chief of staff and later Obama CIA director Leon Panetta remarked with some irony, "I don't think any president walks into their job and starts thinking how they can minimize their authority."[5]

According to historian Stanley Kutler, "Richard Nixon discovered that the nation would tolerate an imperial president, but not an imperious one." However, the line between pushing at the limits of the Constitution and violating them is easily crossed. A decade into the seemingly permanent war against terrorism, the United States has a presidency of newly imperial proportions.[6] George W. Bush's expansive assertions of unilateral authority to deal with new threats to America's security were Nixonian in scope—and to some critics went far beyond those of the thirty-seventh president.[7] Though more restrained in his claims, former constitutional law instructor Barack Obama sustained a terror-age presidency that is largely unmoored from the constitutional principles of the framers.[8] Criticizing Bush's imperial trappings when a candidate for the White House, he affirmed that the president does not have unilateral power to commit forces to combat without congressional approval, but in office he mimicked his predecessor. In unilaterally authorizing U.S. participation in air attacks to assist Libyan rebels in 2011, for example, he defined the bombing raids not as combat missions but as "humanitarian" efforts. By acting first, and defining the narrative first, the president sets the agenda, leaving Congress to respond to his initiatives. As Obama demonstrated, unilateral presidential initiative can institute military intervention that is impossible to undo and politically difficult to resist because opponents would stand accused of not supporting U.S. troops engaged in dangerous military missions.

A constitutional republic is not a self-executing mechanism. The fuel that drives the system is a complex web of interrelationships: an informed and caring public, a strong, involved Congress, a nonpartisan, independent judiciary, a nonpoliticized bureaucracy, a free press, and open, fair elections. When a president eclipses or dominates these elements of the political system, constitutional government is threatened.

This is what Richard M. Nixon attempted; this is what George W. Bush achieved; this is what still remains possible under the successors of the forty-third president. Nixon's failure led to a host of ultimately ineffective legislative efforts to curb the presidential war power, circumscribe presidential budget impoundment, establish new rules for electoral finance, and institutionalize the requirement for ethics in government. Partly because he did not experience the same denouement as the thirty-seventh president and partly because of what one scholar has termed the "security culture"[9] of the war-on-terror presidency, there was no similar reaction in the wake of the forty-third president. Irrespective of contemporary criticism, Bush has therefore established precedents that remain available for presidential use. The observation of Supreme Court Associate Justice Robert H. Jackson in a Roosevelt-era case relating to executive power remains pertinent. A principle once established, he declared, "lies about like a loaded weapon ready for the hand of any authority that can bring forward a plausible claim of early need."[10]

At the time of the formative constitutional debates of 1787, the anonymous Cato predicted that the presidency would develop imperial pretensions. Warning that America could produce tyrants as readily as other nations, he declared, "Your posterity will find that great power connected with ambition...will as readily produce a Caesar, Caligula, Nero, and Domitian in America, as the same causes did in the Roman empire."[11] America's imperial presidents may not have been tyrants in the manner of Roman emperors, but Cato's words still resonate in the wake of Richard Nixon and George Bush. This is not to say that the imperial presidency should become the imperiled presidency that it appeared to be in the post-Watergate late-1970s. America needs a strong president, but—to quote Arthur Schlesinger—"a strong president within the Constitution." In essence, the fundamental problem of the modern presidency is whether it can be empowered to govern effectively without becoming a threat to constitutional democracy. Summing up the paradox of this vital office, one of the coeditors of this volume has remarked elsewhere, "The American presidency is necessary and dangerous, inevitable yet problematic, used for good and for evil, too strong and too weak, a great risk yet a possessor of great hope."[12]

The United States has a government of three branches, not one. When one branch lords over the others, the systemic breakdown produces dysfunctional governing. If it is doomed to repeat the mistakes of the past in this regard, if it fails to learn the lessons of Watergate, America risks more than simply reliving its national nightmare of the Nixon era. It risks losing constitutionalism and the rule of law. This is not hyperbole. The stakes are truly large.

It is not an overstatement to assert that the constitutional republic is at risk. The pressures created by the terrorist attacks of 9/11, the subsequent international war against terrorism, land wars in Afghanistan and Iraq, secret detention centers, Guantanamo, military tribunals, and enhanced interrogation technique (torture) have reintroduced the imperial presidency to the American political landscape. This development poses a direct and significant threat to constitutionalism, the rule of law, and the separation of powers.[13] The United States must come to grips with this, lest the legacy of Watergate comes back to haunt the republic. To do so, today's Americans must come face-to-face with Watergate, examine its legacy, and assess its impact on their political universe.

What Watergate Was

Watergate was the product of presidential personality, historical circumstance, and the structural development of the imperial presidency. As many scholars have noted, Nixon's personality was an important factor in its development. A very able politician, a sophisticated geopolitical thinker, and a leader who did some good things at home and abroad, Nixon was also a strange combination of huge ambition and great personal insecurity.[14] As one of the coeditors has observed elsewhere, "[N]o other leading figure of postwar politics was as lacking in moral scruple as Nixon, lied as often as he did or matched his determination to win at any cost.

No one else was so subject to the allure of power or so prone to misuse it."[15] At the same time, Nixon saw enemies everywhere ready to do him down and prevent him from doing what the nation needed. Such a mind-set justified his determination to take any action to ensure his survival in the political arena. It also generated a mini-industry of psychobiography to explore the life and mind of America's most flawed–and perhaps most fascinating—president.[16] Yet no scholar has better summed up the effect of Nixon's insecurity than Watergate conspirator Jeb Magruder: "The climate of fear and suspicion...had grown up in the White House, an atmosphere that started with the president himself and reached us through [top aides] Haldeman and Colson and others."[17]

Nixon always maintained an "everybody does it" justification of his misconduct in office during his campaign for redemption in the final 20 years of his life. A small band of loyalists have echoed him on this score.[18] As historian Melvyn Small remarked, however, no other president "committed all the illegal acts that constituted Watergate all the time." Historian C. Vann Woodward enumerated these in detail:

> Heretofore, no president has been proved to be the chief coordinator of the crime and misdemeanor charged against his administration as a deliberate course of conduct or plan. Heretofore no president has been held to be the chief personal beneficiary of misconduct in his administration or of measures taken to destroy or cover up evidence of it. Heretofore, the malfeasance and misdemeanor have had no ideological purpose, no constitutionally subversive ends. Heretofore, no president has been accused of extensively subverting and secretly using government agencies to defame and discredit political opponents and critics, to obstruct justice, to conceal misconduct and protect criminals, or to deprive citizens of their rights and liberties. Heretofore, no president has been accused of creating secret investigative units to engage in covert and unlawful activities against private citizens and their rights.[19]

While it is right to emphasize Nixon's uniqueness, it is also important to understand the historical circumstances and structural factors that brought about the Watergate crisis. Nixon's defenders have long argued that his presidency was about more than Watergate. This is true, but more significantly Watergate was also about more than Richard Nixon.

Cold War Foundations

Watergate was a constitutional crisis emanating from the Cold War development of the imperial presidency. In his seminal study of American democracy, published in 1835 when the young republic was far from being a world power, Alexis de Tocqueville observed that the Constitution endowed the president in the foreign policy domain with "almost royal prerogatives which he has no opportunity of exercising." Historical circumstance changed with America's rise to global power in the first half of the twentieth century and its 40-year Cold War struggle with the Soviet Union thereafter. The president's commander-in-chief status and his institutional advantages of "unity, secrecy, decision, dispatch, and superior information" enhanced the authority and responsibility of his office but also fueled its imperial pretensions.[20] Perceiving the Soviet Union as a nuclear threat and a global menace, Nixon's four predecessors were impatient of constitutional restraints on their power to contain it and increasingly sought to circumvent these. To maintain domestic support for their actions, they oversimplified the Cold War as a contest between good and evil, exaggerated the Soviet threat, and invoked a national sense of perpetual crisis. Moreover, they promoted a culture of secrecy not only to hide the scale of America's covert actions—first in Europe, then in Latin America, Asia, and eventually Africa—but also to preempt challenges to the legitimacy of overt military intervention. As a result, presidents were instrumental in creating a Cold War consensus that facilitated the enhancement of their power.[21] It was the Vietnam War's fragmentation of this that precipitated the crisis of the imperial presidency.

Vietnam was a presidential war. In 1965 Lyndon B. Johnson authorized a massive escalation of U.S. military involvement to preserve South Vietnam from a Communist insurgency backed by North Vietnam without seeking a congressional declaration of war. With the war stalemated in evident contradiction of his many declarations that victory was near and the peace movement growing, Johnson decided not to seek reelection for another White House term in 1968. Determined that Vietnam should not destroy his presidency, Nixon had campaigned for office in 1968 on a promise of peace with honor, but achieving this proved difficult. Intent on uniting Vietnam under Communism, North Vietnam's leaders had no interest in accepting peace terms that preserved South Vietnam and were confident that domestic opposition to continued involvement in the war would eventually force the United States to withdraw. However, Nixon would not terminate America's involvement without a settlement that upheld its great power credibility, which he deemed essential to follow through on his bold plans for achieving détente with the Soviet Union and the People's Republic of China.[22]

Nixon eventually pursued a dual approach in his quest for an acceptable peace. To appease war critics, he authorized steady withdrawal of American ground forces, beginning with the removal of 25,000 troops in June 1969, while building up South Vietnam's capacity for self-defense. Meanwhile, he undertook tactical escalations to keep North Vietnam guessing about his intentions and put pressure on it to negotiate. To ensure a free hand in pursuit of this strategy, he engaged in expansive assertions of presidential authority that brought the imperial presidency to a new peak. In March 1969, U.S. B-52 bombers began to raid Communist supply-lines in neutral Cambodia that were used to support military operations in neighboring South Vietnam. Nixon sought to keep this secret by authorizing adjustments in their computerized navigational systems and provision of two sets of flight plans, one to support the lie that the targets bombed were in South Vietnam, the other revealing the real targets for National Security Council (NSC) use.

When a *New York Times* reporter broke the true story of the secret bombing on May 9, Nixon and National Security Adviser Henry Kissinger were convinced that information had been leaked from within the administration. Ordered to find the culprit, the Federal Bureau of Investigation (FBI) tapped the phones of 11 suspects and four journalists, but never caught the informant. The president claimed legal authority for such warrantless surveillance on the basis of the Crime Control Act of 1968, an assertion later rejected by the Supreme Court, and was reassured by FBI director J. Edgar Hoover that his predecessors had ordered such action to find leakers. However, Nixon knowingly stepped into illegal terrain when Hoover refused to tap reporter Joseph Kraft, who had merely written a critical article about his Vietnam policy. Accordingly, a secret White House intelligence unit, created in April 1969 and headed by private investigator Jack Caulfield, undertook the job, gaining fraudulent access to Kraft's home to do so.[23]

The White House invoked national security interest for keeping the Cambodia bombing secret, but its real motive had been to hide the extension of the air war from the American people. To limit dissent, Nixon continued troop withdrawals, culminating in the removal of 150,000 military personnel in April 1970. A week later, however, he authorized a ground force invasion of Cambodia to hit Communist sanctuaries, invoking his commander-in-chief prerogative in justification of not seeking congressional approval of this. The incursion, as Nixon called it, provoked a furor of student protests that had tragic consequences. On May 4, National Guardsmen fired on demonstrators at Kent State University, Ohio, killing four students, and on May 15, police fired on students at the predominantly black Jackson State University, Mississippi, killing two. On the weekend of May 9–10, 100,000 protesters converged on Washington DC, resulting in extraordinary security measures to prevent any assault on the White House itself.

The Huston Plan

Top Nixon aide Charles Colson, who went to prison for Watergate-related crimes, acknowledged that the president and his men were increasingly gripped by a siege mentality as a result of the antiwar protest. "It was 'us' against 'them,'" he recalled. "Gradually as we drew the circle closer round us, the ranks of them began to swell." Reflecting his Cold War beliefs, Nixon was convinced that Communists were behind the peace movement. He also regarded the increase in bombing atrocities and other forms of armed violence by radical groups like the Weathermen as an "epidemic of unprecedented domestic terrorism...[by] highly organized and highly skilled revolutionaries dedicated to the violent destruction of our democratic system."[24] To deal with the perceived threat, the president ordered a reassessment of the government's domestic-intelligence-gathering capability. On June 5, 1970, he convened a meeting of top aides and intelligence agency chiefs to coordinate operations against subversive organizations. It was agreed to form the Intelligence Evaluation Committee coordinated by White House aide Tom Huston and nominally chaired by J. Edgar Hoover (who delegated a deputy to represent him). After several meetings this group produced the so-called Huston Plan.

This project called for opening of mail and tapping of telephones without warrants, breaking into homes and offices, and spying on student groups. Huston admitted that "covert [mail] coverage is illegal and there are serious risks involved," and that surreptitious entry "is clearly illegal; it amounts to burglary. It is also highly risky and could result in great embarrassment if exposed." Despite this Nixon would have gone ahead with the project but withdrew approval when Hoover signaled his opposition to illegal operations, mainly out of fear that his agency would become the focus of media attention and congressional anger if these were discovered.[25] Accordingly, the Intelligence Evaluation Committee was maintained as a purely White House operation under the leadership of Attorney General John Mitchell, but could do little without FBI cooperation. Nevertheless, the Huston plan revealed the growing mind-set that the White House could operate above the law in the national interest. When it became public knowledge in 1973, Nixon defended its necessity to coordinate operations against subversive groups. Regarding its illegality, he told David Frost four years later that when the president "approves an action because of national security, because of a threat to internal peace...the president's decision...is one that enables those who carry it out to carry it out without violating a law."[26]

The Pentagon Papers

The dangers that the stillborn Huston plan signaled became reality in the *Pentagon Papers* case. Watergate conspirator Egil Krogh, among others, later adjudged that the White House's actions in this matter "caused the downfall of the administration."[27] Formally entitled "History of U.S. Decision-Making Process on Vietnam Policy," the top-secret study was commissioned in 1967 by Secretary of Defense Robert McNamara, who had become disillusioned with the war, and was completed in early 1969. The 47-volume report, of which only 15 copies were made, detailed how Presidents John F. Kennedy and Lyndon Johnson, in particular, had misled the Congress and the public about U.S. involvement in Vietnam. Seeking to alert Americans to this, one of the experts who worked on the study, former hawk-turned-dove Daniel Ellsberg, photocopied it for distribution to the media. The *New York Times* began publishing excerpts on June 13, 1971, but the White House, acting through the Justice Department, got the

Federal District Court for the Southern District of New York, to issue a temporary injunction against the newspaper on grounds that the dissemination of the secret report did "irreparable and immediate damage" to national security. Other newspapers that had started to publish extracts were also served with judicial restraints. The case quickly got to the Supreme Court, which issued a judgment on June 30 that the First Amendment guarantee of a free press overrode the administration's claim of an inherent power to prevent publication of material on national security grounds.

Although the *Pentagon Papers* exposed the deceits of Democratic presidents, this still constituted a threat to Nixon's imperial presidency. Firstly, the report vindicated those who questioned the necessity, wisdom, and morality of the ongoing war that Nixon insisted was still essential to America's interests. Aware of Ellsberg's links with Democratic anti-war critics, the president ranted to Charles Colson, "We've got a counter-government here and we've got to fight it. I don't give a damn how it is done."[28] Equally important, Ellsberg's whistle-blowing created a precedent for other leakers to embarrass Nixon's foreign policy, particularly in his dealings with the Communist world and his plans for détente. In reality, as the White House privately acknowledged, most of the *Pentagon Papers'* revelations hardly merited a "top secret" classification. However, the parts of the report that did were sufficient to worry the president that the Soviets and Chinese would become more circumspect about the back-channel talks currently going on. National Security Adviser Henry Kissinger reinforced his concerns on this score. Accordingly, Nixon was of the view, as he told Secretary of Defense Melvin Laird, "The era of negotiations can't succeed w/o [without] secrecy."[29]

In this frame of mind the president authorized a secret effort to defame Daniel Ellsberg as a way of deterring other leakers and discredit the anti-war movement. Unable to rely on the FBI, he instructed top aide John Ehrlichman to see that a White House group did the job. An expanded version of the political intelligence unit that Ehrlichman had set up in 1969 was entrusted with the task under the leadership of Egil Krogh and David Young. Charles Colson also had authority to command its services. He arranged for the transfer of former CIA officer Howard Hunt to the unit. The addition of one-time FBI operative Gordon Liddy completed the staff of the Special Investigations Unit, who became known as the Plumbers because their job was to stop unauthorized government leaks.

The actions of the Plumbers would entrap Nixon in a web of illegality that he had knowingly entered. The Watergate tape of July 1, 1971, records him telling chief of staff H. R. Haldeman, "We're up against an enemy, a conspiracy. They're using any means. *We are going to use any means.* Is that clear?" Nixon wanted the Plumbers to get the dirt not only on Ellsberg but also his other critics ("enemies" as he called them) in order to counterleak against them in the press. This, he asserted, was how he had operated as a young congressman in the face of an executive branch cover-up to protect Alger Hiss, a former high-ranking State Department official under House Committee on Un-American Activities investigation as a suspected Communist agent in 1948.[30] As part of the campaign against Ellsberg, the Plumbers broke into the Los Angeles office of his psychiatrist, Lewis Fielding, on September 3, 1971, in the vain hope of finding damaging information about him. Whether the president had authorized this specific enterprise is unclear, but he had certainly demanded the burgling of the Brookings Institution in the belief that it held Democratic papers with embarrassing revelations about the 1968 Vietnam peace initiative, an order that was never implemented. Accordingly, the Plumbers were acting in the belief that they had his mandate to undertake such illegal operations. As Krogh later remarked of their role, "We were going after an espionage ring, not just Daniel Ellsberg!"[31]

Anxious to avoid other episodes that could be traced back to the White House, Ehrlichman wound up the Plumbers unit in late 1971. The administration consequently had to rely mainly on legal means to discredit Ellsberg, who had been indicted for theft of government property and unauthorized possession of defense documents on June 28, 1971. A federal judge dismissed the case when it eventually came to trial in early 1973 because the White House would not release information about the newly revealed Fielding break-in and the NSC wiretaps. The Los Angeles burglary constituted a vital link to the Watergate break-in of June 1972 that involved some of the same key operatives. Nixon insisted on covering up the later crime in part because he feared that its investigation would turn up evidence of White House involvement in the Ellsberg-related burglary.[32]

Four decades later, the U.S. government pursued another high-profile effort to prevent publication of classified documents by WikiLeaks, the antisecrecy Internet outlet that specializes in dissemination of leaked information, in 2010. While it certainly did not engage in the kind of illegal activities perpetrated by the Nixon administration regarding the *Pentagon Papers*, there were some parallels between the two cases. Daniel Ellsberg himself compared his persecution with the hounding of WikiLeaks chief Julian Assange and the harsh treatment of Private Bradley Manning for leaking classified documents pertaining, among other things, to U.S. policy in the Iraq war. The Obama administration, he declared, "was on the wrong side of history."[33]

Subverting a Democratic Election

The essence of a constitutional democracy is the right of the people to change their government through free and fair elections. As Nixon speechwriter William Safire commented, however, "Watergate was essentially an abuse of the power of the government to affect an election." Nixon would win reelection in 1972 by a landslide but few had predicted this a year earlier. There was no end in sight to American involvement in Vietnam, the glittering successes of détente diplomacy lay in the future, and the economy was in the doldrums. Having scraped home in 1968 with the lowest share of the popular vote for a winning candidate since 1916, Nixon's prospects of victory in 1972 looked uncertain. To safeguard against the democratic chance of being ejected from office through the ballot box, Nixon and his men engaged in a systematic campaign of illegal activities to assist his reelection. They had no difficulty, Charles Colson later remarked, in rationalizing this "as being in the interests of the country." Caught up in its Cold War mind-set, the White House effectively regarded its Democratic opponents as traitors. Haldeman remarked on national television in early 1972 that critics of the president's Vietnam policy were "consciously aiding and abetting an enemy of the United States" and were "in favor of putting a Communist government in South Vietnam."[34]

The Nixon White House's tendency to see its critics as enemies found initial expression in presidential counsel John Dean's memorandum of August 16, 1971, to Haldeman, entitled "How We Can Use the Available Political Machinery to Screw Our Enemies." This addressed "how we can maximize the fact of our incumbency in dealing with persons known to be active in their opposition to our Administration." The list of enemies eventually grew to include more than 200 names, in which liberal Democrats, media figures, and Hollywood progressives featured prominently. In the first instance, the administration looked to use the Internal Revenue Service to audit the tax returns of these individuals for possible irregularities, but Nixon was not satisfied with the results. The tape of the president's conversation of September 15, 1972, with Dean captures him threatening much greater vengeance on his opponents in his second term: "They are asking for it and they are going to get it.... things are going to change now."[35]

To burnish his reputation in the history books as a great foreign policy president and to take revenge on his opponents, Nixon had to win reelection. The first requirement for this was money, the lack of which he blamed for his 1960 defeat by John F. Kennedy. The Committee to Reelect the President, better known as CREEP, became the vehicle for raising funds. Established as a separate entity from the regular Republican Party financial operations in March 1971, it eventually raised and spent more money (over $60 million) than any previous presidential campaign in history, much of this through illegal means. Associate chair Herb Kalmbach, formerly the president's lawyer, later went to prison for being at the heart of the criminal malpractice. Signed into law on February 7, 1972, but not operational until April 7, a new Federal Election Campaign Act imposed tighter regulations on political contributions and their disclosure. In the 60-day interval before its implementation, CREEP operatives raised $20 million Kalmbach and his team then advised contributors on how to circumvent the new restraints after April 7. In addition, they established a "tithing" system of fixed contributions from companies doing business with government or looking for special favors, which was in violation of legal prohibitions on corporate contributions. Although promising federal employment in return for political contributions was also illegal, Kalmbach put a sliding scale on ambassadorships, starting at $250,000 as Nixon instructed. CREEP similarly violated statutory prohibition against accepting contributions from foreign government or their agents, taking money from the likes of the Shah of Iran and President Marcos of the Philippines.[36]

In an effort to hide illegally raised money, some of it was laundered in various ways. American Airlines, for example, sent funds from a U.S. bank to a Swiss account of an agent in Lebanon, back to another U.S. bank, then to CREEP. Still other firms gave money from slush funds, and sometimes airlines sold bogus tickets and sent the cash to CREEP. The most common route to launder money was through a Mexican bank. Some of this was used to finance election dirty tricks and, most significantly, the Watergate break-in of June 17, 1972. The need to prevent the FBI from tracing the cash found on the burglars back to the Mexican bank, a trail that would eventually lead to CREEP and then the White House, was instrumental in Nixon first becoming actively involved in the criminal cover-up to obstruct justice on June 23.[37]

The White House also funded a dirty tricks campaign directed by Donald Segretti to disrupt and distort the Democratic presidential primaries. It had already set the tone for this in its surveillance of Senator Edward Kennedy (D-MA), whom it expected to run in 1972, but he kept out of the race because of doubts about his conduct in the 1969 Chappaquiddick car accident that cost the life of his female passenger. Segretti then focused on undermining early front-runner Senator Edmund Muskie (D-ME). The White House already had him under surveillance because it had maintained the wiretaps imposed on NSC officials Anthony Lake and Morton Halperin, ostensibly to find the Cambodia bombing leaker in 1969, when they left government to help in the senator's presidential campaign. The next targets were centrist candidates like Senator Hubert Humphrey (D-MN) and Senator Henry Jackson, (D-WA). The clear intention was to assist the nomination of Senator George McGovern (D-SD), an antiwar liberal considered Nixon's weakest opponent. The effect of the dirty tricks, many of them little more than pranks, is difficult to gauge. McGovern's winning of the nomination probably benefited more from the rule changes governing Democratic candidate selection in 1972. What is not in question, however, is that the president and his aides had approved and arranged funding for illegal activities to undermine the electoral process. Representative Thomas P. (Tip) O'Neill (D-MA), the future House Speaker, was right to adjudge Nixon's reelection campaign "a new kind of dirty politics."[38]

Alongside the illegal money operations and dirty tricks, CREEP's political surveillance schemes constituted a third element of electoral criminality. With help from Howard Hunt and another former CIA man, James McCord, Gordon Liddy ran what was the organization's intelligence branch. Nixon knew of its existence and was impatient for it to deliver results. However, CREEP chair and Attorney General John Mitchell was reluctant to support Liddy's grandiose scheme for electronic eavesdropping, political burglaries, kidnapping of anti-Nixon demonstration leaders, disrupting Democratic gatherings, and deploying prostitutes to compromise Democratic convention delegates. Instead of the nation's highest law enforcement officer rejecting the illegal project out of hand, the former Plumber was bidden to come up with a less expensive plan than the 1 million dollar cost of the original. Through Hunt, Liddy enlisted Colson to let the CREEP hierarchy know that "the president wanted...to get this thing off the dime."[39] On March 30, Mitchell finally approved a scaled-down scheme for disruption, espionage, and wiretapping, which cost a mere $250,000. Among the targets was Larry O'Brien, chair of the Democratic National Committee, whose office was located in the Watergate complex. Nixon had long suspected him of possessing damaging evidence of his dealings with reclusive billionaire businessman Howard Hughes.

The Watergate Break-In

All the other campaign misdeeds paled in significance in comparison to the Watergate break-in. In the early hours of June 17, police arrested five men in the DNC offices after being alerted to the criminal entry by a nightwatchman. They were wearing rubber surgical gloves, and carrying walkie-talkies, electronic eavesdropping equipment, cameras, and other tools. One of them, James McCord, a former CIA operative, was the security chief of CREEP; the other four were Cubans who had CIA connections. Meanwhile, Howard Hunt and Gordon Liddy were discovered coordinating the operation from a hotel room opposite the Watergate complex.

The motive for the break-in has never been established, prompting a number of conspiracy theories.[40] However the most common-sense explanation is the obvious one, though it is not definitively documented. According to Nixon aide Leonard Garment, "The burglars were there because Nixon and the political men around him had an insatiable thirst for campaign intelligence.... The results they demanded could be achieved only by breaking the law. In the environment of this particular campaign, such lawbreaking seemed not only necessary but natural." This was the burglars' second illegal entry into the DNC office, so they were likely engaged in a multipurpose operation to sweep files, photograph sensitive materials, and tap phones. In retrospect, the high-risk venture appeared wholly unnecessary because Nixon was now well in front in the polls, was making progress towards ending the war in Vietnam, and had achieved spectacular diplomatic triumphs in lessening tensions with the Soviet Union and China. As to why it went ahead, the Watergate break-in testified to White House hubris about getting every scrap of information to pulverize rather than just defeat the Democrats. Colson recalled, "We wanted a coronation; we wanted the power that went with the greatest landslide in history." Nevertheless, presidential insecurity was also a factor because Nixon was anxious to discover what dirt the opposition party had on him.[41]

The combination of initially limited media interest, popular inattention, and the success of the White House cover-up prevented the break-in from affecting the election. On September 8, an eight-count indictment was handed down against the Watergate seven, but nobody in the administration was implicated. Two months later Nixon was reelected with 97 percent of all electoral votes, and over 60 percent of the popular vote, a landslide second only in presidential history to Franklin D. Roosevelt's 1936 victory. White House satisfaction at containing the damage from the Watergate break-in was short-lived, however. After the election, a series of press reports built up to an avalanche of bad news that revealed the wide range of criminal and unethical acts committed on behalf of the president.

The Cover-Up

There is no evidence that Nixon had authorized the break-in. There is speculation based on circumstantial evidence that he had advance knowledge of CREEP's intelligence plans from unrecorded private meetings with John Mitchell in the presidential living quarters. A later comment by Mitchell seemed to bear this out: "I never did anything without his permission." H. R. Haldeman similarly suggests that Charles Colson told Nixon of the break-in plan. Such allegations lack convincing proof of their veracity. In particular, the White House recordings offer no support for these contentions.

What is not in doubt, however, is that Nixon was immediately and deeply involved in a criminal conspiracy to cover up White House association with the Watergate burglars. Why a cover-up? Why didn't the president simply come clean early and cut his losses? Why was there virtually no discussion of *not* covering up? In part the answer is that Nixon and his aides were confident of being able to get away with this illegal project. However, the key concern that drove the cover-up was their need to keep the lid on all the White House's other illegal and unethical activities that might be revealed through investigation of its involvement in the break-in. These included: warrantless wiretaps, the Fielding break-in, the illegal raising of campaign funds, and sabotage of elections. What this meant was that there simply could not *not* be a cover-up.

Vacationing in Key Biscaine when the break-in occurred, Nixon returned to Washington on June 20. In his absence aides had already started the task of removing and destroying White House and CREEP files that contained incriminating evidence. However, there were already press reports linking Hunt to Colson, thereby suggesting a White House connection. It was also evident that FBI tracking of the money in the burglars' possession was getting close to discovering its CREEP source. Nixon discussed the matter with Haldeman, Mitchell, and Colson but the taped evidence is incomplete (notably the 18 ½ minute gap in the recording of his conversation with the chief of staff that a panel of experts later concluded was the result of five separate manual erasures).[42]

It is the June 23 tapes that provide the smoking gun evidence of the president's involvement in a criminal cover-up to obstruct justice. They record him conspiring with Haldeman to enlist the CIA's help in persuading the FBI to halt its investigation on grounds that it threatened to open up "the Bay of Pigs thing again" (Nixon's words in reference to the agency's disastrous effort to overthrow Cuban leader Fidel Castro in 1961). Almost certainly the president and his top aide would never have contemplated this had not J. Edgar Hoover's death on May 2 opened the way for the appointment of Nixon loyalist Patrick Gray as acting director. The outcome of their ploy was the worst of both worlds for the White House. After a meeting with Haldeman, CIA deputy director Vernon Walters, another Nixon ally, delivered the message that the investigation threatened to expose some of the agency's covert operations, but later withdrew it for fear of compromising agency integrity. After some hesitation, Gray authorized the continuation of the investigation, signaling this to the president on July 6. Convinced that Nixon was an innocent party in the attempted deceit, he warned that White House staff efforts to inveigle the FBI and CIA could "mortally wound" him.[43]

In his memoirs, Nixon explained the events surrounding the June 23 meeting as the first steps in the end of his presidency. Admitting that he did enlist the CIA's help in limiting the FBI investigation, the president nonetheless defended his actions as a pragmatic way of containing the scandal rather than covering it up.[44] Regardless of this being a distinction without a difference, the unsuccessful effort to manipulate the FBI and CIA only drew him deeper into the pit of illegality. Familiar with CIA procedures, the seven Watergate defendants expected their superiors to post bail, provide legal services, and pay salaries. On June 26, the agency emphatically rejected a White House request that it should provide this assistance. Needing to look elsewhere for hush money, the president and his aides turned to CREEP. On June 29, Kalmbach told Maurice Stans, chair of the organization's financial committee, that he was "on a special mission on a White House project and I need all the cash I can get."[45] Over the coming months, he would get $350,000 (including some from Haldeman's White House funds) for this purpose. Well aware of what was going on, Nixon was recorded saying on August 8, "Well…they have to be paid. That's all there is for that. They have to be paid."[46]

The Cover-Up Unravels

The cover-up began to unravel even before Nixon's reelection. Although the media was generally inattentive, *Washington Post* reporters Carl Bernstein and Bob Woodward kept the Watergate pot boiling with their stories pointing to the involvement of senior administration officials in illegal activities. Meanwhile, Howard Hunt was virtually resorting to blackmail to ensure a satisfactory flow of hush money on threat of blowing the whistle on White

House involvement. The disintegration of the cover-up then proceeded very rapidly from the start of Nixon's second term.[47]

On January 30, 1973, the trial of the Watergate burglars resulted in guilty verdicts against each of them (James McCord on all eight counts, the others on six). However, presiding judge John J. Sirica declared himself not satisfied that the full Watergate story had been revealed. Awaiting sentence, McCord, a CIA loyalist, wrote to Sirica on March 19 that the agency was not involved in the affair. He further asserted that the defendants were under pressure to remain silent and witnesses in the trial had perjured themselves to cover up others involved in the operation. A tough law-and-order Republican, the judge read McCord's letter in open court on March 23 prior to handing maximum sentences to his codefendants (40 years for the Cubans, 35 for Hunt, and 20 for Liddy) in the hope of encouraging them and others to reveal all they knew.

In the meantime, the administration had to battle on another front following the creation on February 7 of the Senate Select Committee on Presidential Campaign Activities. In response, White House aides decided to pursue a strategy of public cooperation with this body while working quietly to discredit it. This plan never stood much of a chance. Firstly, the Ervin Committee, so known after its chair, Senator Sam Ervin (D-NC), would employ 97 people at its peak. The White House defense, which also had to deal with Justice Department investigations, was simply outgunned in terms of resources. Secondly, the Ervin Committee's 37 days of hearings between May 17 and August 7 became big television events that attracted huge audiences. Finally, the Sirica sentences had the desired effect of encouraging some cover-up conspirators to become whistleblowers.

The key figure in the unraveling of the cover-up turned out to be presidential counsel John Dean. Though little known outside the White House, he had effectively been put in operational charge of the cover-up from its start. Initially Dean reported to Haldeman and other top aides rather than Nixon, whom he had not seen since September 15, 1972. This arrangement changed abruptly when the cover-up began to fray. Over the course of a 25-day period beginning on February 28, Dean and Nixon spoke on the telephone or met in person a total of 31 times. At the first of these meetings the president received assurances that the cover-up would continue to hold up. On the same day, however, FBI director-designate Pat Gray let slip during his Senate confirmation hearings that he had handed over bureau files on the Watergate investigation to Dean despite knowing he and other White House aides numbered among its subjects. To preempt Dean being called to testify on this, Nixon added another layer to the cover-up. On March 12, he issued what one scholar termed "a blunt statement asserting the nature and broadening power of executive privilege." In this he insisted on the necessity to protect internal executive branch communications regarding vital national concerns lest their revelation should threaten the candor of discussion and decision-making. The main effect of this invocation of privilege ("Very bad word" Nixon acknowledged in conversation with Haldeman four days later) bred the impression that he had something to hide.[48]

Dean began to doubt that the cover-up could be sustained as his role became more exposed. On March 13, he warned the president, "There are dangers...There is a certain domino situation. If some things start going, a lot of things are going to start going."[49] The March 21 meeting between the two was pivotal in the Watergate story.[50] At this, Dean gave Nixon a comprehensive overview of the criminal complicity of Mitchell, Haldeman, Ehrlichman, Magruder, Colson, Kalmbach, and himself in the Fielding and Watergate break-ins and consequent cover-ups. He also reviewed all the other illegal activities pertaining to the election and the instances of perjury before various courts. "We have," he declared, "a cancer within, close to the Presidency, that's growing. It's growing daily. It's compounding, it grows geometrically now, because it compounds itself." In essence Nixon was fully informed on Watergate, its roots, and the ongoing cover-up, the potential criminal liability among his top aides, and the unraveling of the cover-up. Many of the details he already knew, of course, but plausible deniability was no longer an option.

Rather than clean up the mess, the president henceforth assumed charge of the cover-up. He instructed in how to commit perjury, asserted the need for stonewalling, approved of hush money to maintain the silence of the Watergate defendants, and orchestrated a new cover-up plan based on finding a sacrificial lamb to take the blame. On March 22, as a counter to the Gray revelations, Nixon suggested that Dean should write a report explaining why he had not only received the FBI files but also sat in on FBI interviews pertaining to the Watergate investigation. "You were our investigator," he advised. "You were directed by the President to get me all the facts." The report, Nixon insisted, should conclude that neither the president nor any member of the White House staff had been involved in Watergate. This would be sent to the Ervin Committee, which would be offered the opportunity to question staff "on an informal basis," a construct that implicitly relaxed without formally surrendering the expansive concept of executive privilege recently invoked.[51]

It was all in vain, because Nixon was so evidently trying to save his own skin at the expense of others. The McCord letter and his fear that Nixon was setting him up with the continued pressure to write a "Dean report" convinced the presidential counsel that it was time to spill the beans in hopes of cutting a deal. Announcing through his lawyers on April 2 that he was willing to cooperate, he began talking to Justice Department prosecutors a week later. With the writing plainly on the wall, Jeb Magruder soon followed suit.

All Fall Down

Nixon still hoped that someone would take the fall with prosecutors. On April 14, John Mitchell dashed presidential hopes that he would do so. The next day, the other intended patsy, John Dean, informed his boss that he was cooperating with prosecutors. Knowing that the whistleblowers were already implicating Haldeman and Ehrlichman, Nixon required their resignations and dismissed Dean. Announcing this in a television address on April 30, he continued to deny personal involvement in the break-in or cover-up but conceded that "there had been an effort to conceal facts." Nixon claimed that aides misled him into believing that nobody in his administration or campaign organization was involved. In his memoirs, he admitted that his words were less that truthful, giving the false impression that he was unaware of the cover-up until March 21. Instead of "exerting presidential leadership," he confessed to embarking upon an "increasingly desperate search for ways to limit the damage."[52] The immediate effect of the firings was that Nixon had little option but to bow to the already strong pressure on him to appoint a special investigator to examine Watergate misdemeanors. Attorney General Elliot Richardson announced that former solicitor general and Harvard law professor Archibald Cox would serve in that capacity. The appointment opened up a yet another new front in the White House battle to preserve the cover-up.

Meanwhile Nixon's personal financial malpractice came under the spotlight. On May 14 a House subcommittee reported that the government had spent as much as $10 million on his vacation White Houses in California and Florida. It was subsequently revealed that he had only paid $878 in taxes in 1971 by backdating a gift of his vice presidential papers, which permitted a huge write-off. The discovery that Nixon's San Clemente property was funded with a loan from friendly financier Robert Abplanalp raised further doubts about the propriety of his personal tax manipulations. Finally obliged to respond to the charges, Nixon asserted his innocence on November 17 with the ill-chosen words that soon became a staple of comedians' jokes: "People have got to know whether or not their president is a crook. Well, I am not a crook." In April 1974 the Joint Congressional Committee on Taxation ruled that he owed $482, 737 in back taxes, money that he never fully repaid.

Embarrassing though this sideshow was, Nixon's all-important fight was now with the Ervin Committee. On the first day of the hearings on May 17 it heard extremely damaging evidence from CREEP-connected witnesses Jeb Magruder, James McCord, and Maurice Stans, among others. In response, the president issued on May 22 a 4,000-word statement denying any involvement in the Watergate cover-up. It included seven categorical statements of innocence, six of which new chief of staff Alexander Haig later admitted were barefaced lies.[53] However this was only the warm-up to the star attraction of John Dean's testimony that began on June 25. He read a 245-page statement that blew the lid off the entire gamut of criminal misdemeanors undertaken in the president's name. It opened with these words: "To one who was in the White House and became somewhat familiar with its interworkings, the Watergate matter was an inevitable outgrowth of a climate of excessive concern over the political impact of demonstrators, excessive concern over leaks, an insatiable appetite for political intelligence, all coupled with a do-it-yourself White House staff, regardless of the law." There was no documentation to corroborate the bombshell testimony, however. It was a matter of Dean's word against Nixon's, but the means to resolve his dilemma soon became clear.

On July 16, in preliminary questioning ahead of his Ervin committee appearance, White House staffer Alexander Butterfield revealed the existence of the presidential recordings that was known to only three other Nixon aides. At Nixon's behest, it was he who had directed the Secret Service to install and activate a voice-operated taping system in mid 1971. The recordings would provide the evidence to determine whether Nixon or Dean was telling the truth. From this juncture, the main focus of the Watergate investigation was to secure their release.

Both the Ervin committee and the special prosecutor requested the tapes. When the president refused to hand them over, they subpoenaed several recordings. Nixon still stonewalled, citing executive privilege in justification. The Ervin Committee and Archibald Cox consequently pursued their case in court, winning a ruling from Judge John Sirica on August 29 that the president should turn over the subpoenaed tapes. On October 12, the U.S. Court of Appeals upheld this judgment against the president's appeal. Rather than risk further defeat by taking the matter to the Supreme Court, Nixon trained his guns on Archibald Cox in a most ill-judged attempt to use executive power to head off the investigation. Several close aides and figures from the president's past also recommended this course of action. "This guy Cox will use anything and everybody," warned longtime mentor Murray Chotiner, "It has to be taken away from him."[54]

Before matters came to a head with the Special Prosecutor, however, attention focused on the problems of Vice President Spiro Agnew. Though innocent of any involvement in Watergate, he had come under Justice Department investigation for taking cash kickbacks while a county official in and later governor of Maryland. A civil court later determined that he had received $147,000 in bribes, of which $15,500 were paid to him when vice president. Although Agnew wanted the House of Representatives to investigate the case against him, he accepted a plea bargain negotiated by his attorneys after their review of the evidence. Under its terms, he resigned office, pleaded *nolo contendere* (literally no contest but effectively the full equivalent of a guilty plea) to one charge of income tax evasion, and escaped a prison sentence (but the Justice Department entered the evidence against him into the public record). Two days after Agnew became the first vice president to resign in disgrace. On October 10, Nixon nominated Gerald Ford as vice president.

To some cynics, Nixon's best hope of escaping impeachment disappeared with Agnew because there would have been almost universal abhorrence to his succession as president. The vice president would probably have fought his case if encouraged to do so, but the president did not want him impeached for fear of creating a precedent injurious to his own cause.

Moreover, Agnew's going opened the way for another counterattack in the Watergate war. "Now that we have disposed of that matter," Nixon reportedly told Elliot Richardson, "we can go ahead and get rid of Cox."[55] This proved to be a miscalculation of the first order.

Nixon asserted that the special prosecutor was technically part of the executive branch, so he had to desist from using the courts to force president disclosure of the tapes. In addition, he offered a compromise of having the specific tapes sought by Cox reviewed for incriminating evidence by a trusted intermediary, the hawkish and conservative Senator John Stennis (D-MS). When Cox signaled that he would continue to use legal means to secure the tapes, Nixon ordered Elliot Richardson to fire him on October 20. Richardson and his deputy, William Ruckelshaus, resigned rather than execute the order. Eventually Solicitor General Robert Bork did the firing, while also abolishing the special prosecutor's office and having the FBI seal Cox's headquarters to prevent removal of any files. Carried out in the president's name, these actions embodied a clear constitutional threat of his assertion to be above the law and the courts. Nixon had taken comfort in the belief that ordinary Americans would rally to his support as the victim of a partisan conspiracy to destroy his presidency, but the popular outcry following the Cox firing shattered this illusion. A shaken president quickly retreated, authorizing the reestablishment of the special prosecutor's office. Appointed to the post on November 1, Leon Jaworski continued the quest for the tapes safe in the knowledge that it was politically impossible for Nixon to order his dismissal as he had done Cox's.[56]

Facing unrelenting pressure to release the recordings, the president announced he would not hand over further tapes because it would violate confidentiality and could have an adverse effect on the Watergate trials. This attempted finger in the dike did nothing to stem the investigatory tide. On February 6, 1974, with only four dissenting votes, the House of Representatives adopted H.R. 803, directing its Judiciary Committee to begin consideration of whether grounds existed to impeach the president. This body then joined in the effort to secure release of the tapes. On April 29, in a national television address, Nixon announced that he would supply the Judiciary Committee with "edited transcripts" of the subpoenaed tapes to "once and for all, show that what I knew and what I did with regard to the Watergate break-in and cover-up were just as I have described them to you from the very beginning...as far as the President's role with regard to Watergate is concerned, the entire story is there."[57] However, the transcripts proved incomplete, inaccurate, and highly sanitized.

Meanwhile Jaworski had built a strong case that persuaded a federal grand jury to issue indictments on March 1 against seven former top presidential aides—Mitchell, Haldeman, Ehrlichman, Colson, Robert Mardian, Kenneth Parkinson, and Gordon Strachan—for lying to the FBI and to the grand jury, and for paying hush money to the original defendants. He had contemplated including Nixon in their ranks, but was uncertain whether a sitting president could be indicted in a criminal case. In the opinion of his legal staff, this entailed issues of "propriety" but there was "no explicit or implicit constitutional bar." However, Jaworski could not bring himself to indict a sitting president.[58] Instead, the grand jury unanimously voted to name Richard Nixon an "unindicted co-conspirator" in the criminal case.

Impeachment Maneuvers

Based on their recent experience as British colonists, the founders viewed tyranny and abuses of power as real dangers. Accordingly, they had made constitutional provision for the removal through impeachment of all civil officers of government, including the president, found guilty of "high crimes and misdemeanors." Devised by James Madison, this was a construct that the constitutional convention of 1787 had no difficulty understanding. The Constitution endowed the House with sole authority to recommend impeachment and the Senate to try all cases, which required a two-thirds majority for a conviction. This was recognized as a political process that could fall prey to the interest of faction but was still deemed appropriate for political crimes. As Alexander Hamilton remarked in *Federalist 65*, it was an acceptable method of "national inquest" into the conduct of public officials, including the head of government. In the words of Stanley Kutler, "The framers knew that men were not angels; they had no reason to bet differently on presidents."[59]

On February 21, committee counsel John Doar submitted a report to the House Judiciary committee entitled "Constitutional Grounds for Presidential Impeachment." A long, often heated, and sometimes eloquent debate over the evidence against the president ensued. The House's only previous impeachment of a president, Andrew Johnson in 1868, was a partisan Republican effort to remove an obstacle to Radical Reconstruction. This was largely responsible for the Senate failing to return a guilty verdict by a one-vote margin.[60] The lesson that Judiciary Committee chair Peter Rodino (D-NJ) drew from history was that Nixon's impeachment required bipartisan support to be deemed legitimate. While he did not have full control of his committee, he worked effectively to bring about agreement not only between Democratic and Republican members but also the various factions among the party blocs.

On July 27, the House Judiciary committee voted on Article I of impeachment, which accused the president of engaging in a "course of conduct" designed to obstruct justice in attempting to cover up Watergate. This passed by a 27-11 vote, with six Republicans joining all 21 Democrats in the majority. The next day, Article II, charging Nixon with abuse of power, passed 28-10. The following day, the third article of impeachment, charging the president with unconstitutionally defying a congressional subpoena for White House tape recordings, carried 21-17. Two other articles, dealing with concealing the bombing of Cambodia and with income tax evasion, both failed to pass by a 26-12 vote.[61]

The release of the presidential tapes was still considered essential for presidential impeachment, however. With Nixon continuing to stonewall against this, the Supreme Court agreed to hear the case, thereby putting itself at the center of a legal *and* political storm. It was not a foregone conclusion that the president would obey a Court ruling. Nixon had already warned that he would only obey a "definitive" ruling. Signifying the inherent danger of this, presidential lawyer Charles Alan Wright declared, "The tradition is very strong that judges should have the last word, but in a government organized as ours is, there are times when that simply cannot be the case." *United States of America v. Richard Nixon* revolved around the question of who decides whether a president obeys a subpoena—the Congress, the courts, or the president himself? On July 24, in an 8-0 decision, the Supreme Court ruled that President Nixon had to hand over the tapes to Judge Sirica because they were evidence in a criminal case. Despite acknowledging a heretofore-unrecognized constitutional basis for the claim of executive privilege, the Court ruled that it did not apply in this case.

The unanimous ruling made it virtually impossible for Nixon to stonewall further on the tapes, but their release on August 5 sealed his fate. The June 23, 1972, recording, which became known as the "smoking gun," provided undeniable evidence of his criminal complicity. When its content became known, the president's defense utterly collapsed. It was now evident that he had lied, covered up, and obstructed justice for reasons not of national security but self-protection. Public opinion, which had been turning against the president since the Cox case, was now overwhelmingly unfavorable to him. Impeachment by the House and conviction by the Senate had become virtually certain.

The Dénouement of Watergate

In a 15-minute television address delivered on the evening of August 8, 1974, the president announced that "I shall resign the presidency effective at noon tomorrow." Nixon showed little remorse in explaining his reason for leaving: "In the last few days it has become evident to me that I no longer have a strong enough political base in the Congress to justify continuing in office." He added, "I regret deeply any injuries that may have been done in the course of the events that led to this decision. I would say only that if some of my judgments were wrong—and some were wrong—they were made in what I believed at the time to be in the best interest of the nation." Nixon neither protested his innocence nor admitted his guilt.

On August 9, 1974, shortly before noon, Nixon's letter of resignation, something that no other president had written, was delivered to Secretary of State Henry Kissinger. It read in its entirety: "Dear Mr. Secretary: I hereby resign the office of President of the United States. Sincerely, Richard Nixon." In a postscript, the Judiciary Committee filed its report and impeachment recommendation, now supported by all 38 members; the House accepted both by a vote of 412-3 on August 20.

The question remained whether Nixon would have to face criminal charges. Other Watergate perpetrators, major and minor, went to prison for varying stretches. Nixon did not join them. On September 8, 1974, Gerald Ford called a news conference to announce that he had granted his predecessor "a full, free, and absolute pardon...for all offenses against the United States which he, Richard Nixon, has committed, or may have committed or taken part in during the period" he was president. Fearing that a trial would prolong the national trauma, the new president wanted to end the "American tragedy" of Watergate and let the process of healing begin. However, his act of clemency aroused intense suspicion that his predecessor had struck a secret deal to save himself before handing the presidency over. There is no evidence of such a pact, though Nixon had certainly tried to get one. Acknowledging his misjudgment of the popular mood in his memoirs, Ford commented that the American people "wanted to see [Nixon] drawn and quartered publicly."[62] The error was a factor in Ford's failure to win reelection as president against Democrat Jimmy Carter in 1976. A quarter-century later, journalist Bob Woodward, who helped expose the Watergate conspiracy, adjudged that he had been right to pardon Nixon but should have better prepared the public, the media, and Congress for his decision, especially by requiring the former president to sign a statement of guilt for release with the pardon. For the rest of his life, Ford would carry in his wallet a Supreme Court opinion in *Burdick v. United States* (1915) that a pardon "carries imputation of guilt, acceptance a confession of it."[63]

In reality, however, Ford's pardon of Nixon had unintentionally become part of the Watergate cover-up. In failing to specify what Nixon was guilty of, it enabled him to deny any culpability for wrongdoing. This became the springboard for his last and greatest political campaign to seek rehabilitation from his Watergate disgrace.[64] It also meant that the full extent of Watergate as a constitutional crisis rather than a scandal was never firmly planted in the popular memory. The focus on Nixon's personal obloquy shrouded the greater significance of Watergate as an outgrowth of the imperial presidency's tendency to flout the Constitution in the public mind. The lessons of the past therefore went unlearned, making it likely that they would be soon repeated. This book looks to make some of these more understandable to a generation of readers for whom Watergate is truly history rather than lived experience.

Notes

1. *Time*, August 19, 1974; Gerald Ford, "Remarks on Taking the Oath of Office," August 9, 1974, in John T. Woolley and Gerhard Peters, *The American Presidency Project* [*APP*] (Santa Barbara: University of California), www. presidency.ucsb. edu.

2. Widely recognized as the best study of Watergate is Stanley I. Kutler, *The Wars of Watergate: The Last Crisis of Richard Nixon* (New York: Norton, 1992). More accessible for those new to the subject are: Michael Genovese, *The Watergate Crisis* (Westport, CT: Greenwood, 1999); and Keith Olson, *Watergate: The Presidential Scandal That Shook America* (Lawrence: University Press of Kansas, 2003). For a good journalistic account, see Fred Emery, *Watergate: The Corruption of American Politics and the Fall of Richard Nixon* (New York: Random House, 1994). The best historical study of the Nixon presidency is Melvin Small, *The Presidency of Richard Nixon* (Lawrence: University Press of Kansas, 1999). The same author has also edited a comprehensive collection, *A Companion to Richard M. Nixon* (Hoboken, NJ: Wiley-Blackwell, 2011). For contrasting assessments, see Michael Genovese, *The Nixon Presidency: Power and Politics in Turbulent Times* (Westport, CT: Greenwood, 1990), and Joan Hoff, *Nixon Reconsidered* (New York: Basic Books, 1994).
3. Kutler, *The Wars of Watergate*, 618.
4. Andrew Rudalevige, "George W. Bush and the Imperial Presidency," in Mark Rozell and Gleaves Whitney, *Testing the Limits: George W. Bush and the Imperial Presidency* (Lanham, MD: Rowman and Littlefield, 2009), 245–246; Richard E. Neustadt, *Presidential Power and the Modern Presidents* (New York: Free Press, 1990), ix; Edward Corwin, *The Presidency: Office and Powers* (New York: New York University Press, 1957), 29–30.
5. Quoted in David Nather, "New Handshake, Same Grip," *CQ Weekly*, December 17, 2007, 3702.
6. For discussion, see Michael A. Genovese and Lori Cox Han, *The Presidency and the Challenge of Democracy* (New York: Palgrave, 2006).
7. Peter Irons, *War Powers: How the Imperial Presidency Hijacked the Constitution* (New York: Metropolitan Books, 2005); and Charlie Savage, *Takeover: The Return of the Imperial Presidency and the Subversion of American Democracy* (Boston: Little, Brown, 2007).
8. Michael A. Genovese, *Presidential Prerogative: Imperial Power in an Age of Terrorism* (Palo Alto, CA: Stanford University Press, 2010).
9. John Owens, "Bush's Congressional Legacy and Congress's Bush Legacy," in Iwan Morgan and Philip John Davies, *Assessing George W. Bush's Legacy: The Right Man?* (New York: Palgrave, 2010), 51–78.
10. *Korematsu v. U.S.* 323 U.S. 214 (1944)
11. Cato, "Letter V," *New York Journal*, November 22, 1787, available at www.constitution.org/afp/cato_05.htm.
12. Arthur M. Schlesinger, Jr., *The Imperial Presidency* (Boston: Houghton Mifflin, 1973), x; Genovese, *Presidential Prerogative*, 8.
13. See, in particular, James Pfiffner, *Power Play: The Bush Administration and the Constitution* (Washington, DC: Brookings Institution, 2008).
14. Despite being one of the most written about presidents, Nixon still lacks a definitive biography. To date, the best remains Stephen E. Ambrose's three volume study, *Nixon: the Education of a Politician, 1913–62, Nixon: The Triumph of a Politician, 1962–72,* and *Nixon: Ruin and Recovery, 1973–1990* (New York: Simon & Schuster, 1987, 1989, and 1991). Conrad Black's mammoth tome, *Richard Milhous Nixon: The Invincible Quest* (London: Quercus, 2007) is the best of the pro-Nixon biographies. For those seeking a short biography, consult Iwan Morgan, *Nixon* (London: Arnold, 2002).

15. Morgan, *Nixon*, 194.
16. The best of these is Vamik Volkan, Norman Itzkowitz, and Andrew Dod, *Richard Nixon: A Psychobiography* (New York: Columbia University Press, 1996). For a review of the genre, see David Greenberg, *Nixon's Shadow: The History of an Image* (New York: Norton, 2003), chapter 6.
17. Jeb Stuart Magruder, *An American Life: One Man's Road to Watergate* (New York: Atheneum, 1974), 5.
18. See, for example, Victor Lasky, *It Didn't Start with Watergate* (New York: Viking, 1976).
19. Small, *The Presidency of Richard Nixon*, 273; C. Vann Woodward, "The Conscience of the White House," in Woodward, ed., *The Responses of the President to Charges of Misconduct* (New York: Dell, 1974), xxvi.
20. Arthur Schlesinger, "The Imperial Presidency Redux," in Schlesinger, *War and the American Presidency* (New York: Norton, 2005), 46–47; Schlesinger, *The Imperial Presidency*, 7.
21. Olson, *Watergate*, chapter 9; Robert Johnson, *Improbable Dangers; U.S. Conceptions of Threat in the Cold War and After* (New York: St Martin's, 1994).
22. For Nixon's Vietnam policy see: Robert Schulzinger: *A Time for War: The United States and Vietnam, 1941–1975* (New York: Oxford University Press, 1997); Jeffrey Kimball, *Nixon's Vietnam War* (Lawrence: University Press of Kansas, 1998); Larry Berman, *No Peace, No Honor: Nixon, Kissinger and Betrayal in Vietnam* (New York: Touchstone, 2002).
23. Ambrose, *Nixon: Triumph*, 272–273; Olson, *Watergate*, 9–12. The latter calculates that Nixon's three predecessors had ordered taps on a total of two government officials and no newspersons other than those working for the communist *Daily Worker*.
24. Charles W. Colson, *Born Again* (Old Tappan, NJ: Chosen Books, 1976), 41; Leonard Garment, *In Search of Deep Throat: The Greatest Political Mystery of Our Time* (New York: Basic Books, 2000); Richard Nixon, *RN: The Memoirs of Richard Nixon* (New York: Grosset and Dunlap, 1978), 471.
25. Ambrose, *Nixon: Triumph*, 361–362, 367–369; Richard Gid Powers, *Secrecy and Power: The Life of J. Edgar Hoover* (London: Hutchison, 1987), 453–456.
26. David Frost, *"I Gave Them a Sword:" Behind the Scenes of the Nixon Interviews* (New York: William Morrow, 1978), 183. In his memoirs, Nixon also asserted that critics who called the scheme repressive and unlawful "did not face the exigencies of a critical period in which the President, whose paramount responsibility is to ensure the safety of all citizens, was forced to consider measures that would undoubtedly be unacceptable in more tranquil times." See *RN*, 475.
27. Quoted in Tom Wicker, *One of Us: Richard Nixon and the American Dream* (New York: Random House, 1990), 660. For a discussion of the case, see David Rudenstine, *The Day the Presses Stopped: The History of the Pentagon Papers Case* (Berkeley: University of California Press, 1996).
28. H. R. Haldeman with Joseph diMona, *The Ends of Power* (New York: Times Books, 1978), 115.
29. Ambrose, *Nixon: Triumph*, 446–48; Kutler, *The Wars of Watergate*, 109.
30. For the transcript, see Stanley I. Kutler, ed., *Abuse of Power: The New Nixon Tapes* (New York: Free Press, 1997), 7–8. This collection provides edited

transcripts of 201 hours of Watergate tapes, released in November 1996. Nixon, and then the Nixon estate after his death, had conducted a legal battle against release of the recordings. However, as a result of the suit brought by Stanley Kutler and Public Citizen, a binding agreement was struck with the National Archives and the Nixon estate providing for eventual release of 3,700 hours of tapes.

31. Kutler, *The Wars of Watergate*, 111–116; Krogh quoted in C. L. Sulzberger, *The World and Richard Nixon* (New York: Prentice-Hall, 1987), 368.
32. Kutler, *The Wars of Watergate*, 116; Small, *The Presidency of Richard Nixon*, 238.
33. Ellsberg: "EVERY attack now made on WikiLeaks and Julian Assange was made against me and the Pentagon Papers at the time," December 8, 2010, Daniel Ellsberg website, http://www.ellsberg.net.
34. Quotations from Olson, *Watergate*, 175–176.
35. Larry Berman, *The New American Presidency* (Boston: Houghton Mifflin, 1987), 174 (this also produces the full enemies' list on p. 279); Kutler, *Abuse of Power*, 150.
36. Small, *The Presidency of Richard Nixon*, 264–266; Kutler, *The Wars of Watergate*, 227–232.
37. Kutler, *Abuse of Power*, 67–68.
38. Rick Perlstein, *Nixonland: The Rise of a President and the Fracturing of America* (New York: Scribner, 2008), chapters 29–32; Anthony Summers, *The Arrogance of Power: The Secret World of Richard Nixon* (London: Hutchison, 2000); Tip O'Neill with William Novak, *Man of the House: The Life and Political Memoirs of Speaker Tip O'Neill* (New York: St. Martin's Press, 1987), 281.
39. Summers, *The Arrogance of Power*, 402.
40. Hoff, *Nixon Reconsidered*, 304–312 reviews the main conspiracy theories.
41. Garment, *In Search of Deep Throat*, 77; Summers, *The Arrogance of Power*, 402.
42. Kutler, *Abuse of Power*, 47–49.
43. Kutler, *Abuse of Power*, 67–70; Garment, *In Search of Deep Throat*, 83–86; Powers, *The Man Who Kept the Secrets*, 263.
44. Nixon, *RN*, 646, 773.
45. Stanley Kutler, ed, *Watergate, The Fall of Richard M. Nixon* (St. James, NY: Brandywine Press, 1996), 50; Small, *The Presidency of Richard Nixon*, 277–278.
46. Kutler, *Abuse of Power*, 111.
47. The details below are largely drawn from Kutler, *Abuse of Power*; Emery, *Watergate*; and Olson, *Watergate*.
48. Kutler, *The Wars of Watergate*, 272; Kutler, *Abuse of Power*, 33–34.
49. John Dean, *Blind Ambition* (New York: Simon & Schuster, 1976), 146.
50. For the full transcript, see Kutler, *Abuse of Power*, 247–57.
51. *The Presidential Transcripts* (New York: Dell, 1974), 170, 176.
52. Nixon, *RN*, 849–851.
53. Stephen Ambrose, *Nixon: Ruin and Recovery*, 148–149; Alexander Haig with Charles McCarry, *Inner Circles: How America Changed the World* (New York: Warner, 1982), 348.
54. Quoted in Kutler, *The Wars of Watergate*, 401.

55. Elliot Richardson, *The Creative Balance: Government, Politics, and the Individual in America's Third Century* (New York: Holt, Rinehart, 1976), 38.

56. For fuller discussion of this episode, see Clodagh Harrington's essay in this volume.

57. "Address to the Nation Announcing Answer to the House Judiciary Committee Subpoena for Additional Presidential Tape Recordings," April 29, 1974, *APP*.

58. Richard Ben-Veniste and George Frampton, Jr., *Stonewall: The Real Story of the Watergate Prosecution* (New York: Bantam, 1974), 161.

59. Kutler, *The Wars of Watergate*, 472–475 [quotation p. 475].

60. Eric Foner, *A Short History of Reconstruction 1863–1877* (New York: Harper & Row, 1990), chapters 5–7.

61. Kutler, *The Wars of Watergate*, 455–456, 48–82, 498, 516–526.

62. Gerald Ford, *A Time to Heal: The Autobiography of Gerald R. Ford* (New York: Harper & Row, 1979), 178.

63. Bob Woodward, *Shadow: Five Presidents and the Legacy of Watergate* (New York: Simon & Schuster, 1999), 37–38.

64. For discussion of this, see the chapter in this volume by Iwan Morgan.

Chapter Two

Revisiting Arthur Schlesinger's The Imperial Presidency: Richard Nixon, George W. Bush, and Executive Power

Jon Herbert

The Imperial Presidency is widely recognized as one of the most important and influential books written on the American presidency. First published in 1973, it explained Watergate's significance even before Richard Nixon had left office. In his best-selling work, eminent historian Arthur M. Schlesinger, Jr. (1917–2007) characterized the "third-rate burglary" of Democratic National Committee (DNC) offices as a peripheral element within a revolutionary project to undermine America's constitutional democracy. In Schlesinger's assessment, the main significance of the botched break-in was to highlight the threat of the imperial presidency. Regardless of Nixon's fate, Schlesinger warned that this "imperial" entity would continue to endanger America's constitutional system because the structural factors that underpinned its development remained in place. George W. Bush's extensive assertions of presidential authority, which some analysts characterized as a "new imperial presidency," appeared to fulfill this prediction.[1] Yet, the matter of causation remains open. Did the structural forces that Schlesinger identified as driving the original version also impel development of the new imperial presidency? This chapter examines his thesis and assesses its continued applicability regarding early twenty-first-century assertions of enhanced executive authority.

Schlesinger's *Imperial Presidency*

Arthur Schlesinger made an unlikely critic of presidential aggrandizement. He had served as special assistant to President John F. Kennedy, and his academic work celebrated the reformist role of strong presidents in Prize-winning studies of Andrew Jackson, Franklin D. Roosevelt, and John F. Kennedy.[2] By his own admission, his scholarship had contributed "to the rise of the presidential mystique."[3] However, concerns about the geopolitical and moral wisdom of the Vietnam War and the threat to democracy at home from sweeping assertions of executive authority made him a critic of the "imperial presidency."[4]

Schlesinger argued that a "revolution" was taking place. The Founding Fathers had carefully constructed a separated system of government that rendered the presidency accountable to and coequal with other branches. Post-1945 presidents, however, had propagated a reinterpretation of the Constitution that breached this intent. According to political scientist Andrew Rudalevige, Schlesinger had three substantive purposes in coining the term "imperial presidency." It linked presidential abuses of power with the imperialistic pretensions of America's Vietnam-era foreign policy; eschewing partisanship, it placed the debate over presidential power within the preoccupations of the founders; and it captured a sense of constitutional borders crossed and governmental authority annexed. As such, it spoke "to the timeless tension between a Constitution that makes limited and vague assignations of [presidential] power and the press of threatening events that riddle real-world politics."[5] To this might be added a fourth concern that use of the "imperial presidency" term should highlight the executive's inordinate claims of power before a general revulsion set in against presidential leadership, thereby harming the nation's capacity to handle future problems. As Schlesinger remarked, "We need a strong presidency – but a strong presidency *within the Constitution.*"[6]

In Schlesinger's assessment, the "perennial threat to the constitutional balance...arises in the field of foreign affairs."[7] As the global Cold War struggle between the United States and the Soviet Union developed, presidents had usurped congressional power to declare war, asserting that their commander-in-chief responsibility amounted to a grant of substantive war-making authority. The interbranch consultation over foreign affairs desired by the founders had fallen into disuse. Nixon, for example, willfully mistranslated his responsibility to guarantee U.S. armed forces' safety in the field into a presidential-command power to justify the 1970 invasion of neutral Cambodia. The claim that presidents had constitutional authority to repel sudden attacks on American interests, howsoever they defined these, particularly exercised Schlesinger. In his view, its logic was to free the president of any obligation to consult Congress before taking military action.[8]

When the White House did communicate with Congress on sensitive international issues, it frequently engaged in deliberate misinformation. National security concerns provided the often-spurious justification for this deceit. Such a claim afforded the nation's chief executive the right to lie, as evidenced by the 1969–1970 secret air war against Cambodia that involved some 3,600 B-52 raids on communist sanctuaries. When leaks revealed these attacks, an angry Nixon ordered wiretaps of National Security Council (NSC) staff and at least four reporters to find the source. Nixon acted without seeking legal authorization. Attorney General John Mitchell asserted "inherent" presidential power to wiretap in the interests of national security.[9]

The imperial presidency was also a domestic phenomenon. Schlesinger bemoaned the systematic White House assault on congressional prerogatives that undermined the core constitutional principle of separate powers. In particular, Nixon's impoundment of funds, effectively refusing to spend monies that Congress had allocated to programs of which he disapproved, undermined the legislature's power of the purse. While conceding the authority of Congress to make appropriations, he asserted the president's right not to spend them. The consequent underfunding of programs amounted to enhanced presidential capacity to shape the policy priorities of the national government, in defiance of congressional preferences.[10]

The thirty-seventh president further asserted that the Constitution endowed him with discretionary authority to refuse to execute laws approved by Congress. His refusal to enforce Title VI of the 1964 Civil Rights Act, which mandated cutting off federal funds from school districts that practiced racial discrimination, fell foul of the courts. Creative use of rule and regulation writing also enabled the White House to interpret legislation differently from the intent of its congressional authors. Using reorganization plans to control federal government activity was another instrument of presidential aggrandizement. Furthermore, Nixon's innovative use of the pocket veto prevented some bills becoming law without risk of a formal veto being overridden.[11]

The administration worked to maximize White House control over domestic policy, while minimizing congressional influence. It reinterpreted presidential appointing power to avoid congressional constraints upon selection of executive-branch personnel, especially by announcing appointments when the legislature was in recess. Nixon also pursued a "calculated disparagement of the cabinet," concentrating executive policy-making and management in the White House.[12] He significantly expanded the Executive Office of the President, particularly its White House staff component, with the result that operating costs effectively doubled during his first term. For Schlesinger, the main consequence was increased politicization of the executive bureaucracy. He particularly objected to the Bureau of the Budget's redevelopment in 1970 into the Office of Management and Budget (OMB) with enhanced powers over executive budgeting and policy review in service of the president's goals.[13] As one political scientist later remarked, the restructured agency was "more a member of the President's own political family and less a broker providing independent analytic service to every president."[14]

Mechanisms to increase presidential control of policy would have had less effect if constrained by stringent congressional oversight. However, Nixon's team made extensive claims of executive privilege that amounted to demands for uncontrolled discretion to withhold information from the legislature. In April 1973, for example, Attorney General Richard Kleindienst asserted that the president possessed this right if disclosure "would impair the proper exercise of his constitutional functions," adding that Congress therefore had no authority to compel testimony from any executive-branch official over his objection.[15] In parallel, Schlesinger noted, the White House operated a "secrecy system" that justified extensive classification of documents in the name of national security.[16]

While deceiving Congress through misinformation and withholding information, the administration also attempted to limit press freedom. For the first time, the executive branch tried to impose prior restraint on the publication of news in the Pentagon Papers case. The president also ordered that reporters suspected of receiving leaked information from within the administration should have their telephones wiretapped. Meanwhile, the White House conducted a campaign of disinformation to deceive press and public about its actions in Vietnam. Media critics also found themselves threatened with antitrust prosecution and nonrenewal of local television station licenses. In the words of Senator Sam Ervin (D-SC), chair of the Senate committee established to investigate Watergate, "The Administration assaulted the very integrity of the press and called into question its right to disagree with official views."[17]

Roots of the Imperial Presidency

According to Schlesinger, a number of structural factors drove the imperial presidency's development. As recognized in Federalist 64 and 75, the Constitution endowed the president with inherent advantages in foreign policy. Alongside commander-in-chief status, Article II granted general executive power that gave the president free rein to exploit his institutional advantages of "unity, secrecy, decision, dispatch, superior sources of information."[18] This endowed him with enhanced authority to defend the nation in an emergency. The more acute the crisis, the more power would consequently flow to his office. In this regard, the Cold War's mutation from temporary emergency into prolonged struggle allowed exceptional presidential powers associated with wartime to become "authority claimed by presidents as constitutionally inherent in the presidential office."[19]

Schlesinger also detected domestic structural factors in the imperial presidency's rise. The New Deal had institutionalized presidential responsibility for economic management, marginalizing Congress in this policy domain. Meanwhile, decay of the traditional political party system left the presidency standing alone as the "central focus of political emotion, the ever more potent symbol of national community."[20] The rise of radio and television enhanced the president's capacity to speak to and for the American people, giving him greater power to rally public support than any other political actor. Finally the larger, politicized presidential staff offered greater control over the executive branch. These developments weakened presidential accountability to other institutional actors in the political system.[21] In Schlesinger's assessment, the effect was to establish a plebiscitary presidency subject to the sole constraint of quadrennial national elections.[22]

Schlesinger was dismayed at elite and popular tolerance of the imperial presidency's overt challenge to longstanding constitutional doctrine. He berated "the chicken-heartedness of Congress, the acquiescence of most of the press and the predilections of the American lower middle class."[23]The legislature had surrendered its constitutional powers of purse, war, and oversight with little fight. The public had bought into Nixon's "silent majority" rhetoric that exploited "middle-class fear of left-wing militancy" to assist his assault upon constitutional traditions.[24]

While emphasizing structural factors, Schlesinger also argued that Nixon's deeply flawed personality contributed to the imperial presidency's climax.[25] A "singular confluence of the job with the man" placed the enlarged presidency in the hands of a president "whose inner mix of vulnerability and ambition impelled him to push the historical logic to its extremity."[26] Driven by his "agitated psyche," Nixon craved the expansion of power, the elimination of enemies, and the affirmation of reelection.

The Covert Dimension of the Revolution

Schlesinger argued that the imperial presidency had a covert dimension that responded to the same "pathologies" as the public one. A member of the wartime Office of Strategic Services (OSS), the precursor to the Central Intelligence Agency (CIA), he detailed with some authority many of the Nixon White House's illegal practices. These included the burgling of offices, dirty tricks against political opponents, forging of historical documents, unauthorized electronic surveillance and wiretapping, perjury and its subornation, bribery, obstruction of justice, destruction of evidence, and conspiracy to co-opt other government agencies into wrongdoing. In Schlesinger's early assessment, vindicated by later revelations, Nixon's appointees had undertaken a host of indictable activities.[27] If anything, he underestimated the administration's misuse of federal agencies, including the Internal Revenue Service (IRS), FBI, CIA, and National Security Agency(NSA), for its own political espionage.

For Schlesinger, Nixon's illegal activities were a natural extension of the imperial presidency. Convinced of his own virtue and certain that the republic was in mortal danger from internal enemies, Nixon conflated defending the nation and defending his presidency. The latter was needed to preserve the former, so exerting every power to defend the administration became legitimate. Invoking threats to national security and the inherent presidential power to defend the nation, Nixon justified the presidency setting itself above the Constitution and ultimately the law.

The covert activities were primarily significant, from Schlesinger's perspective, for their illumination of the overt campaign to strengthen the presidency. Exposure of the Watergate break-in and cover-up, merely a criminal by-product within the broader campaign, laid the administration's imperial purpose bare and legitimized resistance to it. Press revelations, congressional hearings, and criminal cases prompted national discussion of the president's role and both congressional and media reassertion intended to curtail presidential power. In essence, therefore, the burglary and cover-up were not integral to the imperial presidency, but triggered the demise of Nixon's version.[28]

Of course, there are other explanations of Watergate. Some scholars emphasize Nixon's character more than the structural context in which he operated.[29] Others, by contrast, highlight the indictable actions of previous administrations to place Nixon's misdeeds in perspective. Keith Olson has detailed the excessive secrecy, loose campaign ethics, and misuse of federal agencies for political espionage by other presidents.[30] Revisionist scholar Joan Hoff also attested that Watergate was "a disaster waiting to happen, given the decline in political ethics and practices during the cold war."[31] Schlesinger's arguments are particularly interesting, however, as they can be projected onto later expansions of presidential power. For him, the aberration and exposure of Watergate did not eliminate the structural forces sustaining imperial development. Far from proving that the system worked, Nixon's downfall was primarily personal, not institutional. The imperial presidency was consequently interrupted but assertions of its demise were premature. Hence, remembering Watergate requires consideration of the Schlesinger thesis as it pertains to presidential development thereafter.

Bush's "New Imperial Presidency"

Andrew Rudalevige perceived a gradual reassertion of presidential power after Watergate, choosing the term "new imperial presidency" to underscore the parallels between the assertions of the pre- and post-Watergate presidencies. However, he argues that the terrorist attacks of September 11, 2001, generated a "tidal wave accelerating this process" of reassertion that lifted executive power to new heights.[32] This assessment invites a comparison between the Bush and Nixon imperial presidencies. Parallels in foreign policy are considered briefly below, before more extended analysis of executive assertions in the domestic arena.

Schlesinger's analysis had decried Nixon's usurpation of Congress's war powers. Similarly asserting the constitutional legitimacy of unilateral presidential power to prosecute military conflict, the Bush administration initiated conflicts in Afghanistan and Iraq without formal congressional declarations of war and ordered rocket attacks on the Federally Administered Tribal Areas of America's ally, Pakistan. Despite subsequently citing the congressional Authorizations to Use Military Force (AUMF) against terrorists (September 2001) and Iraq (October 2002) as sources of legitimacy, the administration also asserted the right to act without such permission.[33]

The parallels between the two imperial presidencies were also evident regarding domestic surveillance. As the *New York Times* revealed in late

2005, the Bush administration authorized the NSA to wiretap telephone calls for evidence on terrorist activities. It routinely flouted the Foreign Intelligence Surveillance Act of 1978 (FISA), which required that a specialist FISA court issue a warrant for each tap on American citizens. Bush and his advisers insisted these practices were legal on grounds that the president had "inherent power in his constitutional role as commander-in-chief and on authority implicit in the congressional resolution authorizing the use of military force."[34] They employed the same argument to validate the opening of Americans' mail by investigators, despite specific prohibitions in the Postal Service Act of 2006.[35]

Going further than anything attempted by the Nixon administration,[36] the Bush administration also restricted the rights of enemy combatants and U.S. citizens suspected of terrorism. America habitually classified captured enemy fighters as prisoners-of-war possessing attendant rights under the Geneva conventions and guaranteed detained U.S. citizens *habeas corpus* rights preventing indefinite incarceration and guaranteeing appeal against detention through the court system. Citing the president's commander-in-chief status and the September 2001 AUMF as justification, the Bush administration asserted its power to classify detainees in ways that compromised their rights. Designating foreign detainees as "unlawful enemy combatants" denied them the attendant protections of prisoner-of-war status. Reclassifying detained U.S. citizens as enemy combatants plucked them out of the standard judicial process. Many found themselves being held for indefinite terms at the Guantanamo Bay Detention Center. Despite executive, legislative, and judicial maneuvering over such reclassifications, the administration continued to claim the authority to hold alleged terrorists, even if acquitted at trial or having served their sentence.

The military tribunals established to try detainees were also contentious. Citing the Uniform Code of Military Justice (UCMJ), the president's commander-in-chief powers, and the AUMF as justification, the administration bypassed the normal judicial system. The inability of defendants to appeal decisions outside the military chain of command and the use of evidence derived from harsh interrogation practices earned the tribunals sharp criticism. Despite Supreme Court resistance, in the *Hamdan v. Rumsfeld* (2006) and *Boumedienne v. Bush* (2008) decisions, a modified tribunals system survived Bush's term.[37]

The administration also rode roughshod over U.S. and international law in its treatment of suspected terrorists in detention. Its use of "extraordinary rendition" allowed transfers of detainees to states that habitually use torture as an interrogation technique. Furthermore, Bush issued a classified directive, and later an executive order, authorizing CIA establishment of so-called "black sites," secret detention centers for high-value terror suspects. Sometimes, the administration practiced "ghosting," which entailed refusal to recognize officially these suspects' detention, with the consequence of placing them outside any normal regime of protection under U.S. or international law. In parallel, the administration sanctioned use of extraordinary interrogation tactics by American forces on grounds that "unlawful enemy combatants" lacked prisoner-of-war rights. The notorious "torture memo," authored by Office of Legal Counsel official Jay Bybee in August 2002, redefined the level of force permissible in interrogating detainees to permit such brutal techniques as waterboarding. When the Detainee Rights Act of 2005 sought to ensure humane standards of interrogation, Bush claimed presidential authority to ignore its provisions if national security required and to define what constituted "cruel, inhumane or degrading" treatment.[38]

Like Nixon's, the Bush imperial presidency extended its sway beyond security policy, using executive authority to challenge congressional preferences and prerogatives in domestic policy. Both employed "administrative presidency" techniques to control executive-branch activity through selective implementation of laws, increased control over rule and regulation writing, and politicization of the executive branch.[39] To support its version of this, the Bush administration developed the "Unitary Executive" doctrine. As described by the American Bar Association, this asserted that "the president has the sole power to control the execution of powers delegated to him in the Constitution and encapsulated in his Commander-in-Chief powers and in his constitutional mandate to see that 'the laws are faithfully executed.' "[40] In essence, the administration claimed that Congress lacked constitutional authority to influence either the implementation of the laws or the president's conduct as commander-in-chief. A radical innovation, this doctrine had few supporters, academic or legal, but the administration cited it regularly to defend assertions of executive authority and resist congressional encroachments.[41]

While Article II of the Constitution required the president to "take care that the laws be faithfully executed," Nixon and Bush both refused to enforce certain statutes that they deemed unconstitutional. Charged with guarding presidential authority, Vice President Richard Cheney's office assiduously reviewed new legislation for possible infringements. Often, Bush delivered signing statements to announce his preferred interpretation of new laws to assert presidential power. Conventionally a matter of record to influence subsequent Supreme Court deliberations, signing statements became a line-item veto in the hands of the forty-third president. Though not a Bush innovation, more were issued in the first six years of his presidency than the entire total for his 42 predecessors.[42]

Building on Nixon's precedents, Bush increased control over rule and regulation writing by the federal bureaucracy. His administration transformed the role of the Office of Information and Regulatory Affairs within OMB, establishing tighter White House control over the review process for new rules, regulations, and guidance documents issued by the executive branch. In addition, the president appointed new regulatory policy officers in each federal agency to ensure loyalist vetting of decisions by policy experts. The administration also intervened in rulemaking directly, notably by rewriting Clean Air Act antipollution regulations, after legislative efforts to change these had failed.[43] In this case, and others including health, energy, worker safety standards, and product safety disclosure, regulatory frameworks were developed to undermine the purpose of original statutes.[44] According to the respected and independent Congressional Research Service, Bush's frequent practice of ignoring the law as written constituted the "strongest assertion of presidential power in this area in at least 20 years."[45] Executive orders were also integral to Bush's administrative presidency, notably in underpinning his faith-based initiative after congressional refusal to enshrine it in legislation.[46] Bush's strategy moved well beyond Kenneth Mayer's characterization of benign executive orders as "taking advantage of gaps in constitutional and statutory language that allow [presidents] to fill power vacuums and gain control of emerging capabilities".[47]

Like Nixon before him, Bush was condemned for politicizing the executive branch. Criticism peaked with the dismissal of nine Department of Justice attorneys in 2006, allegedly for failing to handle cases with partisan implications in a manner that suited Republican leaders. The administration stood accused of replacing talented nonpartisan attorneys with ideological loyalists, in defiance of federal law. An internal justice department investigation and a separate special prosecutor investigation both concluded that politically motivated firing did occur.[48] Partisan considerations shaped other hiring and firing decisions within the department and decisions on the enforcement of voting rights legislation. Bush's use of recess appointments, most famously that of neoconservative John Bolton as Ambassador to the United Nations, echoed Nixon's disregard for congressional prerogative. Like his disgraced predecessor, he also came under attack for abusing his power to reorganize the executive branch. The forty-third president especially wooed controversy in legislative battles to create the Department of Homeland Security(DHS) and reorganize the senior intelligence community.

Both Nixon and Bush's assertions of expanded presidential authority depended on shielding the executive branch from oversight and investigation by Congress. Accordingly, the latter's administration managed the flow of information to the legislative branch, often asserting executive privilege to refuse requests for intelligence, reports, and testimony. Such claims began with Vice President Cheney's early refusal to provide documentation to a congressional investigation of his Energy Task Force, continued through the conflicts in Afghanistan and Iraq, and quickened after the Democrats took control of Congress in 2007. The administration ignored House committee subpoenas for documents that supported Bush's preinvasion claim that Iraq had been attempting to buy uranium yellowcake. It dismissed congressional subpoenas for documents and White House staff testimony on the dismissal of justice department attorneys. Multiple congressional investigations into the leaking of CIA agent Valerie Plame's identity also encountered administration claims of executive privilege when trying to access reports on FBI interviews with White House staff. According to political scientist Mark Rozell, Bush administration assertions of executive privilege were "almost Nixonian in breadth...[at] the mere utterance of the phrase...no other branch has recourse".[49]

The administration also developed a "secrecy system". Through executive orders, it widened the application of classification and gave former presidents and vice presidents the power to bar release of their documents.[50] It tightened Freedom of Information Act regulations to make disclosures more difficult and more expensive. It also used the state-secrets privilege aggressively in the courts. Normally invoked to avoid disclosing specific information that might jeopardize national security, Bush cited this privilege to dismiss entire legal suits, including those challenging administration practices of rendition and domestic surveillance. Denied necessary information, the suits were dropped as it became impossible to judge the legality of administration conduct. This typified Bush's broadly successful record of protecting his administration from congressional and court scrutiny.

Much as Nixon had misrepresented U.S. operations in Cambodia, the Bush administration used false intelligence to misrepresent the activities of America's enemies and so justify military action, most obviously in its claim that Iraq possessed weapons of mass destruction. A 2008 Senate Intelligence Committee report established that the administration had been warned by the intelligence agencies of the unreliability of sources alleging that Saddam Hussein's regime had attempted to buy uranium yellowcake from Niger. It is also likely that aluminum tubes, intercepted before reaching Iraq and alleged by the administration to be integral to a nuclear weapons program, were intended for conventional weaponry. The 9/11-investigation commission contended that no credible evidence supported administration claims of collaboration between Al Qaeda and Saddam Hussein. Terrorism specialist Richard Clarke provided further proof of the administration's politicization of intelligence. He recounted that when FBI and CIA experts produced a report that did not confirm ties between Iraq and the September 11 terrorists, senior administration officials demanded a further draft to make the connection clear.[51]

The administration's selective use of information stretched beyond intelligence. It consistently understated the costs of the Iraq war, which was largely funded through supplemental appropriations rather than the more heavily scrutinized annual appropriations process. As a prescription drug benefit was debated in 2003, Medicare's chief administrator and Bush appointee Thomas Scully ordered chief actuary Richard Foster to suppress his estimates that the administration's plan would cost a third more than claimed.[52] Scientific experts had their reports edited by administration appointees and, according to Dr. James Hansen of the National Aeronautic and Space Administration(NASA), were discouraged from expressing policy views that did not correlate with administration positions. In essence, the administration treated intelligence and expertise as resources for manipulation rather than means to make informed policy choices.

The Overt and Covert Bush Revolution

Schlesinger's designation of the Imperial Presidency as a "revolution" represented the idea that Cold War presidents had subverted the Constitution by reallocating power within the federal government. Political scientist Joel Aberbach echoed this understanding pertaining to Bush:

> The history of the...administration should be seen as a concerted attack on the original model of the American political system, which was meant to produce a system of checks and balances, consultation, and bargaining that would protect against rash decisions and the ambitions and arbitrariness of rulers...[this government is] centralized, highly secretive, its clean direct lines of authority unencumbered by information or consultation and not much constrained by the existing law.[53]

Much of this revolutionary campaign was overt. Executive and legislative measures to bolster the presidency often attracted media, and sometimes public, attention. The covert elements of the Bush revolution may not be fully known, as yet, but they include black sites, illegal domestic surveillance, extraordinary rendition, torture, and misrepresentation of intelligence. Mainly due to the 'War on Terror' environment, few of these actions triggered Watergate-style criminal procedures against the Bush presidency. Instead, legal challenges focused on events tangential or unrelated to security concerns.

Investigations of the US attorney sackings noted that Attorney General Alberto Gonzales came perilously close to perjury through inaccurate and misleading statements in testimony. However, only the so-called "Plamegate" scandal resulted in a Bush-era conviction reminiscent of the Watergate era. In February 2002, former ambassador Joseph Wilson had visited Niger on a semiofficial mission for the CIA to investigate the claims of Iraqi efforts to buy uranium yellowcake. Wilson's findings largely dismissed the claims, a conclusion which he made public in June 2003 as it became clear that Iraq had not possessed weapons of mass destruction. To preserve its credibility, the White House needed to establish its ignorance of Wilson's visit, which various spokesmen scrambled to portray as a perk arranged by his wife, senior CIA operative Valerie Plame. In the process, at least four administration members leaked Plame's identity to the media in violation of the Intelligence Identities Protection Act of 1982. Administration efforts to cover up the leaking of Plame's identity produced a new cycle of lies to FBI investigators and a grand jury, notably on the part of Vice President Cheney's chief of staff, Lewis "Scooter" Libby. He was eventually convicted for obstruction of justice, perjury and related felonies, receiving a 30-month prison sentence. Bush commuted the sentence, saving the disgraced aide from jail without actually pardoning him. In words carrying echoes of Watergate, House Speaker Nancy Pelosi (D-CA) bluntly decried the president's action as a "betrayal of trust" in putting his administration above the law.[54]

The Causes of the Bush "Revolution"

Citing the Cold War, the Constitution, the president's growing economic powers, and the acquiescence of domestic political institutions as causes of the original imperial presidency, Schlesinger worried that these forces would sustain a post-Watergate manifestation. Each element is assessed below to ascertain its value in explaining Bush's imperial presidency.

The Cold War and The "War on Terror"

For Schlesinger, the prolonged Cold War underpinned the expansion of executive power, allowing temporary and exceptional assertions to harden into permanence. In Bush's case, it is hard to argue that the "War on Terror" generated steady accretions in presidential power. The Bush assertions, in contrast, came thick and fast after the September 11 attacks. Nevertheless, he based his claims of enhanced authority on a broad interpretation of the commander-in-chief power reminiscent of Nixon's Cold War imperial presidency. For Schlesinger, the latter's justifications for the invasion of Cambodia in 1970 equipped him with "so expansive a theory of the power of the Commander in Chief and so elastic a theory of defensive war that he could freely, on his own initiative, without reference to Congress, as a routine employment of unilateral executive authority, go to war against any country containing any troops that might in any conceivable circumstance be used in an attack on American forces."[55] Bush's doctrine of preemption had unambiguous parallels with this assertion, but his war against terror carried greater potency in committing to defense of America's homeland and people as well as its military forces.

The Constitution

Bush's imperial presidency signified that the Constitution endowed it, like the Cold War original, with the structural advantages in crisis times of unity, secrecy, stability of purpose, and dispatch. Less applicable to Bush, however, was Schlesinger's contention that the post-1933 president's power also grew out of his constitutional status as the only nationally elected official, which enabled him to become "the ever more potent symbol of national community"[56] in an era of party decline and electronic media development. The rise of partisanship since the 1980s is well recorded. While the traditional party system has not been reconstructed, party weakness is an unconvincing explanation of the imperial presidency's revitalization. Indeed, Bush benefited greatly from the revival of party discipline manifest in Republican support for his assertions.[57] Equally, scholarship suggests that the electronic media are less significant sources of presidential power than in the Nixon years. The golden age of presidential television appears over and even when presidents get coverage, their messages may fall on deaf ears.[58]

Economic and Budgetary Power

The trend towards a managed economy that Schlesinger perceived as enhancing presidential power was reversed in the 1980s and beyond. The deregulatory impulse reduced presidential capacity to micromanage the economy. The Federal Reserve chair replaced the president as the chief manager of prosperity with the emergence of monetary policy as the principal instrument of economic management. Even in fiscal policy, Congress reequipped itself to contest budgetary priorities with the presidency in the post-Watergate period through reforms of the budgetary committee process and establishment of the Congressional Budget Office.[59] Few allege that Bush practiced Nixon-style impoundment, even though his signing statements could sometimes have this effect.[60]

Initially, therefore, Schlesinger's economic case seems irrelevant to the Bush period. Nevertheless Bush did make substantial assertions of presidential fiscal-and-economic power that should be considered part of his new imperial presidency. His securing of funding for two wars is notable. His use of Congress' supplemental appropriations process to fund the Iraq war hid its true financial costs from proper scrutiny. Furthermore, Bush resisted congressional efforts to use the power of the purse to limit U.S. military involvement in Iraq. Instead, he engineered the surge, defying the Democrat-led 110th Congress and the antiwar mandate it appeared to have received from the 2006 elections.

In October 2008, Bush received an extraordinary grant of economic power in the form of the Troubled Assets Relief Program (TARP). Congress appropriated $700 billion to support executive actions to prevent a collapse of the banking system. This sum was remarkable, but so was the subsequent freedom the administration generated to allocate funds. Eleven days after Congress approved TARP, Bush and Treasury Secretary Henry Paulson announced program revisions. Two months later, Bush declared his authority to spend TARP money in any manner Secretary Paulson judged necessary to avoid economic collapse.[61] With the nation seemingly facing economic disaster, Congress deferred to this presidential claim of extraordinary spending power.

Congress

Schlesinger condemned congressional "chicken-heartedness" in response to Nixon's imperial assault. Facing Bush's assertions, Congress was certainly spectacularly tolerant, often facilitating presidential aggrandizement. The AUMFs of 2001 and 2003 bypassed the formal process for declaring war, allowing the president to make broad claims pertaining to his commander-in-chief powers. The USA Patriot Act of 2002 delegated new law-enforcement powers to the presidency. The Detainee Treatment Act of 2005 and Military Commissions Act of 2006 can be interpreted as retrospective approvals of presidential assertions. Congress rewrote the FISA, validating elements of previous administration behavior. Repeatedly, the presidency requested more power and the legislature obliged. Furthermore, until 2007, Congress operated a lax oversight regime and launched few investigations of alleged administration misconduct, thereby allowing executive assertions to pass unchecked.[62] In particular, Congress imposed remarkably few constraints on how funds appropriated for the Iraq war should be spent and expected scant reporting on their expenditure.

Parallels with overt aspects of the original imperial presidency appear clear. The key difference is that Bush marginalized his own congressional party. Nixon's transgressions can be portrayed as the conduct of an "opposition presidency" seeking executive enhancement to circumvent a liberal Democrat Congress.[63] In contrast, Bush's party was dominant in Congress for the first six years of his presidency, only losing control of the Senate for 18months after James Jeffords (R-VT) assumed independent status in mid-2001. Notwithstanding the resulting diminution of its authority, the GOP-led legislature usually supported Bush's imperial assertions, even when these contradicted libertarian and small-government beliefs. As Norman Ornstein commented, "[T]he Republican leaders in both houses of Congress made the decision that they were going to be field soldiers in the president's army, rather than members of an independent branch of government."[64]

In part, congressional Republicans' support for the administration reflected the broader phenomenon of greater party discipline that trumped their loyalty to Congress.[65] Amid intense partisan conflict, defending the administration's conduct, and therefore their own party label, was a matter of self-interest for GOP legislators. Bush's immense popularity after the 9/11 attacks made him an electoral asset worth defending. His intervention in the 2002 elections, effectively turning them into a referendum on his "war on terror" leadership, reinforced this impression as he helped his party to regain control of the Senate and expand its House majority. With limited incentives for the Republican majority to challenge Bush's assertions of enhanced authority, the imperial presidency thrived by partisan permission.

The Democrats' recapture of Congress in the 2006 elections seemed likely to produce a challenge to Bush's imperialism. What followed was an education in the contingent nature of executive power. In theory, Congress should have been able to force Bush to agree to a timetable for withdrawal from Iraq by using its power of the purse to dictate a specified date when funds would be cut off. Instead, there ensued a contest for public opinion in which GOP admonitions against leaving American troops under-resourced in the line of fire spiked Democratic threats to defund the war. Long wary of looking weak on national security and facing Bush's veto as a further obstacle, Democratic leaders did not carry through their plans. Instead, they granted the president's supplemental requests in return for fig-leaf concessions that made continued funding dependent on the Iraqi government meeting certain benchmarks pertaining to democratization.[66]

Consequently, the Democrats shifted focus to highlight Bush's abuses of power through the oversight process. Among their investigatory targets were the administration's initial case for the Iraq war, the detention and interrogation of alleged terrorists, the leaking of Valerie Plame's identity, and the justice department attorney sackings. As detailed above, these encountered the buffer of presidential claims of executive privilege. However, they did bring about the resignation of administration officials in some instances and more broadly enabled the Democrats to depict Bush as secretive and resistant to accountability. As such, their effect was to damage the Bush presidency and tarnish the Republican party as a whole.

This congressional reassertion hardly matched that following Nixon's downfall, but it did suggest that the institution was not helpless in the face of an imperial presidency. With suitable partisan and electoral incentives in place, the legislature could act. Nevertheless, the tendency to look to the presidency for leadership during crisis had not abated. The same Congress that tried to clip Bush's imperial wings also delegated extraordinary fiscal authority to him as the banking crisis unfolded.

The Press

Schlesinger's accusation that inadequate press vigilance contributed to the original imperial presidency found echoes in accounts of Bush's presidency. The media, including well-reputed outlets, were certainly deferential to presidential leadership and even appeared to promote administration messages in the aftermath of the 9/11 attacks.[67] As the Iraq war unfolded and weapons of mass destruction (WMD) remained undiscovered, however, the press questioned its own standards. Both the *New York Times* and *Washington Post* published *mea culpas* in 2004 detailing their failure to question administration WMD claims adequately.[68] Subsequently, the media appeared to compensate for its passivity as the administration's image of managerial competence floundered, courtesy of Hurricane Katrina and the insurgency in Iraq. Importantly, the now-critical press covered aspects of the imperial presidency: the torture scandal at Abu Ghraib, the domestic surveillance program, the US attorneys scandal, and the legal action against Scooter Libby were all subject to high profile investigatory reporting.

Despite this critical outburst, the administration continued to assert its authority, suggesting that media ability to constrain the White House was limited. Bush operated a "pressless presidency" based on the calculation that the national media no longer mattered to presidential success.[69] The administration treated the fourth estate as another interest to be managed,

rather than a check on its conduct. The tightly run White House communications operation concentrated on promoting its agenda, often through
new outlets in a media industry undergoing rapid transition. Fragmentation
of media audiences across technologies and producers allowed the administration to bypass criticism from the conventional press corps. Furthermore,
the rise of the conservative media provided means to rally the administration's party and ideological base and, to a degree, shape popular perception
of issues. Fox News, conservative talk radio, and an assertive conservative
presence online provided friendly audiences for the White House agenda.
Where Schlesinger considered the media monolithic, Bush confronted a far
more complex environment that offered scope to promote his agenda.

The Public

Schlesinger's argument that the American public, particularly the lower
middle-class, tolerated Cold War presidential assertions in return for promises of security appeared to find parallels in the "War on Terror". As one
analyst commented, "Americans who watched large jets fly into Manhattan
skyscrapers...need little convincing that this is their war, that the threat
is real and imminent, and that a vigorous response is essential." A public
recognizing the danger would, it was assumed, tolerate executive actions to
attack the enemy and ensure homeland security, but the reality was more
complex.[70]

Opinion surveys portrayed a public wary of imperial assertions, however. The majority of respondents (59 percent) in a 2006 CBS–*New York
Times* poll agreed that it was a "bad idea" that the president should "have
the authority to make changes in the rights usually guaranteed by the
Constitution...in the current campaign against terrorism."[71] The same
year, a *Newsweek* survey asked whether the "Bush-Cheney administration" had "gone too far in expanding presidential power." 57 percent of
respondents answered that it had.[72]

Polling data on some Bush actions are scarce, but public attitudes on
civil liberties issues were assessed extensively and reveal skepticism over
the administration's behavior. On whether or not it was preferable to violate basic civil liberties to prevent acts of terrorism in the United States,
a majority of respondents to the CNN–*USA Today*–Gallup survey chose
the latter option, and by unambiguously clear margins after June 2002.[73]
In 2005, 73 percent of those surveyed opposed any enhancement of federal
authority to read mail, e-mail, or tap phones without the knowledge of
those under surveillance. Substantial majorities also opposed allowing the
government to imprison U.S. citizens suspected of terrorism without putting them on trial for years, and allowing the government to collect phone
records from phone companies to establish databases on calling records.[74]
The polls indicated popular ambivalence on other issues. On wiretapping
suspicious phone conversations without a court order, numbers waxed and

waned over the year after the Bush surveillance program was exposed.[75] Using torture drew differing public responses depending on question phrasing: only 38 percent considered "torture" reasonable in pursuit of information about future terrorist attacks against the US, but 55 percent considered the use of "harsh interrogation techniques" justified.[76] Other actions drew unambiguous approval. Excepting a rare moment as Barack Obama won office, the public supported keeping Guantanamo open.[77] Americans also favored military tribunals over civilian courts as a venue for combatants' trials.

Instead of thoughtlessly accepting any White House assertion, the public mind captured in the polls was complex. Nonetheless, a majority of respondents to a Gallup survey thought the administration had not gone far enough or had been "about right" in restricting people's civil liberties in order to fight terrorism.[78] Significantly, as repeatedly demonstrated by Gallup's Most Important Problem surveys, issues pertaining to civil liberties and executive assertions had low salience for the public. Although the majority of Americans disagreed with, or were ambivalent concerning, certain policy specifics, their attention focused primarily on terrorism, the Iraq war, the economy, healthcare, and immigration. As such, the public could be said to have tolerated Bush's renewal of the imperial presidency.

Conclusion

Schlesinger demanded that Watergate be remembered as a warning of the presidency's potential to violate the Constitution. He saw it as the product of systemic pathology rather than individual aberration. The Bush presidency did much to validate this concern. The reemergence of the imperial presidency implied structural problems and casts Watergate within a recurring pattern of presidential assertion.

However, Schlesinger's diagnosis of that pathology applies only partially to Bush's imperial presidency. It manifests distinct differences from Nixon's version, most obviously the increased influence of party politics. Partisan incentives can, on occasion, assist or hinder presidential assertion in ways that Schlesinger did not describe. Party calculation replaced chicken-heartedness as a cause of congressional deference to executive power. The growth of partisanship in the media also warrants attention as it provides a platform for justifying executive assertion to the president's party and ideological bases.

Simply replacing Schlesinger's understanding with one based on the influence of congressional partisanship ignores a more complex picture, both in the conduct of the imperial presidency and scholarship on the subject. During the latter part of Bush's second term, Congress concurrently resisted his assertions and delegated substantial authority to him. Instead of broad-brush explanations that ignore political complexity, executive assertion is better considered, rather like policy, as a product of complex contests between interested players. Exemplifying this approach, William Howell and Jon Pevehouse emphasize the contingent nature of executive power in their work, which suggests that outcomes of contests over executive assertions are derived from a myriad of factors that shape participants' incentives and opportunities.[79]

Investigation of path dependency's contribution to understanding the imperial presidency is also required. Contrasting old and new imperial presidencies highlights differences in timescale: the gradual accretion of power highlighted by Schlesinger against Bush's all-but-instantaneous assertions. Arguably, previous assertions laid the groundwork for such rapid reassertions. Path dependency scholarship could be used to investigate how the actions and decisions of the Bush administration were shaped by actions and decisions taken by preceding administrations, including Nixon's. Certainly, a similar assumption underpins concern that legal precedents set in the Bush years could sustain later presidential imperialism. As James Pfiffner observes, "Executive claims to constitutional power ratchet upwards."[80] According to Gordon Silverstein, Republicans have campaigned consciously and over the long term to establish such a legal framework.[81] Legal foundations are only one element in such path dependencies. There is also a case for assessing institutional memory's role in presidential assertions, particularly through examination of Dick Cheney's executive-branch experience in the Nixon, Ford, and Bush 41 administrations. The very presence of the imperial presidency's history equips successors, potentially of either party, to make cases for imperial assertion by providing familiar narratives for use in Washington and to broader publics. One set of experiences shape those that follow.

Finally, while path dependency and proper accounting for the politics of executive assertion may help in understanding the imperial presidency, the role of events also demands attention. Though it is standard to assert that crisis engenders executive power, scholarship on the impact of specific events in shaping the nature of executive assertions is limited. The nature of the crisis explains idiosyncrasies of the assertions, such as the terrorist threat engendering Bush's policies on the holding of "combatants." Forms of imperial assertion almost certainly remain latent in the presidency, awaiting events that will trigger their realization. Accordingly, the next wave of presidential imperialism will likely have its own unique dimensions.

Notes

1. Examples include Andrew Rudalevige, *The New Imperial Presidency: Renewing Presidential Power after Watergate* (Ann Arbor: University of Michigan Press, 2005); Peter Irons, *War Powers: How the Imperial Presidency Hijacked the Constitution* (New York: Metropolitan Books, 2005); and Charlie Savage, *Takeover: The Return of the Imperial Presidency and the Subversion of American Democracy* (Boston: Little, Brown, 2007).

2. Arthur M. Schlesinger, Jr., *The Age of Jackson* (Boston: Little, Brown, 1945), *The Age of Roosevelt*, 3 vols. (Boston: Houghton Mifflin, 1957–1960), and *A Thousand Days: John F. Kennedy in the White House* (Boston: Houghton Mifflin, 1965). For autobiographical detail, see Arthur M. Schlesinger Jr., *A Life in the Twentieth Century: Innocent Beginnings, 1917–1950* (Boston: Houghton Mifflin, 2001), and *Journals: 1952–2000* (New York: Penguin, 2007). For insightful assessments, see John P. Diggins and Michael Lind, *The Liberal Persuasion: Arthur Schlesinger Jr. and the Challenge of the American Past* (Princeton: Princeton University Press, 1997); and Daniel Teller, "Arthur M. Schlesinger, Jr.," in Robert A. Rutland, *Clio's Favorites: Leading Historians of the United States, 1945–2000* (Columbus: University of Missouri Press, 2000), 156–169.

3. Arthur M. Schlesinger, Jr., *The Imperial Presidency* (Boston: Houghton Mifflin, 1973), ix.

4. Arthur M. Schlesinger, Jr., *The Bitter Heritage: Vietnam and American Democracy 1961–1968*, rev. ed. (Boston: Houghton Mifflin, 1968).

5. Andrew Rudalevige, "George W. Bush and the Imperial Presidency," in Mark J. Rozell and Gleaves Whitney, eds., *Testing the Limits: George W. Bush and the Imperial Presidency* (Lanham, MD: Rowman and Littlefield, 2009), 244.

6. Schlesinger, *The Imperial Presidency*, x.

7. Arthur M. Schlesinger, Jr., *War and the American Presidency* (New York: Norton, 2005), 45.

8. Schlesinger, *The Imperial Presidency*, 177–207.

9. Schlesinger, *The Imperial Presidency*, 256–257, 356–357.

10. Schlesinger, *The Imperial Presidency*, 235–240, 397–400.

11. Schlesinger, *The Imperial Presidency*, 240–245.

12. Schlesinger, *The Imperial Presidency*, 252.

13. Schlesinger, *The Imperial Presidency*, 219–223.

14. Hugh Heclo, "OMB and the Presidency—The Problem of Neutral Competence," *Public Interest* 38 (Winter 1975), 87.

15. Schlesinger, *The Imperial Presidency*, 246–252; quotation from 248.

16. Schlesinger, *The Imperial Presidency*, 227–232, 349.

17. Schlesinger, *The Imperial Presidency*, 227–231, 331–334, 346–347; quotation from 231.

18. Schlesinger, *The Imperial Presidency*, 7.

19. Schlesinger, *The Imperial Presidency*, x.

20. Schlesinger, *The Imperial Presidency*, 209–210.

21. Schlesinger, *The Imperial Presidency*, 209–210.

22. On this concept, see Theodore Lowi, *The Personal President: Power Invested, Promise Unfulfilled* (Ithaca, NY: Cornell University Press, 1986)

23. Schlesinger, *The Imperial Presidency*, 266.

24. Schlesinger, *The Imperial Presidency*, 258.

25. For similar critiques, see: James David Barber, *The Presidential Character: Predicting Performance in the White House,* (New York: Prentice Hall, 1972); Bruce Mazlish, *In Search of Nixon: A Psychohistorical Inquiry* (New York: Basic Books, 1972).

26. Schlesinger, *The Imperial Presidency*, 216.

27. Schlesinger, *The Imperial Presidency*, 256–263, 379.

28. Schlesinger, *The Imperial Presidency*, 377.

29. Mazlish, *In Search of Nixon*; Anthony Summers, *The Arrogance of Power: The Secret World of Richard Nixon* (New York: Viking, 2000).

30. Stanley Kutler, *The Wars of Watergate: The Last Crisis of Richard Nixon* (New York: Norton, 1990); Keith Olson, *Watergate: The Presidential Scandal That Shook America* (Lawrence: University Press of Kansas, 2003), 168–75.

31. Joan Hoff, *Nixon Reconsidered* (New York: Basic Books, 1994) 341.

32. Rudalevige, *The New Imperial Presidency* (quotation p. 212).

33. John C. Yoo, "The President's Constitutional Authority to Conduct Military Operations Against Terrorists and Nations Supporting Them: Memorandum Opinion for the Deputy Counsel to the President," September 25, 2001; http://www.justice.gov/olc/warpowers925.htm. See too the same author's "War Powers in the Bush Administration," and Louis Fisher, "Bush and the War Power: A Critique from the Outside," in Rozell and Whitney, *Testing the Limits*, 131–156, 157–175.

34. Joel Aberbach, "Supplying The Defect of Better Motives?: The Bush II Administration and the Constitutional System," in Colin Campbell, Bert Rockman, and Andrew Rudalevige, eds., *The George W. Bush Legacy* (Washington, DC: CQ Press, 2008), 121–122..

35. "Editorial: The Imperial Presidency 2.0," *New York Times*, January 7, 2007.

36. In May 1971 the administration organized the arrest of several thousand members of the People's Coalition, a radical antiwar group that was intent on shutting down Washington through a week of civil disobedience actions, and detained them in ways that violated their constitutional rights, for which it was later fined. See Melvin Small, *Johnson, Nixon, and the Doves* (Rutgers, NJ: Rutgers University Press, 1988), 217.

37. James P. Pfiffner, *Power Play: The Bush Presidency and the Constitution* (Washington, DC: Brookings Institution Press, 2008), chapter 5.

38. James P. Pfiffner, *Torture as Public Policy: Restoring U.S. Credibility on the World Stage* (Boulder, CO: Paradigm, 2010); Jay S. Bybee, "Memorandum for Alberto R. Gonzales, Re: Standards of Conduct for Interrogation under 18 U.S.C. §§ 2340–2340A," August 1, 2002; www.findlaw.com.

39. Richard P. Nathan, *The Plot That Failed: Nixon and the Administrative Presidency* (New York: Wiley, 1975).

40. Aberbach, "Supplying The Defect of Better Motives?," 118.

41. John C. Yoo, *The Powers of War and Peace* (Chicago: University of Chicago Press, 2005), vii; Christopher S. Yoo, Steven G. Calabresi, and Anthony J. Colangelo, "The Unitary Executive in the Modern Era: 1945–2004," *Iowa Law Review*, 90:2 (2005), 601–731.

42. Aberbach, "Supplying The Defect of Better Motives?," 116–120; Phillip J. Cooper, "George W. Bush, Edgar Allan Poe, and the Use and Abuse of the Presidential Signing Statements," *Presidential Studies Quarterly*, 35 (September 2005), 515–532; T.J. Halstead, "Presidential Signing Statements: Constitutional and Institutional Implications," Congressional Research Service Report RL33667, http://www.fas.org/sgp/crs/natsec/RL33667.pdf., September 17, 2007; Government Accountability Office, "Presidential Signing Statements Accompanying The Fiscal Year 2006 Appropriations Acts," June 18, 2007, http://www.gao.gov/decisions/appro/308603.pdf.

43. Joel D. Aberbach, "The Political Significance of the George W. Bush Administration," *Social Policy and Administration*, 39 (April 2005), 130–149.

44. Joel Brinkley, "Out of Spotlight, Bush Overhauls US Regulations," *New York Times*, August 14, 2004.
45. Curtis W. Copeland, "Statement to Subcommittee on Commercial and Administrative Law of the House Judiciary Committee, 2008," cited in House Committee on the Judiciary Majority Staff Report to Chairman John Conyers, Jr., *Reining in the Imperial Presidency: Lessons and Recommendations Relating to the Presidency of George W. Bush*, January 13, 2009, http://judiciary.house.gov/hearings.
46. Aberbach, "The Political Significance of the George W. Bush Administration," 142–143; Amy E. Black, *Of Little Faith: The Politics of George W. Bush's Faith-Based Initiatives* (Washington, DC: Georgetown University Press, 2004).
47. Kenneth R. Mayer, *With the Stroke of a Pen: Executive Orders and Presidential Power* (Oxford: Princeton University Press, 2002), 223.
48. Eric Lichtblau, "Prosecutor's 2006 Firings Won't Result In Charges," *New York Times*, July 21, 2010.
49. "Editorial: Power Without Limits," *New York Times*, July 22, 2007.
50. Rudalevige, *The New Imperial Presidency*, 239.
51. Interview with Richard A. Clarke, *60 Minutes* (CBS Television broadcast, March 21, 2004), www.cbsnews.com/stories.
52. For discussion of military and Medicare cost manipulations, see Iwan Morgan, *The Age of Deficits: Presidents and Unbalanced Budgets from Jimmy Carter to George W. Bush* (Lawrence: University Press of Kansas, 2009), chapter 7.
53. Aberbach, "Supplying The Defect of Better Motives?," 115 and 130.
54. Joe Wilson, "What I Didn't Find in Iraq," *New York Times*, July 6, 2003; Valerie Plame-Wilson, *Fair Game: My Life as a Spy, My Betrayal by the White House* (New York: Simon & Schuster, 2007). For brief review, see Clodagh Harrington, "The Ethical Record of the Bush Presidency," in Iwan Morgan and Philip Davies, eds., *Assessing George W. Bush's Legacy: The Right Man?* (New York: Palgrave, 2010), 110–13.
55. Schlesinger, *The Imperial Presidency*, 192.
56. Schlesinger, *The Imperial Presidency*, 210.
57. Gary C. Jacobson, *A Divider, Not a Uniter: George W. Bush and the American People* (London: Pearson Longman, 2006); Sarah A. Binder, "The Dynamics of Legislative Gridlock, 1947–96," *American Political Science Review*, 93 (September 1999), 519–533; John Owens, "American-Style Party Government: Delivering Bush's Agenda, Delivering Congress's Agenda," in Iwan Morgan and Philip Davies, eds., *Right On? Political Change and Continuity in George W. Bush's America* (London: Institute for the Study of the Americas, 2006), 131–160.
58. Matthew A. Baum and Samuel Kernell, "Has Cable Ended The Golden Age of Presidential Television?" *American Political Science Review*, 93 (March 1999), 99–114; George C. Edwards III, *On Deaf Ears: The Limits of the Bully Pulpit* (New Haven, CT: Yale University Press, 2003).
59. James L. Sundquist, *The Decline and Resurgence of Congress* (Washington, DC: Brooking Institution Press, 1981).
60. A Government Accountability Office review of 19 Fiscal 2006 appropriation measures found that six had not been fully implemented. See "Presidential Signing Statements Accompanying the Fiscal Year 2006 Appropriations Acts," June 18, 2007, hpp://www.gao.gov/decisions/appro/308603.pdf.

61. George W. Bush, "Remarks on the American Auto Industry," December 19, 2008, in John Woolley and Gerhard Peters, *The American Presidency Project* (Santa Barbara: University of California), www.presidency.uscb.edu.

62. See, in particular, John Owens, "Bush's Congressional Legacy and Congress's Bush Legacy," in Morgan and Davies, *Assessing George W. Bush's Legacy*, 51–78.

63. David A. Crockett, *The Opposition Presidency: Leadership and the Constraints of History* (College Station: Texas A&M University Press, 2002).

64. Jonathan Mahler, "After the Imperial Presidency," *New York Times*, November 9, 2008.

65. Thomas E. Mann and Norman J. Ornstein, *The Broken Branch: Why Congress Is Failing America and How To Get It Back On Track* (New York: Oxford University Press, 2006); Owens, "Bush's Congressional Legacy and Congress's Bush Legacy."

66. Jonathan Weisman, "Liberals Relent on Iraq War Spending," *Washington Post*, March 23, 2007; David Stout and Sheryl Gay Stolberg, "Citing 'Rigid' Deadline, Bush Vetoes Iraq Bill," *New York* Times, May 2, 2007; Morgan, *The Age of Deficits*, 240–244.

67. Susan D. Moeller, *Media Coverage of Weapons of Mass Destruction*, http://cissm.umd.edu/papers/display.php?id=32; Last Accessed, December 12, 2010.

68. "From The Editors: The Times and Iraq," *New York Times*, May 26, 2004; Howard Kurtz, "The *Post* on WMDs: An Inside Story," *Washington Post*, August 12, 2004.

69. Ryan Lizza, "The White House Doesn't Need The Press," *New York Times Magazine*, December 9, 2001; John Anthony Maltese, "Communication Strategies in the Bush White House," in Andrew Wroe and Jon Herbert, eds., *Assessing the George W. Bush Presidency* (Edinburgh: Edinburgh University Press, 2009), 216–238.

70. G. Calvin MacKenzie, "Old Wars, New Wars and the American Presidency," in George C. Edwards III and Philip John Davies, eds., *New Challenges for the American Presidency* (London: Pearson Longman, 2004), 208.

71. CBS/*New York Times* Poll, August 17–21, 2006; www.pollingreport.com.

72. Newsweek Poll, May 11–12, 2006; www.pollingreport.com.

73. CNN/USA Today/Gallup Poll, December 16–18, 2005 (and preceding); www.pollingreport.com.

74. Lydia Saad, "Americans Reject Extreme Anti-Privacy Security Measures," August 8, 2005, gallup.com; CNN/USA Today/Gallup Poll, Dec. 16–18, 2005; www.pollingreport.com.

75. Lydia Saad, "Public Opinion Mixed On Bush Anti-Terrorism Agenda," September 21, 2006, gallup.com; CBS News Polls, February 22–26 and May 16–17, 2006, both www.pollingreport.com; CBS Polls particularly revealed the suggestibility of the US public: two-thirds majorities consistently opposed the monitoring of "ordinary Americans" but monitoring of "Americans that the government is suspicious of" was approved by a similar proportion of the public. A narrow majority disapproved of wiretaps without warrants, but mention of terrorism in the question reversed the narrow margin.

76. Frank Newport, "Americans' Complex Take on the Interrogation Debate," April 27, 2009, www.gallup.com.

77. For example, CNN/USA Today/Gallup Poll, June 16–19, 2005, www.pollingreport.com.

78. Gallup Polls May 12–13, 2006 (and preceding), "Civil Liberties," www.gallup.com.
79. William G. Howell, *Power Without Persuasion: The Politics of Direct Presidential Action* (Princeton: Princeton University Press, 2003); William G. Howell and Jon G. Pevehouse, *While Dangers Gather: Congressional Check on Presidential War Powers* (Princeton: Princeton University Press, 2007).
80. Pfiffner, *Power Play*, 243.
81. Gordon Silverstein, "The Law: Bush, Cheney and The Separation of Powers: A Lasting Legacy?," *Presidential Studies Quarterly*, 39 (December 2009), 878–895.

Chapter Three

Watergate and the Decline of the Separation of Powers

Nancy Kassop

> The constitutional separation of powers...is a political as well as a legal principle.[1]

Whether by conscious intent or by the unpredictable unfolding of events in office, the Nixon administration bears heavy responsibility for affecting the operation of the twin principles of separation of powers and checks and balances in the succeeding decades, right up to the present time. Separation of powers and checks and balances function as two opposite sides of a coin: the concept of "separation of powers" refers to the allocation of constitutional authority to each of the three coordinate branches—executive, legislative, and judicial—and the manifestation of "checks and balances" occurs either by the shared authority of two branches for certain, designated constitutional functions (e.g., the legislative, appointment, impeachment, and amendment processes) or in the monitoring of the actions of each branch by one or both of the others (e.g., judicial review of legislative or executive actions, or, conversely, legislative or executive reactions to judicial decisions).

As the opening quotation aptly indicates, political factors play an equally determinative—and consequential—role as legal ones in the ultimate way in which these twin principles work. A primary legacy of the Nixon administration is the setting in motion of a more hostile, cynical, and contentious relationship among the three branches of government, making far more difficult and uncertain the interbranch accommodation so essential to James Madison's constitutional design and, thus, to effective governance.

The scope and sweep of the "fall-out" from the actions of one administration, as we reflect in hindsight almost 40 years later, are quite staggering, impacting the way we approach war powers, foreign intelligence activities, oversight of the executive branch by Congress (and investigation of high-level political misdeeds by special prosecutors), the pardon power, campaign finance regulations, budgeting authority, judicial appointments, access to presidential records, impeachment, the treaty power, and claims of executive privilege, all areas of constitutional interpretation that provided sources of political tension during the Nixon era, and whose lingering effects are still

evident today. Searing conflicts between the branches in each of these areas
took root under the Nixon presidency, and they resulted in dramatically
changed procedures for the future as well as an entrenched wariness among
all three governmental units, as each one now glances suspiciously towards
the others, effects that have lasted for the long-term and that have contributed to the intransigent political environment that bedevils us today.

To assert that there has been a "decline" in the separation of powers means
that the moderating, or oversight, functions to be performed by each branch
that Madison incorporated into his governmental system are no longer reliable. We cannot depend on Congress to "check" an aggressive president
who is determined to begin offensive military operations, even when public
support is weak or not forthcoming (i.e., Congress's open-ended authorization to President George W. Bush in October 2002 to invade Iraq at a time
of his choosing and under circumstances that he alone could determine);
nor can we rely upon the courts to operate with their traditional distance
from affecting the outcome of major political processes, in one case, the
most consequential decision a nation can make—the determination of the
winner of the presidential election (i.e., the 2000 Supreme Court decision in
Bush v. Gore). Neither can we rely on the executive branch to insure that
the federal courts are operating at full strength, when it is locked in partisan
combat with an opposition party in the Senate (when that opposition party
is *either* a majority *or* a minority) that is unwilling to allow floor votes on
judicial confirmations (e.g., in 1996 and in 2010–2011).

Can we blame President Nixon directly for all of these actions? Obviously
not, but the larger point here is that the seeds of the political environment
that made these outcomes possible were planted during the Nixon era by
the intensity of the polarized atmosphere among the branches and between
the political parties that emerged at that time, and that was, itself, the
product of an unprecedented perspective on the constitutional contours of
executive power. The longer-term effects are visible today in two ways: (1)
in the deep, stinging divide between the two political parties; and (2) in
the exceptionally aggressive and expansive interpretations of presidential
power advanced by President Nixon 40 years ago, dubbed memorably by
Arthur M. Schlesinger, Jr. as "the imperial presidency," that have, in large
part, been relied upon by succeeding presidents of both parties, with mini-
mal pushback from the public and the other branches.[2]

It is these two remarkable features—an excessively confrontational
political environment and an aggrandized presidency—that owe their origins to the Watergate era. They are the hallmarks of a "politics" and a
political process today that have traveled far from Madison's vision, where
each branch took seriously its good-faith obligation to oversee the actions
of the others, in order to maintain an approximate equilibrium of governmental power. Poisonous politics and an outsized presidency, in short, have
fueled the absence of reliable "checks" among the branches. Thus, the dual
concepts of separation of powers and checks and balances have both been
weakened in ways that have been costly to American political life.

In the Beginning...

The June 17, 1972, break-in into the Democratic National Committee(DNC) headquarters in the Watergate apartment-office complex in Washington, DC by five men, who acted at the direction of members of the president's staff, was the opening act for what would culminate just two years later in August 1974 in the first resignation in disgrace from office by a sitting president. The House of Representatives cranked up the presidential impeachment machinery in the summer of 1974 for the first time since its efforts in 1868 against President Andrew Johnson, who was impeached by the House but narrowly escaped conviction in the Senate by one vote. The catalyst that sparked the process against President Nixon towards its dizzying conclusion was the July 24, 1974, decision (8-0) by the Supreme Court that ordered him to turn over to the Watergate Special Prosecutor nine audiotapes of conversations between the president and his advisers that were recorded in the Oval Office in the days immediately following the Watergate burglary.[3] Within a week of the Court's decision, the House Judiciary Committee, on a largely party-line vote, approved three articles of impeachment against Nixon, charging him with obstruction of justice, abuse of power, and contempt of Congress for refusing to supply the House with subpoenaed information.

When public release of the audiotapes on August 5 revealed that the president had participated in a cover-up, support for him among fellow Republican Party members in Congress eroded quickly, to the point where senior party members informed him that he could expect to be impeached by the full House and convicted and removed from office by the Senate. Neither the full House nor the Senate ever had the chance to formally consider these impeachment charges, since, on August 8, 1974, President Nixon announced in a brief televised address from the White House that "I shall resign the presidency effective at noon tomorrow."[4] Vice President Gerald Ford was sworn in immediately, under the first use of the Twenty-Fifth Amendment provision that elevates a sitting vice president to the office of president, upon the removal, death, or resignation of the president. A peaceful transfer of power, under the most extraordinary of circumstances, was accomplished. Four weeks later, on September 8, 1974, President Ford announced a pardon of Richard Nixon "for all offenses against the United States which he...has committed, or may have committed, or taken part in during the period from January 20, 1969, through August 9, 1974."[5]

Features of American Government
Highlighted during the Watergate Period

This remarkable, cascading series of events and processes brought to the surface many key features of the American political system. First, a president and his staff were suspected of engaging in behavior that could be

both criminal as well as in contravention of constitutional norms, and triggered the need for an investigation into the facts and a determination of the
governmental processes that would be used to address an unprecedented
set of circumstances. Thus, Congress opened hearings to find the facts and
to decide how government should respond, and the Department of Justice,
through attorney general-designate Elliot Richardson, pledged to appoint
an independent prosecutor (since former justice department officials from
the Nixon administration had been implicated in the cover-up, and a prosecutor independent of the department was necessary to avoid a conflict of
interest) to evaluate whether laws were broken, and if criminal prosecution
of executive-branch officials close to the president was warranted.

These actions by Congress and the justice department resulted in the
use of the impeachment process and in the creation of the office of Special
Prosecutor with authority to investigate and subpoena *any* executive-
branch official, including the president. That exact scenario occurred
in October 1973 when Special Prosecutor Archibald Cox subpoenaed
President Nixon for evidence needed by the government in the criminal
conspiracy case against the cover-up defendants. Nixon's refusal to comply with the subpoena led to a showdown between the president and Cox,
culminating in the breathtaking "Saturday Night Massacre," during which
Nixon approached three justice department officials, in descending order
of seniority, demanding that each dismiss Cox. After Attorney General
Richardson and Deputy Attorney General Ruckelshaus refused to carry out
the president's order (and both promptly left office: Richardson resigned
because he was asked to compromise the assurance of independence for
the Special Prosecutor that he had promised Congress he would respect,
and Ruckelshaus was fired before he had a chance to resign), Robert Bork,
the Acting Solicitor General at the time, performed the deed, which then
led to a further refinement by Congress of the appointment and removal
processes for the office of the Special Prosecutor and the naming of Cox's
replacement, Leon Jaworski. Jaworski, then, picked up where Cox had left
off: further legal conflicts ensued between Jaworski and the president over
the demand for documents for use at trial, ending with the July 24 decision
of the Supreme Court that ordered the president to deliver nine subpoenaed
tapes of Oval Office conversations to Jaworski.[6]

In the wake of this unfolding drama, the political, legal, and constitutional issues began to mount: at a minimum, these included
(1) impeachment—questions about the process and about what constitutes
an "impeachable offense"; (2) special prosecutors—questions about when
they are needed, how they should be created, and what authority they
should possess; (3) executive privilege—under what circumstances may a
president invoke it, and what is the scope of its protection?; and (4) the pardon power—questions surrounding its use against a president *after* leaving
office and against whom no criminal charges were ever brought (Nixon
was never charged with a crime, but, rather, was labeled an "unindicted
co-conspirator" in the cover-up case).

It's déjà vu, All Over Again...

The answers to each of these questions laid the groundwork for the reappearance of *all* of them at some point over the succeeding 40 years. When the Republican Congress moved to impeach Bill Clinton in 1998, it referred back to the Nixon precedent for guidance as to the process. Use of special prosecutors continued under the independent counsel provisions of the Ethics in Government Act of 1978 (until Congress declined to renew it in 1999), which was, itself, a product of lengthy and complex debates in Congress over how best to provide for such an office in a way that would avoid the pitfalls from the Nixon era. The Supreme Court treatment of "executive privilege" in its 1974 *U.S. v. Nixon* decision remained relevant for successive presidents, as (a) President Reagan and his legal counsels determined whether to draw upon it when Iran-contra independent counsel Lawrence Walsh subpoenaed Reagan's diaries in the 1987 inquiry;[7] (b) President Clinton attempted unsuccessfully to assert a variety of privilege claims during the investigation of his personal relationship with Monica Lewinsky, including attorney-client privilege, government lawyer-client privilege, and Secret Service protective privilege;[8] and (c) Vice President Dick Cheney successfully invoked executive privilege in the suit brought against him by watchdog groups and the Comptroller-General seeking to learn the identity of private persons who met with him to influence energy policy in the George W. Bush administration.[9] The pardon power has been used by every president, although never again in a case where a president was the recipient, since there has not been a president after Nixon who was implicated in a criminal case (the Clinton legal battles were mostly civil, not criminal, cases, although one of the impeachment charges was for perjury before a grand jury).[10]

Thus, impeachment, investigation by special prosecutors, judicial interpretation of the scope of executive privilege, and the pardon power were all essential aspects of the Watergate episode, and all have had a continuing presence in American politics, shaped heavily by the role each played in that earlier era.

An Era Defined by Watergate and Vietnam

But, if these were the most immediate and most critical features that rose to prominence as the specific consequences of the Watergate scandal, they were not the only ones from that time that have left a continuing and deep resonance in the flow of politics that grew out of that formative and consequential period. The constitutional and legal issues arising out of the Watergate break-in dominated *domestic* politics in 1973–1974, but that scandal erupted on the heels of an already fiercely divided nation over the continuing, controversial military commitment in Vietnam that had dragged on by that time for ten years.

Although the official commitment of significant U.S. forces began under Lyndon Johnson, Nixon was elected in 1968, promising to have a "secret plan" to end the war. But, instead, worsening conditions on the ground in Southeast Asia, failure to achieve a negotiated settlement with north Vietnam, and a sustained, round-the-clock secret bombing campaign of north Vietnam in 1969, and the invasion of neutral Cambodia in April 1970 all contributed to even more heightened antiwar sentiment at home and explosive protests on college campuses throughout the late 1960s until the American pullout by President Ford in April 1975. In fact, Vietnam had become "Nixon's war," and, in the minds of his political opponents, it came to symbolize all that was wrong with him as a leader. Despite its authorization by Congress through passage of the Gulf of Tonkin Resolution in August 1964, the increasing unrest among and high visibility of the war's critics and the repeated, unsuccessful attempts by Congress to cut off funding for the war soon led many to conclude that this war was being carried on by a defiant president who had become isolated from public opinion, and was determined to continue the commitment of U.S. military forces against the waning support of Congress and growing public opposition.

By October and November 1973, Watergate and Vietnam had become intertwined, with the advent of twin political showdowns. October 20 was the date on which the memorable "Saturday Night Massacre" occurred, when Nixon ordered the firing of Special Prosecutor Archibald Cox, which prompted public outrage and the introduction of 22 bills in Congress to begin the impeachment process.[11] Then, just two weeks later, on November 7, both houses of Congress overrode Nixon's veto of the War Powers Resolution, enacting into law a proposal intended to insure that future presidents would include Congress in the process to both start as well as to *continue* military engagements.[12] The law was aimed directly at Nixon, as an official rebuke to his disregard for Congress as a constitutional partner in war-making. This law is one of many congressional enactments in the mid-1970s whose passage was fueled by the frustration and resentment of a Democratic Congress that watched as an opposition party president exceeded his constitutional authority across a wide range of policy areas. Congress defended itself by passing one law after another, dubbed collectively as "framework legislation" (because, rather than authorizing a specific policy, they provide, instead, an organizational structure, i.e., "framework," within which Congress and the president both carry out their respective constitutional duties in a variety of policy areas) that all, generally, had similar objectives of (1) reasserting congressional authority in policy areas where the president had excluded Congress, and of (2) reining in presidents by subjecting them to tighter congressional oversight through detailed procedures, such as reporting requirements or legislative vetoes, for exercising governmental decision-making.[13]

The statutes that fit this basic description within this mid-1970s timeframe read today like a bad dream: each one was prompted by presidential overreaching during the Nixon administration, with the hope of reversing and preventing such conduct in the future, and yet, almost every one of them has been thwarted, bypassed, or rendered impotent by later presidents: the Case-Zablocki Act of 1972 (regulating executive agreements); the War Powers Resolution of 1973 (imposing procedural restraints on a president's ability to commit military force); the Congressional Budget and Impoundment Control Act of 1974 (revising the budget process to provide a greater institutional role for Congress and imposing restrictions on a president's ability to impound, or refuse to spend, appropriated funds); the Hughes-Ryan Amendment to the Foreign Assistance Act of 1974 (requiring the president to report to Congress with an explicit "finding" that each covert operation is "important to the national security of the United States"); the Federal Election Campaign Act of 1974 (including, among other provisions, public funding for presidential campaigns as an effort to reduce the undue influence on candidates of large campaign contributions); the National Emergencies Act of 1976 (requiring presidents to declare formally the existence of a national emergency and to identify the specific statutory authority he intends to use, and providing continuing oversight by Congress); the International Emergencies Economic Powers Act of 1977 (imposing controls on executive discretion to declare national emergencies); the Presidential Records Act of 1978 (establishing for the first time that ownership and control of presidential and vice presidential records reside exclusively with the federal government, and outlining procedures for the administration of these official records); the Ethics in Government Act of 1978 (providing procedures and requirements for the appointment of independent counsels to investigate and prosecute designated executive-branch officials in circumstances when the Department of Justice has a real or apparent conflict of interest); and the Foreign Intelligence Surveillance Act of 1978 (providing procedures for requesting judicial authorization for electronic surveillance for foreign intelligence purposes).

Contemporary Vestiges of Watergate and Vietnam

Beyond the fact that Congress enacted this long list of statutes with the common objectives of restricting presidential discretion and of injecting procedures to insure congressional monitoring of presidential actions, perhaps the most defining and lasting characteristic of the Nixon era, and one that has wended its way up to the present day, is the political ill-will engendered by the entire period containing Watergate and Vietnam. That political mistrust and suspicion found its way into the relationship among the three branches of government: (a) scholars and commentators adopted Schlesinger's phrase of "the imperial presidency" as a succinct way to label the conduct of a chief executive who had attempted to gather exclusive and absolute power into his office, thereby, usurping the legitimate constitutional authority of the other branches; (b) Congress responded, as described above, with a series of legislative enactments, in efforts to "reclaim" power the president had taken from it (or, that Congress had, concededly, permitted to slip through its fingers) and to lay down new constraints on presidents, prompted by Nixon's overreaching actions; and (c) judicial decisions that left a legacy of interpretation by the federal courts of the scope of executive power, including *New York Times v. U.S.* (often referred to as the Pentagon Papers case), *U.S. v. Nixon*, and *Nixon v. Administrator of General Services*, to name only a few from that immediate era.[14] Later separation of powers cases, some of which addressed the constitutionality of the 1970s legislation, included decisions such as *Buckley v. Valeo* and *Morrison v. Olson.*[15] Additionally, there were many lower federal court decisions during the early 1970s, such as *Berk v. Laird*, *Orlando v. Laird*, *Mitchell v. Laird*, and *Holtzman v. Schlesinger*, contesting the president's authority to prosecute the Vietnam War,[16] and an even greater number of efforts (without any conclusive outcome), many during the 1980s, to determine the constitutionality of the War Powers Resolution, in such cases as *Crockett v. Reagan*, *Sanchez-Espinoza v. Reagan*, *Lowry v. Reagan*, and *Dellums v. Bush.*[17]

One other practice by Nixon that symbolized his disdain for Congress and that blossomed more fully under later presidents was his use of the signing statement to direct executive agencies to decline to enforce selected parts of a law: in effect, this amounted to the equivalent of a line-item veto, a power that presidents do not possess. Nixon engaged in this practice, for example, in 1969 when he directed the Department of Health, Education, and Welfare to decline to implement a portion of the Civil Rights Act of 1964 that required the denial of federal funding to colleges that had not desegregated, a position that was rejected by a lower federal court in *Adams v. Richardson*;[18] and in 1971 when he signed the Mansfield Amendment to the Military Procurement Authorization Act that asserted that current U.S. policy was to end the American involvement in Vietnam "at the earliest practicable date."[19] His signing statement declared that this language was "without binding force or effect" and that the enacted law "will not change the policies I have pursued and that I shall continue to pursue..."[20]

The political ill-will mentioned above as the overriding legacy of Watergate and Vietnam, insinuated itself into the interstices of all three branches during the 1970s, and it has not receded. The Nixon presidency set in place an arrogance on the part of the chief executive, that was then countered by efforts, largely unsuccessful, by Congress and the courts, to clip the president's constitutional overreaching. The election in 1980 of Ronald Reagan brought with it a fresh zeal to push back against these legislative and judicial restrictions: additionally, the ineffectiveness of these restraints or, alternatively, the recognition that some of the language in laws and judicial decisions that purported, at their inception, to restrain further presidential excesses, in fact, either legitimized such conduct or, at the very least, failed to fulfill their intended objectives (e.g., as in the War Powers Resolution, Hughes-Ryan Amendment, and the Federal Election Campaign Act). Other laws have been amended by later presidents to undo or undermine their initial purpose (e.g., FISA, amended in 2009, and Executive Order 13233 issued by George W. Bush in November 2001 that substantially weakened the Presidential Records Act although the Bush order was eventually overturned by a later executive order issued by Barack Obama in 2009), while the independent counsel provision of the Ethics in Government Act was completely eliminated through Congress's decision to decline to renew it in 1999.

The Reagan administration brought forth new tensions among the branches, but ones that were traceable back to the Nixon era. Once again, executive-branch officials took actions in violation of the law, justifying them as consistent with the president's policy preferences. National security advisor John Poindexter and Lieutenant Colonel Oliver North were initially convicted of conspiracy and other charges stemming from the Iran-contra scandal in 1985–1987 (although these charges were ultimately overturned on appeal, due to prior congressional grants of immunity), where Congress, in a series of enactments sponsored by Democratic member of Congress Edward Boland between 1982 and1986, had prohibited the use of funds by the CIA, the defense department, or any other "agency...involved in intelligence activities" to support the rebel contras in Nicaragua. Poindexter and North ignored these legislative restrictions, and carried out plans to sell arms to Iran and to secretly transfer the profits from these sales to the contras, as part of a covert operation that was later revealed to the American public in November 1986, when a foreign newspaper published the story.[21]

Other Reagan administration actions perpetuated some of the same interbranch dynamics that had grown out of the Nixon era. Reagan asserted, in similar fashion as Nixon, that the War Powers Resolution was an unconstitutional infringement on his powers as commander-in-chief, and he refused to comply with the law's requirements, stating in reports to Congress on his use of force in Lebanon, Chad, Libya, Grenada, and the Persian Gulf that he was reporting "consistent with the War Powers Resolution" but never "pursuant to it" (there was a singular exception in the Multinational Force in Lebanon Resolution in 1983, when Reagan and Congress agreed, under the War Powers Resolution, to an authorization for U.S. Marines to remain as a peacekeeping force in Lebanon for 18 months, although the troops were withdrawn prematurely after the suicide bombing of the Marines barracks there), language that has been used by every president since Nixon, indicating the continuing refusal of presidents to comply with its specific provisions.[22]

On the domestic side, Reagan expanded the use of signing statements, succeeding in 1986 in having them published in the *United States Code Congressional and Administrative News* (USSCAN) in its "Legislative History" section, thus providing him an authoritative context to claim that his interpretation of the meaning of a law ("executive intent") carried equal weight and status with the traditional "legislative intent" used by courts in statutory interpretation. He also used signing statements to decline to enforce parts of laws that he signed, provoking challenges in the courts that resulted in judicial rebukes to his administration (*Lear Siegler* and *Ameron*), but this practice has continued and has expanded exponentially through succeeding administrations of both parties up to the present.[23]

The Final Frontier in the Breakdown of Separation of Powers: The Judicial Appointment Process

There is one other area that seems to have absorbed the greatest concentration of ill-will between the branches from the past four decades. Controversy over Nixon's appointments to the Supreme Court and the lower federal courts may seem mild today, in comparison to later clashes, but his administration set the stage for what came later—and for what is, today, the most serious example of a separation of powers breakdown.

Nixon had the opportunity to fill four vacancies on the Supreme Court, although these came from a total of eight attempts. He entered office in January 1969 against the backdrop of former President Lyndon Johnson's failed effort in June 1968 to appoint Associate Justice Abe Fortas as a replacement for retiring Chief Justice Earl Warren. When the Senate refused to move the nomination of Fortas to a floor vote, Fortas asked the president to remove his name from nomination, and Warren, in return, remained on the Court until May 1969, when Nixon had his first shot at a Supreme Court appointment, which went to Warren Burger. Nixon had campaigned on a pledge to appoint "law and order" judges, those who would "strengthen the peace forces as against the criminal forces of the land," and who would be "strict constructionists" who would understand "their duty as interpreting law and not making law."[24] Some of these criteria have a familiar ring to them, as the debate over whether judges should interpret or make law has been an ongoing source of controversy for decades, and remains, still, the key question confronting every judicial nominee at Senate confirmation hearings. Warren Burger fulfilled these prerequisites, and his confirmation as chief justice was smooth and quick.

Immediately prior to Burger's successful appointment, Fortas resigned from the Court, amid reports of his association with a convicted financier that prompted questions about his judgment and integrity. This opportunity for a second Supreme Court appointment turned into a debacle, after the failed nominations of two southern U.S. Court of Appeals judges, Clement Haynsworth (for financial improprieties, as well as opposition expressed by labor and civil rights groups for some of his positions) and G. Harold Carswell (for overtly racist comments made two decades earlier, and, also, for the growing sense that he lacked sufficient judicial and legal expertise to serve on the nation's highest court, memorialized by Senator Roman Hruska's highly publicized comment about Carswell, that "Even if he is mediocre, there are a lot of mediocre people and judges and lawyers. They are entitled to a little representation, aren't they, and a little chance? We can't have all Brandeises, Cardozos and Frankfurters, and stuff like that there."[25]).

Nixon, then, backed off of his desire to appoint a Southerner, and, instead, turned to Harry Blackmun, a U.S. Court of Appeals judge from Minnesota, who was quickly confirmed by a 94-0 vote.[26]

Upon the retirements in September 1971 of both justices, Hugo Black and John Marshall Harlan II, Nixon was afforded yet two more chances to affect the direction of the Court. What followed was a series of "trial balloons," a list of six names of potential nominees sent to the ABA Committee on the Federal Judiciary for its ratings, of which the first two names on the list, Mildred Lillie and Herschel Friday, were the president's clearly intended choices. The ABA rating of "unqualified" and "not opposed," respectively, for these two, coupled with a plea to the president to "add some people with stature," doomed all six. Nixon followed this with the names of two new nominees whose legal credentials were far higher than the ill-fated six: Lewis Powell, Jr. of Virginia, and William Rehnquist of Arizona. Powell's nomination sailed through easily with an 89-1 Senate vote, but Rehnquist ran into considerably more opposition, especially, from the American Civil Liberties Union (ACLU), which opposed Rehnquist for many of his conservative positions on civil liberties and criminal rights issues as a Department of Justice official. He was eventually confirmed by a vote of 68-26, but not until after a weeklong debate and a filibuster on the Senate floor, led by Senator Birch Bayh (D-IN).[27] The injection into the judicial confirmation process of public opposition by interest groups (ACLU) and obstructionist tactics in the Senate (lengthy debate and a filibuster), though not unprecedented in 1971, nevertheless, was a hint of what was to emerge, full-blown, in the later, turbulent Supreme Court nominations of Robert Bork in 1987 and Clarence Thomas in 1991.

Scholars of the judicial confirmation process have posited conflicting theories as to why "the judicial appointments process has become needlessly acrimonious."[28] The "Big Bang" theory suggests that one event (most often, the Bork nomination is cited) so changed the existing norms of judicial appointment politics as to propel that process into a polarized, hyper-partisan climate that has continued to develop into its present state. The alternative theory, the "nothing new under the sun" perspective, suggests that ideological differences have always affected judicial appointment politics, as presidents view their opportunities to influence the direction of Court decisions as strategic behavior in which we should expect them to engage.[29] Yet, the "new normal" of judicial selection, including unprecedented Senate delays at both the committee and floor stages (and refusals to even bring opposition party nominees to the floor for a vote), filibusters and the 2005 Republican threat of a "nuclear option," has rendered the process so dysfunctional that it has infected lower federal court appointments just as much as those for the Supreme Court. It has also resulted in the negative, twin consequences of an unacceptably high number of judicial vacancies on the federal courts that has led, in turn, to the undesirable effect of undermining public confidence in the capacity of the courts to fulfill their institutional obligations.[30]

Conclusion

As if to confirm that the "imperial presidency" attributed to Richard Nixon has remained rather intact to the present day, presidential scholar Andrew Rudalevige wrote in 2005 that

> The Vietnam/Watergate era has shaped our current era in numerous tangible ways, both in reaction and counterreaction...the framework of presidential-congressional relations established in the wake of Watergate is critically important for understanding a wide range of current issues, from war powers to budgeting to government ethics to executive secrecy....[31]

In noting that the terrorist attacks of September 2001 had prompted government leaders to reconsider many of the issues that were prominent in the 1970s and had also appreciably raised the appeal to them of vigorous presidential leadership, he asked, in short, "Had the imperial presidency returned?"[32]

Perhaps, it never left—or, merely went "underground" temporarily, only to wait for an opportunity to rise to the surface again. Those "opportunities" can be personal, political, or even wholly external to the nation. Post-Nixon, Ronald Reagan emerged as a charismatic president, who refused to chafe under the restraints imposed by the 1970s laws and Court decisions that were reactions to an overzealous presidency. Arguably, he wriggled free of many of those restraints, and in a less confrontational but no less consequential way, presented to the public, once more, the reality of a president who asserted vigorous claims to the prerogatives of the office—from war powers to signing statements to annual pleas to Congress for a line-item veto as a budget-cutting tool to an admittedly concerted and unabashedly political approach for appointing judicial conservatives to the federal courts. In similar fashion, President George H.W. Bush continued many of these same actions,[33] as did President Bill Clinton (even though lower court decisions on executive privilege and a Supreme Court ruling on presidential immunity pared back his claims considerably on these specific counts). The latter's assertions of enhanced presidential power also demonstrated that presidential efforts to protect and expand prerogatives of the office need not be confined to one political party and, rather, can be based on institutional, not partisan, premises.

President George W. Bush may be credited with the fullest and most robust revival of an aggressive presidency, fueling the evocative titles of two popular books published midway through the 2000 decade, Rudalevige's *The New Imperial Presidency: Renewing Presidential Power After Watergate*, and Charlie Savage's *Takeover: The Return of the Imperial Presidency and the Subversion of American Democracy*.[34] No small notice should also be paid to the fact that his vice-president, Dick Cheney, cut his political teeth in the Nixon administration as an aide to Donald Rumsfeld in the Office of Economic Opportunity, and then, in the Ford administration as deputy chief of staff under Rumsfeld, followed by his ascension to that full position when Ford appointed Rumsfeld to Secretary of Defense. By 1979, Cheney was a freshman member of Congress from Wyoming, and throughout the 1980s, watched as Congress continued to tighten the noose against President Reagan's efforts to support the Nicaraguan contra rebels, a vantage point from which Cheney reinforced his own position that the mass of legislation from the post-Watergate Congress had encroached unconstitutionally on the president's powers. His leadership in overseeing the Minority Report of the Iran-contra investigating committee is testament to his belief in an all-powerful presidency in national security matters, a belief that he would have the opportunity to operationalize in the post-September 11 counterterrorism policies for which his office was largely responsible in developing.[35] The imperial presidency was, indeed, back—and with a vengeance. So, too, was the bitter institutional and partisan rancor that had its origins in the Nixon era, now, simply transposed 40 years later.

It was not surprising, then, that the 2008 presidential campaign propelled to prominence a candidate who promised to be a "post-partisan president," who pledged to dial back the excessive claims to executive power of the Bush administration and to respect Congress as an equal constitutional partner in the governing process. Whether such promises prove possible to attain, only history will tell.

Notes

1. Walter Dellinger, "The Constitutional Separation of Powers between the President and Congress," 20 Op. OLC ___, May 7, 1996. Available at: http://www.justice.gov/olc/delly.htm.
2. Arthur M. Schlesinger, Jr., *The Imperial Presidency* (New York: Houghton Mifflin, 1974).
3. *U.S. v. Nixon*, 418 U.S. 683 (1974).
4. John T. Woolley and Gerhard Peters, *The American Presidency Project* [online], (Santa Barbara, CA.) Available from World Wide Web: http://www.presidency.ucsb.edu/ws/?pid=4324.
5. Gerald Ford, "Proclamation 4311, Granting Pardon to Richard Nixon," *Public Papers of the Presidents*, 61: September 8, 1974, 103.
6. *U.S. v. Nixon*, 418 U.S. 683 (1974).

7. Lawrence E. Walsh, *Firewall: The Iran-Contra Conspiracy and Cover-Up* (New York: W.W. Norton, 1997), 227; Bob Woodward, *Shadow: Five Presidents and the Legacy of Watergate* (New York: Simon and Schuster, 1999), 132–135.

8. For a discussion of the efforts by Clinton to claim various privileges during the Lewinsky scandal, see Mark J. Rozell, *Executive Privilege: Presidential Power, Secrecy, and Accountability* (2nd edition, revised) (Lawrence, KS: University Press of Kansas, 2002), 140–144.

9. *Walker v. Cheney,* 230 F.Supp.2d 51 (D.D.C.2002); *Cheney v. U.S. District Court for the District of Columbia* , 542 U.S. 367 (2004) .

10. For a discussion of the presidential pardon power, generally, see Jeffrey Crouch, *The Presidential Pardon Power* (Lawrence, KS: University Press of Kansas, 2009).

11. Christopher H. Pyle and Richard M. Pious, *The President, Congress and the Constitution: Power and Legitimacy in American Politics* (New York: Free Press, 1984), 215–216.

12. Joint Resolution of Nov. 7, 1973, Public Law 93-148, 87 Stat. 555; Message from Richard Nixon to the House of Representatives, Oct. 24, 1973, 9 *Weekly Compilation of Presidential Documents* 1285 (1973).

13. For a discussion of framework statutes, see Harold Hongju Koh, *The National Security Constitution: Sharing Power after the Iran-Contra Affair* (New Haven: Yale University Press, 1990), 69–70.

14. *New York Times v. U.S.,* 403 U.S. 713 (1971); *U.S. v. Nixon,* 418 U.S. 683 (1974); *Nixon v. Administrator of General Services,* 433 U.S. 425 (1977).

15. *Buckley v. Valeo,* 424 U.S. 1 (1976); *Morrison v. Olson,* 487 U.S. 654 (1988).

16. *Berk v. Laird* , 429 F.2d. 302 (Calif. 2 1970); *Orlando v. Laird* , 443 F. 2d.1039 (2d Cir. 1971); *Mitchell v. Laird* , 488 F. 2d. 611 (D.C. Cir. 1973); and *Holtzman v. Schlesinger,* 484 F. Supp. 2d. 1307 (2nd Cir. 1973).

17. *Crockett v. Reagan,* 558 F. Supp. 893 (D.D.C. 1982); *Sanchez-Espinoza v. Reagan,* 770 F.2d 202 (D.C. Cir.1985); *Lowry v. Reagan,* 676 F. Supp. 333 (D.D.C. 1987); and *Dellums v. Bush,,* 752 F. Supp. 1141 (D.D.C. 1990).

18. *Adams v. Richardson* , 480 F. 2d. 1159 (1973).

19. 85 Stat 430, as described in Richard M. Pious, *The American Presidency* (New York: Basic Books, 1979), 402; and as described in Andrew Rudalevige, *The New Imperial Presidency: Renewing Presidential Power after Watergate* (Ann Arbor, MI: University of Michigan Press, 2005), 63.

20. "Statement on Signing the Military Appropriations Authorization Bill," *Weekly Compilation of Presidential Documents* 7 (November 22, 1971), 1531.

21. Lawrence E. Walsh, *Iran-Contra: The Final Report* (New York: Times Books of Random House, 1994).

22. See Nancy Kassop, "The Power to Make War," in Katy J. Harriger, ed., *Separation of Powers: Documents and Commentary* (Washington: CQ Press, 2003), 74–75.

23. *Lear Siegler v. Lehman,* 842 F. 2d 1102 (9th Cir. 1988); and *Ameron Inc. v. U.S.,* 787 F. 2d 875 (3rd Cir. 1986). For discussion of the history and the recent use of signing statements, see Christopher S. Kelley, "The Significance of the Presidential Signing Statement," in Christopher S. Kelley, ed., *Executing the Constitution: Putting the President Back into the Constitution* (Albany: SUNY Press, 2006), 73–89; James P. Pfiffner, "The Power to Ignore the Law: Signing Statements," in James P. Pfiffner, *Power Play: The Bush Presidency and the Constitution* (Washington, Brookings Institution Press, 2008),

194–228; and Charlie Savage, "Power of the Pen: Signing Statements," in Charlie Savage, *Takeover: The Return of the Imperial Presidency and the Subversion of American Democracy* (New York: Little Brown and Company, 2007), 228–249.

24. Henry J. Abraham, *Justices, Presidents and Senators: A History of U.S. Supreme Court Appointments from Washington to Clinton* (Lanham, MD: Rowman and Littlefield, 1999), 9, 253.

25. Abraham, *Justices, Presidents and Senators*, 11.

26. Abraham, *Justices, Presidents and Senators*, 13.

27. Abraham, *Justices, Presidents and Senators*, 269–270.

28. Comment made by Senate Republicans in 2009, as quoted in Sarah Binder and Forrest Maltzman, "Advice and Consent during the Bush Years: The Politics of Confirming Federal Judges," *Judicature*, vol. 92, No. 6, May-June 2009, 320.

29. Sarah Binder and Forrest Maltzman, *Judicature*, 321–322.

30. Sarah Binder and Forrest Maltzman, *Advice and Dissent: The Struggle to Shape the Federal Judiciary* (Washington, DC: Brookings Institution Press, 2009), 127.

31. Rudalevige, *The New Imperial Presidency*, 5.

32. Rudalevige, *The New Imperial Presidency*.

33. For an analysis of the hostility between the White House and Congress during the George H.W. Bush administration, see Charles Tiefer, *The Semi-Sovereign Presidency: The Bush Administration's Strategy for Governing Without Congress* (Boulder: Westview Press, 1994).

34. Rudalevige, *The New Imperial Presidency*; Savage, *Takeover*.

35. Shirley Anne Warshaw, *The Co-Presidency of Bush and Cheney* (Stanford, CA: Stanford University Press, 2009); Barton Gellman, *Angler: The Cheney Vice Presidency* (New York: Penguin Press, 2008); Jane Mayer, *The Dark Side: The Inside Story of How the War on Terror Turned into a War on American Ideals* (New York: Doubleday, 2008).

Chapter Four

Watergate and Scandal Politics: The Rise and Fall of the Special Prosecutor

Clodagh Harrington

The revelations of the Nixon White House's Watergate wrongdoings generated a national sense of mistrust of the ethical standards in America's government. Reacting to this, Congress approved the Ethics in Government Act of 1978 that codified ethical requirements for officeholders in all branches of government and institutionalized in its Title VI the office of special prosecutor to investigate alleged wrongdoing by executive-branch officials. During the debates over its enactment, the measure was widely touted as being necessary to prevent another Watergate. The confidence that it placed in the special prosecutor reflected the hero status that holders of that office had attained for their determined investigation of the misconduct of Nixon and his men. Their successors were expected to shore up the nation's faith in the continued integrity of the process for enforcing the law against the executive. As a Justice Department official acknowledged during the congressional hearings over the 1978 measure, "[I]n the shadow of Watergate,...the appearance of justice is almost as important as justice itself."[1] However, overuse, and sometimes misuse, of the machinery of investigation, combined with the nation's increasingly polarized political culture, brought cries of foul play against post-Watergate special prosecutors. Increasingly perceived as a partisan tool in scandal politics, the office lost the credibility it needed to function effectively.

This chapter examines the special prosecutor's emergence as a Watergate hero and the consequent decline of its reputation to the point that denial of reauthorization led to the office's final expiry in 1999. Its downfall resulted from enmeshment in the politics of scandal that was a legacy of Watergate. The search for wrongdoing in government became embedded into America's political culture as a result of the Nixon administration's misdeeds. Watergate became the prism through which later scandals were interpreted but the issues under investigation were never as clear-cut and unambiguous as in its case. In this more blurred context special prosecutors appeared to be constantly in search of a crime, large or small, without ever finding the smoking gun. As a consequence, the office created to make the political process more ethical in the wake of Watergate inadvertently helped to weaken the ethics in government process.

The Watergate Hero

"And whatever else I shall be, I shall be independent," Special Prosecutor Archibald Cox remarked at his initial Cambridge press conference in May 1973.[2] This was what the nation needed to hear at a time when confidence in America's constitutional democracy was at low ebb. The political circumstances in which Cox was appointed could hardly have been more dramatic. A presidential war in Southeast Asia had already eroded confidence in executive respect for the authority of other branches of government. Now Watergate indicated that the imperial presidency's threat to the constitutional polity had reached new heights. In the words of one analyst, "The presidency itself had become corrupt in the deepest sense."[3] In similar vein, Attorney General Elliot Richardson later remarked, "A government of laws was on the verge of becoming a government of one man."[4] Cox and his successor, Leon Jaworski, played important roles in averting this outcome, but their consequent status as Watergate heroes papered over some shortcomings that would arise in more serious form in later ethical investigations. Firstly, they focused more on the obstruction of justice issues than the abuse of powers that was arguably the more significant element of Watergate. Moreover, Cox became the subject of partisanship allegations that would dog later special prosecutors. In many regards, too, Cox and Jaworski benefited from Nixon's ill-judged counterattacks that tarred him as the villainous foil to their white knight, but later presidents would learn from his mistakes when facing their scandal investigations.

As the Watergate scandal gained momentum in early 1973, Nixon came under increasing pressure to appoint a special prosecutor to investigate executive wrongdoing rather than continue to entrust the task to the Justice Department, which amounted to executive-branch self-investigation. He had little option but to do so in response to the furor over his effective firing of top aides H. R. Haldeman, and John Ehrlichman, and Attorney General Richard Kleindienst on April 30, 1973, in a vain bid to save his presidency. Senate leaders indicated that confirmation of Elliot Richardson as the new attorney general would be conditional on his appointment of a special prosecutor. After being turned down by his preferred candidates, Richardson eventually found his man in Harvard law professor Archibald Cox. In an ironic inversion of history, Cox's great-grandfather, William Evarts, had successfully defended Andrew Johnson in the hitherto sole presidential impeachment trial in 1868. Understanding the symbolic as well as substantive importance of his post, Cox made his acceptance of it dependent on Richardson's agreement to guidelines that ensured his independence and authorized him to contest presidential claims of executive privilege as legitimacy for withholding information. "Somehow," he declared at his first press conference, "we must restore confidence, honor and integrity in government."[5]

Though not the first choice for the job and lacking recent prosecutorial experience, Cox's reputation as a rock-solid, trustworthy, objective, and professional individual preceded him. He had performed effectively as solicitor general in the administration of John F. Kennedy, for whom he had campaigned in 1960, and was now a highly respected scholar specializing in labor law and constitutional law. Although he had reservations about his qualifications to be special prosecutor, an ingrained sense of duty overcame these. As he later remarked, "Somebody clearly had to do it. It is important that everything possible be done to show that a fair enquiry into wrongdoing at the very highest level of government can be conducted under our system."[6] That old-fashioned sense of being called by the nation was a recurring theme with later special prosecutors, but never to the same popular effect because they were continually judged on the basis of the Watergate metaphor.

From the outset Cox recognized that he had both a legal and a political role that were potentially contradictory. Prosecutors were not supposed to go public until they presented an indictment in a court of law. In contrast to Richardson, who was confident of White House cooperation with his investigation, Cox anticipated that Nixon would invoke executive privilege to hinder it. To combat this, the special prosecutor needed to mobilize popular support, a difficult task if he operated in secrecy. As an aide later commented, "The essence of the crime was cover-up, and it would be important to establish early with the press and public that Cox was not part of the cover-up."[7] Accordingly Cox had persuaded Richardson to include in the guidelines for his post the authority to make periodic public reports on his investigation.

Getting the media on his side was critical in Cox's battle for public opinion. However, its response to his appointment was initially mixed out of concern not only whether an Ivy League academic could operate in the Washington political environment of "knives and blackjacks" but also because he had a reputation for arrogance.[8] Recognizing that he needed media-savvy help to court the press, Cox persuaded *Washington Star* correspondent James Doyle to accept appointment as his spokesman. This gambit was so successful that reporters were soon commenting on Cox's moral courage for his persistence in trying to secure release of the White House tapes, whose existence was revealed in congressional testimony by presidential aide Alexander Butterfield on July 16.[9]

The battle over the tapes became the central element in the Watergate drama, with Cox in the starring role. On July 23, the president rejected his initial request for release of relevant tapes. One of Nixon's lawyers informed Cox he had "absolute power to decide what may be disclosed" and, more importantly, was the special prosecutor's superior. Responding to Judge John Sirica's subpoena in support of Cox's request for release of nine specific tapes, Nixon maintained that "the president is not subject to compulsory process from the courts."[10] Such assertions of presidential supremacy challenged the legitimacy and independence of the special prosecutor. In holding his ground, however, Cox was also aware of the danger of a constitutional crisis if he pushed the president too far. Compliance, the notion that a powerful executive official should acquiesce to judicial decree, was a fragile principle.[11]

Cox took comfort in the belief that the legislature stood ready to impeach the president for withholding the Watergate tapes. He had the advantage of being independent of, but supported by, Congress (unlike the Iran Contra special prosecutor). Another factor in his favor, also in contrast to Ethics in Government Act successors, was that having been appointed by Elliot Richardson, he retained the attorney general's backing throughout the crisis. Thanks to the broad support of the media, public reaction against Nixon's refusal to release the tapes also lent credence to Cox's position.[12]

The president's resistance partly reflected the conviction that his Kennedy-connected adversary was engaged in a partisan witch-hunt. He later complained, "No White House in history could have survived the kind of operation Cox was planning." Without doubt Cox did proceed in a manner that appeared oblivious, some might say defiant, to concerns over his impartiality. Not only did East Coast liberals make up most of the Watergate Special Prosecutor's Force (WSPF) staff but also seven of its 11 senior appointees had worked for a Kennedy.[13] To make things worse, the White House became concerned that the Soviet Union's threat of intervention in the renewed war of October 1973 between Israel and its Arab enemies reflected its conviction that Nixon was hamstrung by the Watergate investigation.[14] Matters came to a head when Cox rejected a White House compromise to provide written summaries of the nine tapes under subpoena and have their accuracy verified by Senator John Stennis (D-MS), and refused to desist from further attempts to secure presidential materials through the courts.

On October 20, 1973, Nixon ordered Elliot Richardson to fire Cox but he resigned office rather than do so, as did Deputy Attorney General William Ruckelshaus. Solicitor General Robert Bork finally carried out the president's instruction. With his attention on the Middle East, Nixon reportedly told Richardson that the Kremlin "would never understand if I let Cox defy my instructions."[15] More seriously, however, the American people did not understand or agree with his decision. The ensuing firestorm of protest over what became known as the Saturday Night Massacre prevented Nixon from achieving his avowed goal of abolishing the WSPF. His later claim of only wanting to get rid of Cox rather than the office was unconvincing. After the firing, White House chief of staff Alexander Haig had immediately ordered the Federal Bureau of Investigation (FBI) to seal off the WSPF premises. Televised images of it doing so shocked the nation, prompting comparisons to the Reichstag fire that was instrumental in Adolph Hitler's rise to power in Germany in 1933. Explaining his decision later, Haig remarked, "You would turn the country into a banana republic if you allowed defiance of the President." Three days later Robert Bork signed an order abolishing the WSPF effective from October 21 and incorporating its functions into the Justice Department. These actions signified clear intent to give the president greater control over the Watergate investigation.[16]

The firing of Cox was in many ways the last gasp of Nixon's imperial presidency. In his memoirs, Nixon admitted that it had been a "serious miscalculation" because he was unaware until the "hysterical reaction" just how deeply Watergate's "acid had eaten into the national grain." The president's self-serving words ignored the strong foundations of public anger. His Gallup approval rating plummeted to 17 percent; 450,000 telegrams of protest, the largest traffic in Western Union's history, deluged the White House and Congress. The expression of popular outrage did much to convince Congress of the need for legislation to institutionalize the special prosecutor and endow the office with guaranteed statutory independence.[17]

Cox's sacking by Nixon confirmed their respective status as Watergate hero and villain in the eyes of the public. Criticisms of the special prosecutor's judgmentalism, partisanship, and inflexibility in dealing with Nixon, some of them valid, vanished from orthodox memory of the scandal. In the words of colleague Phil Heymann, "Something amazing happened to Archie's life. He became a permanent American hero."[18] The vast majority of his countrymen may not have been able to explain the finer details of Watergate but they regarded Archibald Cox as embodying the forces worth fighting for—the truth, the presidency, and the Constitution. Obituaries on his death in 2004 testified to the enduring historical image that "his reputation for integrity and fairness led him to play a pivotal role in one of the most turbulent episodes in the nation's history."[19] Nixon himself could take much of the credit for the saintly anointment of his adversary. The Saturday Night Massacre validated Cox's consequent warning that the question now at stake was "whether we shall continue to be a government of laws and not of men."[20] The physical appearances of the two adversaries reinforced their popular imagery. Nixon had the misfortune to look like a crook and liar, while the crew-cutted and ramrod straight Cox with his trademark bow tie seemed representative of the nation's better self. Such clearly defined images, with right and wrong easily distinguishable, were not characteristic of later investigations, so it was impossible for Cox's successors to live up to his reputation.

Backpedaling in the face of national anger, Nixon authorized the reestablishment of the WSPF, which was formally done on November 2. Leon Jaworski, who had turned down Richardson's offer of appointment in May, now agreed to succeed Cox in what was still an ad hoc post. It would take years to enact formal guarantees of special prosecutor independence, but the White House succumbed to demands for new safeguards that all but ensured this for Jaworski, who could only be dismissed for "extraordinary impropriety."[21]

Infuriated by the appointment of the liberal Cox, Nixon was hopeful that the new man would prove more accommodating, but Jaworski proved just as troublesome and was less vulnerable to presidential retribution. A conservative Democrat who had chaired the Texas Democrats for Nixon in 1972, he could not be attacked for partisan bias. Moreover, he had long prosecutorial experience dating back to his involvement in the Nuremberg war-crime trials of Nazi leaders and was widely respected in the legal community as a former head of the American Bar Association.[22] The Texan's memoirs show a man very slow to believe the worst of his president and yet increasingly dogged in his pursuit of the truth. Jaworski's description of how he felt after listening to segments of the subpoenaed presidential tapes testified that cynicism about officeholders had not reached its later levels. "My heart," he said, "was shriveling inside me."[23]

Jaworski's integrity and courage were apparent in his willingness to go beyond other investigatory actors in pursuit of Watergate wrongdoers. Effectively secure from the sack and facing a president very much on the defensive, he could afford to be more assertive and confrontational than Cox. Bringing his case before a Washington grand jury, he secured indictments in March 1974 against former Nixon aides H. R. Haldeman, John Ehrlichman, and Charles Colson, and former Attorney General John Mitchell for their participation in the Watergate cover-up. Though kept secret at the time, this body had also named the president as unindicted coconspirator.[24] However, Jaworski did not allow Nixon to remain outside his dragnet for long because he needed the White House tapes for the trials resulting from the grand jury indictments.

With the president's lawyers attempting to stall him in the Court of Appeals, the special prosecutor asked the Supreme Court to bypass this lower court and adjudge the case in an "imperative public importance" brief. It agreed to do so for only the third time since 1945, hearing arguments in *United States of America v. Richard Nixon* on July 8. Nixon's lawyers claimed that executive privilege and the separation of the powers afforded the president absolute immunity from disclosure. In response, Jaworski contended that the public interest outweighed such vague claims of privilege, particularly as a conspirator made them. On July 24, the Court handed down its verdict by a margin of 8-0 upholding the principle of executive privilege but ruling that it did not apply in this case. Explaining why the tapes had to be released, it declared, "[T]he generalized interest in confidentiality...cannot prevail over the fundamental demands of the due process of law in the fair administration of criminal justice."[25]

The sweeping majority judgment made it impossible for Nixon to refuse to hand over the subpoenaed tapes. The smoking gun evidence of his involvement in the cover up on the June 23, 1972, recording, in particular, sealed his guilt. The House Judiciary Committee approved three articles of impeachment even before the White House released the tape transcripts on August 5. With the whole House now certain to support these and seeing no way to escape a guilty verdict in the Senate, Nixon resigned on August 9, 1974. Ford's pardon on September 8 denied Jaworski the opportunity to indict the former president for his criminal activities. Some of his staff wanted him to challenge the pardon in the courts in order to bring Nixon into the dock, but he doubted that a fair trial would have been possible because of all the publicity that the president's activities had already received.[26]

Believing his job fundamentally done, Jaworski resigned office on October 25. His departure left the WSPF to continue under the leadership of Henry Ruth and later Charles Ruff, until it finally ceased to exist in 1976. Editorial comment generally supported his decision to leave because he was widely credited as the man who had nailed Nixon's guilt, but there were some dissenting voices that his job was not yet finished, notably that of the *New York Times*.[27] This criticism was ironic in view of the seemingly unending nature of later investigations that lasted for years and incurred huge costs. The estimated bill for the WSPF's investigation of the Nixon White House was a relatively paltry $3 million. In contrast, Independent Counsel Lawrence Walsh's almost seven-year investigation of the Reagan administration officials over Iran-contra totaled nearly $48 million.[28]

The importance of Watergate as a political scandal was about more than its dramatic significance. It also illustrated how such scandals are created and maintained. In particular, it highlighted the multifaceted aspects of American scandals, as later illustrated by the Iran Contra and Whitewater/Lewinsky affairs. Emphasis moved from media reports to FBI investigations, court hearings to special prosecutors to congressional committees, and back again. Such variety of input meant that those involved in the scandal had to react with a multipronged approach, making a defense strategy more challenging.[29]

Experienced overwhelmingly by most Americans through television, Watergate sometimes appeared to be more entertainment than reality, but popular interest in its investigation was huge. At a time when there few television outlets, huge audiences daily tuned into the televised Senate hearings in the summer of 1973 and the House Judiciary Committee impeachment hearings in July 1974. When the White House tapes were released, 19 metropolitan newspapers printed the 1,300 pages of transcript as a supplement and within a week, three million copies of the transcript had been put into print.[30]

Understanding that newspaper and television journalists were critical in shaping the public perception of Watergate, Cox and Jaworski assiduously cultivated their support.[31] The media's presentation of them as heroic figures battling for justice against presidential criminality underwrote the capacity of their new office to stand up to the White House. The contrast with its negative portrayal of Nixon and his men provided the public with a strong but simple image of right and wrong. The fact that Cox received numerous anonymous death threats only strengthened his position as moral crusader pursuing justice in the face of adversity. However, the hero status of the Watergate special prosecutors bred unrealistic expectations about the office that could not be sustained in later scandals. In setting an impossible standard to follow, Cox and Jaworski were instrumental in making Watergate the misleading metaphor for understanding the fundamentally different scandals that were to beset American politics in the remaining years of the twentieth century.

Title VI of the Ethics in Government Act 1978

According to Elliot Richardson, the Ethics in Government Act would have been better named the No Ethics in Government Act as it was created on the assumption that no-one in government could be trusted. Congress institutionalized the Special Prosecutor in Title VI of the legislation to investigate wrongdoing by executive officials in the Watergate-inspired belief that only this office could inspire popular confidence that justice would not be politicized. As Deputy Independent Counsel Cary Feldman later remarked, however, once created as a permanent entity, there was almost a need to keep it busy in order to justify its existence. The lack of a public integrity renaissance in Watergate's aftermath ensured that the office would not be idle. Scandal politics provided a new avenue for partisan competition. Often the party controlling Congress would seek advantage through revelation, investigation, and prosecution of perceived wrongdoing, large and small, within an executive branch controlled by the opposition party. In these circumstances, the problems associated with Title VI of the 1978 ethics legislation soon became apparent.[32]

Special prosecutor procedures were initiated a total of 11 times between 1978 and 1982, but in only three cases was one appointed—and even these were trivial in comparison to Watergate. Allegations of cocaine use by two of President Jimmy Carter's aides—Hamilton Jordan and Tim Kraft, resulted in investigations of each. No indictments were made in either case but the negative publicity caused damage to the individuals involved and the administration. Using procedures almost identical to those for Watergate in such cases, which a regular U.S. attorney would likely have ignored, lessened the credibility of the special prosecutor. Urging its limited use only in "special cases" in the wake of the Jordan investigation, the *Washington Star* asserted that an office intended to "slay the dragons of official corruption" was instead being used as "the heaviest of hammers on every gnat of petty rumor."[33] Tim Kraft's lawyers brought a civil suit against Special Prosecutor Gerald Gallinghouse for "exercising executive power in violation of the Constitution of the United States." Gallinghouse found the allegation against Kraft "so unsubstantiated that it did not warrant further investigation" before the counter case went to court. Nevertheless, it was an early indication that the special prosecutor was evolving from David to Goliath in the eyes of some.[34]

Disenchantment with the Ethics in Government Act was evident when Congress began considering its reauthorization in 1981. Ronald Reagan initially opposed renewal based on constitutional and cost objections pertaining to the special prosecutor but relented in recognition that the office ensured the appearance of justice. The measure was eventually reauthorized in 1983 after lengthy wrangling over amendments. These included renaming the special prosecutor as the independent counsel, a more neutral title; allowing the attorney general greater discretion in the decision to name a counsel and to dismiss the officeholder for "good cause;" and provision for reimbursement of attorney fees for investigation subjects who were not indicted.[35]

When another reauthorization debate ensued in 1987, the Reagan administration opposed Title VI renewal more strongly than before, citing its possible unconstitutionality and assailing injustice to those falsely accused under its implementation. However, the pending Iran-contra investigations and separate conflict-of-interest ones of three Reagan aides (the Michael Deaver case produced the first conviction under the Ethics Act) strengthened resistance to change. In these circumstances, supporters of the measure played on memories of Nixon's misdemeanors. They were aided by the Justice Department's insensitivity in reiterating its view that all prosecutors should be responsible to the president on the fifteenth anniversary of the Watergate break-in. The Reagan administration, charged Senator Carl Levin (D-MI), "would have us return to the days of Watergate and Nixon's 'Saturday Night Massacre' when public trust in our criminal system hung in the balance. We don't want to go to the brink again."[36] Popular support for the appointment of an independent counsel to investigate the Iran-contra affair was further cited as proof of need for the measure, which was approved by veto-proof margins and signed by Reagan on December 15, 1987.

Unwilling to accept defeat meekly, the White House supported a constitutional challenge to the office of independent counsel by those presently under investigation. It received support from former Nixon aides who damned the "orgy of investigation." At issue was the power of the executive branch to conduct all criminal investigations. In January 1988, the Court of Appeals invalidated the independent counsel provision as an intrusion on executive authority. However, a relatively conservative Supreme Court thought differently in overturning this verdict by a vote of 7-1 in its *Morrison v. Olson* judgment. For the majority, Reagan-nominated Chief Justice William Rehnquist (initially a Nixon nominee as associate justice) found neither violation of the separation of powers nor congressional usurpation of executive functions in the Ethics Act.[37] The judicial assault on the independent counsel ultimately got nowhere but the political tide would soon turn against it.

Lawrence Walsh and the Iran Contra Affair

Iran-contra occasioned the first really lengthy, expensive, and highly political investigation by the independent counsel. It involved secret foreign policy initiatives by the executive in violation of congressional statute. As part of the Reagan Doctrine strategy of rolling back communism in the third world, the president had authorized covert support for the Contra rebels battling Nicaragua's leftist Sandinista government in late 1981. Having initially funded this venture, Congress placed strict limits against provision of aid intended to overthrow the Nicaraguan government in the Boland Amendment of 1982. Revelations that the Reagan administration was exploiting loopholes in this led to enactment of another Boland Amendment in 1984 prohibiting all U.S. government support for military operations in Nicaragua. To circumvent this, the White House embarked on a complex scheme entailing multiple illegality. In direct violation of the Arms Export Control Act of 1976, Reagan authorized secret weapons sales to Iran in 1985–1986, initially via Israel, in the hope of securing the release of American hostages taken by Iran-backed groups in Lebanon. In parallel with this, some National Security Council (NSC) aides concocted a plan to divert the funds acquired through this enterprise, supplemented by money raised from wealthy conservative Americans and foreigners, to assist the Nicaraguan Contras.[38]

Like Watergate, Iran-contra entailed abuse of power and cover-up of illegal actions, but it remained unclear just how far this was the work of executive officials operating without presidential authorization and knowledge. The furor, when the shroud of secrecy slipped off the project in late 1986, persuaded the White House to appoint a Special Review Board, headed by former Texas Republican senator John Tower, to investigate the NSC staff implicated in the wrongdoing. This was a deliberate effort to preempt an independent counsel investigation. However, the Tower Commission could not compel anyone to appear before it, so the report it released in February 1987 was necessarily incomplete. Accordingly, the Justice Department had little option but to institute independent counsel proceedings. On December19, 1986, a three-judge panel named Lawrence Walsh to the post.[39]

A former district court judge, diplomat, deputy attorney general, and president of the American Bar Association, Walsh seemed an ideal choice as an experienced and well respected jurist. A moderate Republican, he had no political ax to grind against the president. He saw his task as being to uncover violations of the law and, if applicable, to bring to justice the individuals who had committed them. In his opinion, it was the job of the new Senate Select Committee, created to emulate its Watergate predecessor, to provide a full account of the Iran-contra affair.[40]

Iran-contra represented the most significant violation of the constitutional polity since Watergate, but reaction was more muted. Perhaps this was because the shock factor of executive-branch wrongdoing was inevitably less the second time round. It also reflected the efforts of the Reagan administration to avoid becoming enmeshed in another Watergate, which helped to stop the 'gate' suffix becoming part of the terminology of its scandal. Watergate was the metaphor for understanding Iran-contra but in a way that did not disadvantage the White House. The absence of Watergate-style whistle-blowers, the sense that foreign policy interests rather than lust for power was the mainspring of the scandal, and the lack of smoking gun evidence comparable to the Nixon tapes, all helped to obfuscate the seriousness of executive wrongdoing in Iran-contra. Even though his innocence was never absolutely established and his defense relied on effective admission that he was not in control of his White House, there was never a moment when Reagan appeared in real danger of impeachment. As Michael Schudson remarked, the Watergate precedent may well have saved Reagan because what was at stake in Iran-contra rapidly narrowed to whether he had direct knowledge of specific criminal activity, thereby shrouding the broader constitutional violations that it entailed.[41] Walsh himself later told Bob Woodward, "I never had the feeling that he was going to go down."[42]

Instead, of Walsh's investigation dragging down the president, its interminable length, huge cost, and seemingly limited success gave new impetus to criticisms of his office. Paradoxically the independent counselor's hooking of a big fish only earned him accusations of partisan bias rather than plaudits when he reindicted Reagan's Secretary of Defense, Caspar Weinberger, for obstruction of justice just before the 1992 presidential election in which fellow Republican George H. W. Bush was fighting for his political life. Nevertheless, the Watergate metaphor also came to Walsh's rescue in one sense. Bush and Attorney General William Barr were tempted to fire him after the Weinberger reindictment but desisted for fear of generating a public furor comparable to that provoked by Archibald Cox's dismissal.[43]

Notwithstanding the reality that Iran-contra did not become another Watergate, there was a highly significant parallel between them in the evident inadequacy of criminal law and the independent counsel to deal with accusations against the president. As political scientist Katy Harriger suggests, the two scandals illustrated how the separation of powers worked to keep the independent counsel's power in check and offer alternative methods of inquiry. In the case of Watergate, Cox had tried in vain to get the Senate Select Committee hearings called off for fear that these would prejudice a fair trial for the accused and produce immunity for some of the accused in return for evidence against others. Ultimately, the common focus on obtaining the White House tapes and the special prosecutor's sacrosanct status following the Saturday Night Massacre prevented serious fragmentation of the Watergate investigation, but this was more a matter of circumstance than systemic solidity. In contrast the odds were heavily stacked against Walsh in Iran-contra. Although he brought indictments against 14 individuals, only five of these were successful. A procession of pardons, overturned convictions, and immunities undermined his authority. Those pardoned were Assistant Secretary of State Elliot Abrams, former National Security Adviser Robert McFarlane, Caspar Weinberger, and three CIA officials (the case against a fourth was dismissed). National Security Adviser Admiral John Poindexter and another NSC official, Colonel Oliver

North, had their convictions overturned on constitutional grounds that did not absolve them of guilt. Significantly, only five businessmen involved in financial aspects of Iran-contra, had their convictions sustained.[44]

Ironically the separation of the powers that presidents sought to circumvent in their wrongdoing made it difficult to hold them to account. Locating the responsibility for misconduct was difficult. Dispersion of power and accountability in the system created "the problem of many hands [that made it]...difficult even in principle to identify who is morally responsible for political outcomes."[45] Iran-contra provided a textbook example of this. In his defense, Oliver North, the NSC official at the heart of the Iranian arms sales and diversion of the proceeds to the Contras, claimed that he had been following orders and had been operating within and guided by a specific policy framework. In the estimate of investigative analyst Theodore Draper, the criminal justice process brought an unsatisfactory resolution to the case. Reminiscent of the Watergate investigation's obstruction of justice focus, Walsh found himself mainly dealing with the narrow charges that North and Poindexter had misled Congress. Though a serious misdemeanor, this was a small part of Iran-contra. Use of criminal law in pursuit of wrongdoing detracted public attention from the hugely significant constitutional issues of the case, something Walsh's office was acutely aware of. Iran-contra exemplified the difficulties of keeping politics out of high profile investigations. Commenting on this in his final report, Walsh drew attention to the intense pressure he had faced and his lack of support from other actors in the investigation.[46]

Walsh entitled his memoir of the investigation *Firewall* to justify its record and the reputation of his office in the face of virulent criticism, including Republican claims that he was under the control of Democratic lawyers on his staff. In many respects it was his doggedness in contrast to other Iran-contra investigators that brought this reaction. In justifying his pardon of Weinberger, George Bush remarked, "By seeking to craft criminal violations from a political foreign policy dispute, the office of independent counsel was cast in a biased position from the beginning." According to Yale law professor Harold Koh, Walsh's investigation "degenerated into the case of the US versus itself...the Justice Department, the Congressional Committees, the White House and the intelligence agencies all subsequently threw major road blocks into the independent counsel's path."[47] Walsh vented his frustration at this in his final report but this only played into his critics' hands. Even a neutral analyst, Theodore Draper, commented, "[It] was written in a militantly prosecutorial vein and sometimes oversteps the bounds of logic and fair play. It alleges a conspiracy and cover-up that are never made clear or convincing."[48]

In an inversion of Watergate, it was almost as if the villain in Iran-contra was the independent counsel not the perpetrators of the illegal acts, some of whom claimed to be the real heroes of the affair. Richard Nixon's self-justification and self-pity had got him nowhere, but the Iran-contra accused were allowed to present their actions in terms of national security imperatives. Training his guns on Walsh, Oliver North also charged, "[T]he independent counsel is independent alright: independent of financial restraints, independent of time limitations, and independent of any obligations to show results within a given period of time. The office of independent counsel has become a pervasive and powerful machine, a legalistic tank that can roll over and flatten its victims beneath its unlimited time, size and money."[49]

The Whitewater/Lewinksy Investigation

Title VI of the Ethics in Government Act was allowed to expire in 1992. Walsh's Iran-contra investigation was instrumental in this outcome. Republican disdain for it, Democratic apathy now that Iran-contra had afforded them partisan gain, and media frustration at the cost and lack of smoking gun, undermined support for reauthorization. Within a year, however, congressional Republicans discovered new enthusiasm for Title VI as a Democratic president became enmeshed in the Whitewater real estate scandal. The opposition party could hardly challenge them on this for fear of being accused of covering up their leader's alleged transgressions. Accordingly, the statute was renewed in June 1994 with support from both parties in Congress and the Clinton administration.

Five years later the measure was allowed to expire for good out of revulsion against the independent counsel's operations in the scandals that beset the Clinton administration. Lawrence Walsh offered some explanation for this development when reflecting on the history of the office in 1998. "The principal criticism of the investigation of prior independent counsel, including my own Iran Contra matter," he remarked, "has been not only the cost and time required for completion, but also a concern that an independent counsel, preoccupied with a narrow area of investigation, will become obsessive in an attempt to validate his efforts, and will take excessive action that a regularly appointed federal prosecutor would not take."[50]

In conventional investigations, a prosecutor was assigned to investigate a specific crime and to find out what was involved. The independent counsel, however, was instructed to investigate a particular individual and find any crimes he or she may have committed, not just the most serious crimes that he was appointed to investigate. The Whitewater/Lewinsky affair clearly illustrated this, evolving from an investigation into Bill and Hillary Clinton's involvement in a failed 1980s land deal in Arkansas into examination of whether the president had perjured himself whilst testifying about his relationship with White House intern Monica Lewinsky. Clinton became the subject of a seemingly endless series of allegations over a period of years. Independent counsel investigation of these diminished the sense that the office focused on "special situations" and its prolongation increased the pressure to bring misdemeanor charges regardless of whether these pertained to the original purpose.

Once the statute was reauthorized, Kenneth Starr was appointed Whitewater independent counsel in place Robert Fiske, who had been conducting the investigation as ad hoc special counsel. The latter was removed on grounds of perceived conflict-of-interest from being "affiliated with the incumbent administration" through his appointment by Attorney General Janet Reno.[51] A partisan Republican, the new man had a reputation as a moderate, bolstered by his record as a federal judge and Bush administration solicitor general. However, some Democrats expressed concern at his recent closeness to GOP right-wingers connected to Senator Jesse Helms (R-NC). It was not long before he came under attack for conflict-of-interest and bias in his investigation. This intensified into a no holds barred personal assault after the Lewinsky scandal erupted. "I think," declared Clinton adviser James Carville, "he is an abusive, privacy-invading, sex-obsessed, right-wing, constitutionally insensitive, boring, obsequious and miserable little man who has risen further in this life by willingness to suck up to power than his meager talents and pitiful judgment ever would have gotten him."[52]

As had been the case in Watergate and the Reagan era scandals, Starr's investigation provoked legal controversy that had to be settled by the Supreme Court. Writing in 2002, he asserted that the *Jones v. Clinton* (1997) ruling added to the existing judicial validation of presidential accountability to due process. *Nixon v. Fitzgerald* (1982), which held that the president could be sued for decisions taken while in office, cemented the principle that the head of state and government was not above the law. In ruling that the independent counsel provision was constitutional, *Morrison v. Olson* (1988) confirmed that executive power was subject to the limitations that Congress chose to impose. In the Jones case, the Clinton lawyers failed in their argument that the president was too busy to deal with the sexual harassment case brought against him.[53] Paradoxically Starr himself had long harbored doubts about the independent counsel statute. Though recognizing its potential benefits, he deemed the measure unconstitutional at its core because "it intruded improperly into the function of the Executive Branch."[54]

Whatever its legal significance, the Starr investigation of Clinton has gone down in history as fundamentally politicized. Believing that it was improperly seizing on any charge and constantly changing its focus in an effort to destroy the president, the Clinton White House went into full defense mode. In effect, it charged Starr with conducting a personal and partisan vendetta. The bilious commentary from the right-wing media in support of impeachment only encouraged this viewpoint. In remarks on NBC's *Today* program in January 1998, Hillary Clinton famously represented the Starr investigation as part of "a vast right wing conspiracy that has been conspiring against my husband since the day he announced for president." As the investigation moved into the lurid details of Clinton's extramarital sexual activities, its gravitas became increasingly compromised. A disgusted Arthur Schlesinger made plain his belief that Starr was unjustifiably exposing private misconduct to support a failing case of public misdemeanor. He had become, asserted the chronicler of Nixon's imperial presidency, "America's number one pornographer." The public also had little sympathy for the independent counsel, who had a consistently low poll rating in marked contrast to the president as his investigation reached its climax in 1998.[55]

Starr's lack of popular support suggested that he had forgotten the golden rule underlying the initial establishment of his office, namely that the appearance of justice is as important as its reality. The Clinton White House and its supporters succeeded in focusing attention on his investigation's seemingly prurient attention to personal matters, thereby limiting awareness of the legally questionable means the president employed to frustrate it.[56] Starr became the first special prosecutor/independent counsel to be instrumental in the impeachment of a president. The House approved impeachment articles against Clinton on the basis of the charges in Starr's final report that he had lied in sworn deposition about the true nature of his involvement with Lewinsky and had attempted to cover up the affair. However, this was puny stuff by comparison with what Nixon had done. Although Clinton's misdemeanors were certainly less serious than Reagan's in Iran-contra, there was good cause to believe that both had done wrong. Nevertheless, the Watergate metaphor did much to save each of them and frustrate the independent counselor.

Conclusion

Until Iran-contra, the Office of Independent Counsel was viewed as the "jewel in the post-Watergate crown."[57] Cox and Jaworksi had set a gold standard but their successors were destined inevitably to fall short of their heroic stature. Present from its inception, doubts about the independence of the office and whether it violated the separation of the powers had intensified as a result of Iran-contra and reached a new peak during the Lewinsky scandal. There was also growing concern that an office intended to control the executive's tendency to overreach its powers had itself become uncontrollable. Even Lawrence Walsh agreed that he had never had power like it, and yet the unlimited time, mandate, and budget that came with the post were problematic in themselves.[58] The special prosecutor/independent counsel ended up investigating misdemeanors that were not special. As Suzanne Garment noted, there is no plausible evidence of a rise in federal corruption since Watergate commensurate with the phenomenal increase in scandal investigation during the same period.[59] The reality was that the independent counsel could never be truly independent from the scandal politics that both political parties engaged in during the late twentieth century.

The Lewinski affair represented a new low in scandal politics. The independent counsel became a victim of this. In 1999 the office was allowed to expire, apparently for good. Public groups, such as Common Cause and the American Bar Association, that had enthusiastically endorsed its creation in 1978 now opposed its reauthorization. In future cases of executive misconduct, a special counsel would be appointed by the Department of Justice and given broad powers to operate independently. Whether this offers the best way of dealing executive misdemeanor is a matter of debate. As such, one of the troubling legacies of Watergate remains unresolved. The American presidency still harbors imperial pretensions, but as yet, the United States does not appear to have discovered the best means of investigating and punishing executive-branch misdemeanors.

Notes

1. Stanley I. Kutler, *The Wars of Watergate: The Last Crisis of Richard Nixon* (New York: Norton, 1992), 581.
2. George Lardner Jr., "Cox is Chosen as Special Prosecutor," *Washington Post*, May 19, 1973.
3. Suzanne Garment, *Scandal: The Crisis of Mistrust in American Politics* (New York: Random House, 1991), 31.
4. Kutler, *The Wars of Watergate*, 414.
5. Lardner, "Cox is Chosen as Special Prosecutor." For discussion of who initially rejected the post and why, see Kutler, *The Wars of Watergate*, 330.
6. Ken Gormley, *Archibald Cox: Conscience of a Nation* (Cambridge, MA: Perseus, 1997), 240.
7. James Doyle, *Not Above the Law: The Battles of Watergate Prosecutors Cox and Jaworski: A Behind the Scenes Account*, (New York: William Morrow, 1977), 45.
8. Gormley, *Archibald Cox*, 250.
9. Doyle provides his account of the Cox-Jaworski investigations in *Not Above the Law*.
10. Archibald Cox, *The Role of the Supreme Court in American Government*, (New York: Oxford University Press, 1976), 6; Melvin Small, *The Presidency of Richard Nixon* (Lawrence: University Press of Kansas, 1999), 285.
11. Cox, *The Role of the Supreme Court in American Government*, 8.
12. Analysis based on author interview with Cox biographer Ken Gormley, July 6, 2004. See also Katy Harriger, *The Special Prosecutor in American Politics*, 2nd ed. (Lawrence: University Press of Kansas, 2000), 183–185.
13. Richard Nixon, *RN: The Memoirs* (New York: Grossett & Dunlap, 1978), 912; Kutler, *The Wars of Watergate*, 332–333.
14. Small, *The Presidency of Richard Nixon*, 289.
15. Elliot Richardson, *The Creative Balance; Government, Politics, and the Individual in America's Third Century* (New York: Holt, Rinehart, 1976), 39.
16. Doyle, *Not Above the Law*, 193–194; Kutler, *The Wars of Watergate*, 409.
17. Nixon, *RN*, 935–936; Iwan Morgan, *Nixon* (Arnold: London, 2002), 185; Kutler, *The Wars of Watergate*, 406.
18. Ken Gormley, *Archibald Cox*, 390.
19. Quotation from Harvard University obituary on http://www.law.harvard.edu/news/2004/05/30coxobit.php. See also Bart Barnes, "Watergate Prosecutor Faced Down the President," *Washington Post*, May 30, 2004;

"Archibald Cox, 92 is Dead; Helped Prosecute Watergate," *New York Times*, May 30, 2004; Harold Jackson, "Archibald Cox," (London) *Guardian*, May 31, 2004.

20. Fred Emery, *Watergate: The Corruption of American Politics and the Fall of Richard Nixon* (New York: Times Books, 1994), 399.

21. Robert Williams, *Political Scandals in the USA* (Edinburgh: Keele University Press, 1998), 18–20.

22. Kutler, *The Wars of Watergate*, 426–428; Anthony Summers, *The Arrogance of Power: The Secret World of Richard Nixon* (New York: Penguin, 2001), 466.

23. Leon Jaworski, *The Right and the Power: The Prosecution of Watergate* (New York: Readers Digest, 1976) 45–46.

24. Small, *The Presidency of Richard Nixon*, 291–292.

25. *United States of America v. Richard M. Nixon, President* (73-1766, 1974), Cornell University Law School, Legal Information Institute.

26. Doyle, *Not Above the Law*, 371–375.

27. Doyle, *Not Above the Law*, 375.

28. "The Nation: What Price Watergate?" *Time*, February 11, 1974; Jack Maskell, *Congressional Research Service Report for Congress: Independent Counsel Appointed Under the Ethics in Government Act of 1978: Costs and Results of Investigations* (Maryland: Penny Hill Press, 2001), 5.

29. Williams, *Political Scandal in the USA*, 27–28.

30. Michael Schudson, *Watergate in American Memory: How We Remember, Forget and Reconstruct the Past* (New York: Basic Books, 1992), 58.

31. Harriger, *The Special Prosecutor in American Politics*, 36.

32. Robert Roberts and Marion Doss, *From Watergate to Whitewater: The Public Integrity War* (Westport, CT: Praeger, 1997); author interview with Cary Feldman, February 20, 2004; Harriger, *The Special Prosecutor in American Politics*, 195–204.

33. Arthur H. Christy, "Trials and Tribulations of the First Special Prosecutor Under the Ethics in Government Act of 1978," *Georgetown Law Journal*, 86, 6 (1998), 2287–2297; "The Law's Heavy Hammer," *Washington Star*, September 16, 1980, A16.

34. Harriger, *The Special Prosecutor in American Politics*, 75–76.

35. Kutler, *The Wars of Watergate*, 582–583.

36. Kutler, *The Wars of Watergate*, 583–584.

37. Leonard Garment, "Does America Really Need This Orgy of Investigation," *Washington Post*, May 10, 1987; Gordon Krowitz, "Independent Counsels: Quo Vado?" *Wall Street Journal*, February 9, 1988; *Morrison, Independent Counsel, v. Olson, et al.* (U.S. Supreme Court, slip opinion, No 87-1279).

38. For Iran-contra, see: Jane Mayer and Doyle McManus, *Landslide: The Unmaking of President Reagan* (Boston: Houghton Mifflin, 1989); Theodore Draper, *A Very Thin Line: The Iran Contra Affairs* (New New York: Hill & Wang, 1991); and Robert Busby, *Reagan and the Iran-Contra Affair: The Politics of Presidential Recovery* (New York: Macmillan, 1999).

39. Busby, *Reagan and the Iran-Contra Affair*, 118. See also Lawrence Walsh, *Firewall: The Iran-Contra Conspiracy and Cover-Up* (New York: Norton, 1997), 29–30.

40. Harriger, *The Special Prosecutor in American Politics*, 162; author interview with Lawrence Walsh, April 29, 2004.

41. Schudson, *Watergate in American Memory*, 179.

42. Walsh also admitted treating Reagan rather too deferentially, accepting written interrogatories from him in 1987 and only interviewing him in person the following year. See Bob Woodward, *Shadow: Five Presidents and the Legacy of Watergate* (New York: Simon & Schuster, 1999), 168–170 [quotation p. 169].
43. Woodward, *Shadow*, 206.
44. Harriger, *The Special Prosecutor in American Politics*, 215–217; Doyle, *Not Above the Law*, 67–68; author interview with Lawrence Walsh, April 29, 2004.
45. Dennis F. Thomson, *Political Ethics and Public Office* (Cambridge, MA: Harvard University Press, 1987), 40.
46. Draper, *A Very Thin Line*, 583–584; Lawrence Walsh, *Iran Contra: The Final Report* (New York: Times Books/Random House, 1994), xv, xxi.
47. Williams, *Political Scandals in the U.S.A.*, 51; Harold Koh, *The National Security Constitution: Sharing Power After the Iran Contra Affair* (Yale University Press, New Haven, 1990), 23.
48. Quoted in Robert Williams, "The Last Word on the Iran Contra affair: The Final Report of the Independent Counsel," *Crime, Law and Social Change*, 23 (1999), 12.
49. Oliver North, *Under Fire: An American Story* (New York: Harper Collins, 1991), 381.
50. Lawrence Walsh, "Kenneth Starr and the Independent Counsel Act," *New York Review of Books*, March 5, 1998.
51. Bill Clinton, *My Life*, (London: Hutchinson, 2004), 613.
52. James Carville, *And the Horse He Rode In On: The People V Kenneth Starr* (New York: Simon & Schuster, 1998), 10.
53. Kenneth Starr, *First Among Equals: The Supreme Court in American Life* (New York: Warner, 1992), 261,
54. Starr, *First Among Equals*, 259,
55. Robert Busby, *Defending the American Presidency: Clinton and the Lewinsky Scandal* (New York: Palgrave, 2001), 98–99; Molly Andolina and Clyde Wilcox, "Public Opinion: The Paradoxes of Clinton's Popularity," in Mark Rozell and Clyde Wilcox, ed., *The Clinton Scandal and the Future of American Government* (Washington, DC: Georgetown University Press, 2000), 188–189; David Halperin, "Ethics Breakthrough or Ethics Breakdown? Kenneth Starr's Dual Role as Private Practitioner and Public Prosecutor," *Georgetown Journal of Legal Ethics*, 15 (Winter 2002), 2.
56. For critical discussion of this, see in particular Howard Kurtz, *Spin Cycle: Inside the Clinton Propaganda Machine* (New York: Free Press, 1998).
57. Suzanne Garment, *Scandal*, 302.
58. Author interview with Lawrence Walsh, April 29, 2004.
59. Garment, *Scandal*, 6–7.

Chapter Five

Vietnam, Watergate, and the War Power: Presidential Aggrandizement and Congressional Abdication

David Gray Adler and Michael A. Genovese

The crisis of Watergate was both spawned and worsened by America's involvement in the war in Vietnam. Many of the early illegal actions by the Nixon administration rose from fear that opposition to the war would undermine Nixon's efforts to build a new "grand design" in foreign affairs, and once the Watergate crisis became a national scandal, the backlash from the war further deteriorated Nixon's then fragile political position. Further, opposition to the war led to a clash between the president and Congress over the war powers, eventually leading to the passage of the War Powers Act in 1973 over President Nixon's veto. While initially it appeared that Nixon's bold claims of plenary presidential war-powers was discredited, it was not long before Nixon's sweeping assertions of presidential power in foreign affairs and war would be revived, leading to a reemergence of an imperial presidency.[1]

Vietnam as the Beginning of the End

President Richard Nixon, it should be recalled, inherited the Vietnam War. The war had driven Lyndon Johnson from the White House, which destroyed his goal of becoming a "great" president. President Nixon was barely into his first term of office when a wave of antiwar protests swept the nation, decrying his continuation of this "presidential war" and demanding a withdrawal of American troops. Nixon, critics believed, deserved the same fate that had befallen Johnson. The Office of the Presidency, riding high since the days of Franklin D. Roosevelt's assertion of broad executive authority, was under attack; an era of reexamination of presidential power was underway; and president-bashing was, in some quarters, becoming a national sport. To further complicate matters, Nixon faced divided government. Democrats controlled both Houses of Congress. The Democrats, Nixon knew, would be difficult to deal with, particularly in the realm of foreign affairs and national security. It was, to say the least, a challenging time to hold the nation's highest office.

Nixon's "Grand Design" Meets Vietnam

The president had an ambitious "Grand Design" for remaking American foreign policy. It involved detenté with the Soviet Union, opening the door to China, and ending the war in Vietnam. To implement this new approach, Nixon and his quixotic National Security Advisor Henry Kissinger wanted a free hand in shaping America's future.

President Nixon's Grand Design was a complex, daring, ambitious formula that required both short-term and long-term plans. First among the short-term plans was ending the long, divisive war in Vietnam. If a structure of peace was to be built, the first step had to be extricating the United States from Vietnam but with honor. For Nixon and Kissinger, Vietnam became both a personal test of will and a test of America's credibility. Yet, getting out of Vietnam proved to be more difficult than either Nixon or Kissinger anticipated. "Peace with honor" proved elusive. For Nixon's Grand Design to work, American power had to remain a credible force in world politics. Thus, Vietnam became an important—and vexing—piece in the larger puzzle Nixon and Kissinger were trying to piece together.

Prior to taking office, Nixon reviewed a variety of options on Vietnam. A military victory could, he believed, be attained with massive, perhaps even nuclear, bombing, but the domestic and international blowback to such a move would be unacceptable. A conventional escalation could take at least six months—too long a time, Nixon believed. A negotiated settlement was the best option. What of simply pulling out? This option undermined Nixon's larger plans, as it would have abandoned the South to communism, put into doubt America's will and power, and undermined Nixon's own credibility.

At the time Nixon came to be the presidency, the Vietnam war was stalemated, with no victory—or end— in sight. It caused a tremendous amount of domestic strife—protest marches, civil disobedience, the emergence of a counterculture. The war was tearing the nation apart.

It was a long, slow process that got the United States into Vietnam. Decisions by Harry S. Truman, Dwight D. Eisenhower, John F. Kennedy, and Lyndon B. Johnson drew the United States further and further into a Southeast Asian land war that, by 1969, many saw as unwinnable.[2]

The United States had over 500,000 troops in Vietnam when Nixon took office. In fact, a great deal of Nixon's success in the 1968 election was attributed to the failure of Lyndon Johnson and the Democrats to win or effectively prosecute the war. This left the Democrats divided and allowed candidate Nixon to talk of a plan to end the war. Nixon was, in effect, the "peace candidate".

However, Nixon's "plan" to end the war wasn't much of a plan at all. Early efforts at a negotiated settlement did not work, as North Vietnam was determined to gain victory, not compromise. On July 15, 1969, Nixon secretly sent what he thought to be a rather conciliatory letter to President Ho Chi Minh of North Vietnam calling for serious negotiations and an early end to the war.

Simultaneously, Henry Kissinger, without the knowledge of Secretary of State William P. Rogers, was setting up secret back channel negotiations with North Vietnamese officials (notably Xuan Thay). Ho Chi Minh's reply to Nixon's letter, signed on August 25, a week before Ho's death, was disappointing to Nixon. Ho, in effect, blamed the United States for the war, reiterated his determination to settle for nothing less than independence of his country, and called for a complete U.S. withdrawal from Vietnam.

The President did not take Ho's letter seriously. He viewed it as Ho's effort to take a tough initial bargaining position from which he would later back away. Nixon and Kissinger were convinced that, faced with a show of the superiority of America's military might, the North could not long withstand a massive American military barrage. The assumptions of Nixon and Kissinger about Vietnam, reflect both the historically developed "arrogance of American power" and a profound ignorance of Vietnam and its history. Incorrect or faulty assumptions got the U.S. into Vietnam, they would also keep the U.S. there.

The Kissinger-Xuan Thay meeting, held in Paris on August 4, 1969, went nowhere. However, when Ho died, the president hoped for a more encouraging response to his overtures. Again he was disappointed. If the North would not cooperate, if talking wouldn't work, perhaps increased military pressure would. Nixon would not pull out: he would plunge forward.

In an effort to get the Paris negotiations untracked, Nixon decided to play a risky carrot-and-stick game. He would offer incentives to negotiate and disincentives for stalling. The incentive was a phased withdrawal of American combat troops from Vietnam. The stick was massive bombing of the North, the invasion of Cambodia, incursion into Laos, and an intensified effort on North Vietnam's allies, China and the Soviet Union, to persuade the North to end the war.

In notes, Nixon's chief of staff, Bob Haldeman, took at a September 27, 1969, meeting with the president, Nixon says:

VN—enemy
    Misjudges 2 things
        —the time—has 3 yrs + 9 mo
        —the man—won't be 1st P to lose war.[3]

The president's confidence was displayed in notes taken by chief domestic policy advisor John Ehrlichman at an October 7, 1969, meeting with the president in which Ehrlichman wrote that the president said, "War will be behind us by the end of next year...or at least see the end of the Tunnel."[4] Nixon fell into the same trap Lyndon Johnson had fallen into. He could not believe the North Vietnamese would or could hold out much longer. After all, the United States was the mightiest military power in the world. How could a tiny, backward (in Nixon's view) country stand up to such a massive show of military power?

The United States would continue to prosecute the war in Vietnam. Nixon was determined not to be the first president to lose a war! To Nixon, it was a matter of both individual and national pride. He would not be defeated, and the United States could not be defeated.

As the "plan" to end the war evaporated, the protest movement accelerated. Marches became bigger, the crowds, more middle class, and Nixon began to take it very personally.

Nixon knew the war had to be ended and ended soon, lest he be dragged down by it. "I'm not going to end up like LBJ, holed up in the White House afraid to show my face on the street. I'm going to stop that war fast," he said.[5] Vietnam became *the* overriding issue of the first term. Everything else—internationally and at home—was predicated on honorably ending the war in Vietnam. But how?

In late January of 1969, Nixon decided that he could not simply pull out of Vietnam, yet he couldn't prosecute the war as Johnson had. He would execute a gradual withdrawal of American forces—thereby diffusing the antiwar movement at home; end the draft, further dampening the protest movement; seek a negotiated agreement with the North—something that allowed the United States to preserve its honor; and dramatically increase the bombing in Southeast Asia—thereby bombing the North into an agreement.

A New Approach: Vietnamization

The troop pullout from Vietnam was part of what was called Vietnamization, a plan that called for gradually turning the war over to the South Vietnamese. Vietnamization was intended as a sign of good faith being sent to the North. However, the North read this signal as a sign of weakness, and Nixon's announced troop withdrawal only strengthened their resolve. Like his predecessors, Nixon had misunderstood and misread his adversaries. The three-pronged strategy of Vietnamization, a bombing increase, and negotiation was not to work.

Vietnamization was in trouble from the start. There was no way the South could assume fighting responsibility for the war. Yet, Vietnamization had a strong domestic component, and Nixon hoped that announcements of troop pullouts would soften the antiwar criticism and allow the other parts of the Vietnam strategy to take effect. It also allowed Nixon to simultaneously be the dove, with his troop pullout, and the hawk, with increased bombing.

To force the North to the bargaining table and to a negotiated settlement, Nixon was willing to expand the war into Cambodia and Laos and decisively increase bombing of North Vietnam.

So, while American combat troops were being withdrawn, B-52s began bombing the North. "I refuse to believe," Kissinger is reported to have said, "that a little fourth-rate power like North Vietnam doesn't have a breaking point."[6] The bombing targets included Hanoi and Haiphong, as well as other cities, and main roads to the South around the Ho Chi Minh Trail, and the railroads linking the North to China. Between 1969 and early 1973, the United States dropped on Vietnam an average of a ton of bombs each minute. It would be what Nixon and Kissinger called "a savage blow." In the end, it would not be enough.

The War Expands: Cambodia and Beyond

Despite Nixon's promises to wind down the war, the president expanded the war into Cambodia. The president widened the war by secretly bombing North Vietnamese bases inside the neutral nation of Cambodia. In 1970, Nixon sent American troops into Cambodia. It was a bold assertion of a unilateral executive war-making power that suggested an expansive, even imperial, interpretation of presidential authority. The secret war in Cambodia was truly a presidential war, ordered by the executive branch on its own, with no congressional approval or oversight, no public scrutiny, and no democratic controls. It was, for reasons discussed in this chapter, blatantly unconstitutional.

The president's goal in Cambodia was to disrupt enemy supply lines and attack the North Vietnamese in their "safe" havens inside Cambodia. To keep this mission secret, the military had to set up improvised command chains outside of normal military channels, file false reports, and create a dual reporting system. For the operation to be a success, the president felt that the bombing had to be kept secret.[7] But secret from whom?

On March 18, 1969, the first B-52 raid against Cambodia was launched.[8] Operation Menu, the first phase of the bombing, lasted over 14 months. In that period, B-52s flew 3, 875 sorties into Cambodia and dropped 108, 823 tons of bombs. After that, the operation became public knowledge as U.S. troops invaded Cambodia on April 30, 1970. Bombing missions continued until August 1973, when Congress forbade all such bombings. The total tonnage of bombs dropped on Cambodia in approximately four years was 540,000.[9]

On April 30, 1970, Nixon went on television and shocked the nation with his announcement that he had ordered American troops into Cambodia. "The time has come for action," the president asserted. This decision went to "the heart of the trouble." Expressing outrage that the enemy had violated the neutrality of Cambodia by setting up sanctuaries there, he avowed that "American policy had been to scrupulously respect the neutrality of the Cambodian people." He insisted that "neither the United States nor South Vietnam has moved against these enemy sanctuaries, because we did not wish to violate the territory of a neural nation."[10]

The president went on to say that "we live in an age of anarchy both abroad and at home. We see mindless attacks on all the great institutions which have been created by free civilizations in the last five hundred years. Even here in the United States, great universities are being systematically destroyed." The president issued a warning: "If, when the chips are down the world's most powerful nation, the United States of America, acts like a pitiful, helpless giant, the forces of totalitarianism and anarchy will threaten free nations and free institutions throughout the world."

Nixon continued, "We will not be humiliated. We will not be defeated," and "it is not our power but our will and character that is being tested tonight...if we fail to meet the challenge, all other nations will be on notice that despite its overwhelming power, the United States, when real crisis comes, will be found wanting."

The military impact of the invasion of Cambodia was such that it damaged the communists, but not fatally. It did buy some time for Nixon as he pursued Vietnamization, but since Vietnamization did not stand the test of time, such an expenditure of arms, men, and, at home, political capital, proved damaging to the president.

Because of the Cambodian invasion, the war at home heated up beyond anything that Nixon expected. The campuses erupted. Nixon's comment about "bums blowing up campuses" was published and further fired up the already outraged protesters. Four hundred forty-eight colleges declared themselves "on strike". Some rioted. Police had to protect the White House from the over one hundred thousand protesters who converged on the nation's capitol.

A siege mentality captured the president and his aides. Then on May 4, tragedy struck. At an antiwar demonstration at Kent State University, National Guardsmen opened fire on a group of protesters and bystanders. Fifteen people were wounded; four were killed.

The biggest student strike in U.S. history followed. On May 9, over 250,000 demonstrators descended on Washington, and across the country campuses shut down. Clark Kerr, who chaired a Carnegie Commission study on higher education, reported that 89 percent of independent universities and 76 percent of public universities held demonstrations.[11]

Less than two weeks later, two student protesters were killed in Jackson State College in Mississippi.

The War Drags On

President Nixon's efforts to end the war in Vietnam met with frustration. Hanoi was not seriously negotiating, the bombing of the North seemed only to strengthen their resolve, extending the war into Cambodia and Laos had a limited impact, the antiwar movement seemed to grow larger with each passing day, and congressional doves seemed to be undermining the president's position. Would Nixon, like his predecessor, be dragged down and defeated by the Vietnam War?

As the war dragged on with no honorable end in sight, the president began to see Vietnam as a test of both his and America's prestige. America would not be "a pitiful, helpless giant," Nixon said; and H.R. Haldeman's notes of meetings with the president reflect a repeated concern for not appearing weak. On June 2, 1971, Haldeman wrote:

> P. will not go out VN whimpering
> Play hole card in Nov—bomb NV totally
> Unless we get our breakthrough
> (Underlined in original)

In earlier notes taken by Haldeman, the president says, "our purpose is not to defeat NVN—it is to avoid defeat of America" (underlined in original). But "peace with honor" proved no easy goal.

Nixon decided to further escalate. On Monday, May 8, after a lengthy National Security Council (NSC) meeting, Nixon handed his own draft of a speech written at Camp David to speechwriter Ray Price. Nixon would go on national television at nine that evening to announce his plans.

"An American defeat in Vietnam," Nixon said, "would encourage...aggression all over the world...I have...concluded that Hanoi must be denied the weapons and supplies it needs to continue the aggression." He continued, "All entrances to North Vietnamese ports will be mined to prevent access to these ports and North Vietnamese naval operations from these ports."

Nixon would blockade the North. The air force would bomb rail and roadways, along with military targets in the North. The bombing of Hanoi and Haiphong was to begin immediately.

Under the grueling pressure of round-the-clock bombing (Nixon said to his associates, "The bastards have never been bombed like they're going to be bombed this time"),[12] the North finally agreed to resume negotiating.

By the summer of 1972, North Vietnam's politburo made a major concession: they would drop the demand for a coalition government in the South. President Thieu of South Vietnam would be permitted to remain in office. In effect, the North was agreeing to let the United States leave Vietnam and to wait for either the government of the South to collapse or an opportunity to overthrow this shaky regime. From that point on, the negotiations moved ahead. By the fall of 1972, an agreement was in sight. A cease-fire was agreed to, the North was allowed to keep its troops in the South (a major concession by Nixon), all U.S. troops were to withdraw, and an election commission was set up to decide the fate of Vietnam.

South Vietnam was not a party to this agreement, and when Kissinger took the tentative agreement to Thieu in October, things began to fall apart. Thieu recognized the agreement was South Vietnam's death warrant. He refused to allow the North's troops to remain in the South and refused to recognize the legitimacy of the Vietcong.

Nixon and Kissinger pressed Thieu, telling him that this was the best they could do and promising continued U.S. support. On October 26, 1972, Radio Hanoi disclosed the terms of the agreement in hopes of forcing the United States to sign the agreement. Also on October 26, Kissinger announced at a press conference that "peace is at hand." This premature announcement, less than two weeks before the 1972 presidential election, blew up in Kissinger's face. Thieu refused to accept the deal struck by Kissinger and Le Duc Tho. Kissinger urged Nixon to make a separate peace agreement with Hanoi. Nixon refused.

Kissinger and Le Duc Tho met in November of 1972 to try to iron out an agreement, but the introduction of President Thieu's demands led to North Vietnamese objections. Nixon informed the North that if Thieu remained intransigent, he would make a separate deal with Hanoi; further he threatened Theiu with a cutoff of U.S. support if Thieu refused to go along with the agreement. Nixon also promised Thieu that if the North violated the agreement, the United States would "save" South Vietnam from a communist takeover.[13] Finally, Nixon gave Hanoi 72-two hours to seriously resume negotiations or face renewed, and more massive, B-52 bombing.

The President Nixon decided to again step up the pressure. On December 18, 1972, U.S. B-52s began a 12-day, round-the-clock bombing of North Vietnam in which the United States dropped more tons of bombs that had been dropped in the entire 1969–1971 period. The "Christmas Bombing" shocked the nation. It was one of the most brutal examples of force in history, and was a blatant effort to bomb the North into submission. As bombs showered the North, Nixon sweetened the pot for Thieu and the South, giving them an additional billion dollars in military aid, warning Thieu that if he didn't accept the American "peace" terms, Nixon would make his own peace with North Vietnam. In the end, neither side could resist Nixon's ultimatum.

The North returned to the bargaining table, Nixon ordered a halt to the bombing, Thieu acquiesced to U.S. pressures, and in Paris on January 23, 1973, the Agreement on Ending the War and Restoring Peace in Vietnam was initialed by Henry Kissinger and Le Duc Tho. Nixon claimed his "peace with honor."

Two years after the signing of the Paris accords, the Saigon government fell to the communists, in spite of Nixon's promise to President Thieu to "respond with full force" if the North violated the agreements. The North had conquered the South by force. The Khmer Rouge controlled Cambodia.[14]

Congress Awakens: The War Powers Resolution

While presidents tend to dominate the Congress in the field of foreign policy, and while the courts normally grant wide latitude to presidential claims of power in the field of foreign affairs,[15] there are rare occasions in which Congress or the courts will muster a challenge to presidential conduct of the nation's foreign relations. Early in his term, President Nixon faced a Congress frustrated by U.S. policy in Vietnam and impatient for a sign that Nixon was prepared to end the war. After some early scrapes with Congress over issues such as the ABM treaty and military and economic aid proposals, Nixon and the Congress came to loggerheads over the Vietnam War.

Whatever support Nixon had in the Democratic-controlled Congress was shattered by the bombing and invasion of Cambodia in 1970. From that time on, congressional efforts to force an end to U.S. involvement in Vietnam accelerated. Signaling this, the Cooper-Church amendment to the 1970 foreign military sales bill signaled this development to prohibit funds for U.S. forces in Cambodia. In 1973 and 1974 these restrictions were extended to forbid "the use of any past or present appropriations for financing directly or indirectly United States combat activities in or over or from off the shores of North Vietnam, South Vietnam, Laos, or Cambodia."[16]

By 1973, the president's foreign policy stock had fallen dramatically, and a more activist, liberal Congress, emboldened by the miasma of the Watergate scandal and the Saturday Night Massacre, attempted to further codify—and limit—the president's powers in foreign affairs. In November of 1973, over Nixon's veto, the Congress passed the War Powers Resolution, which called for congressional consultation before the president committed troops to combat, limited the time and circumstances of U.S. military involvement without congressional authorization, and gave Congress authority to disengage American troops from hostilities. While all presidents since Nixon, with the possible exception of Barack Obama, have questioned the constitutionality of this act, there has, to date, been no judicial ruling on the constitutional standing of the measure.[17]

Because of what Congress felt were excesses committed by Nixon in the conduct and management of the nation's foreign affairs, the early 1970s, to some observers, represented something of a resurgence of congressional will to become a participant in the design of American foreign policy. Nixon's successor, Gerald Ford, faced a vocal and, in Ford's view, obstructionist Congress in the field of foreign affairs. As Ford explained it, if the presidency had, indeed, become "imperial" in Nixon's time, it had, by force of congressional assertions of power, become shackled, restrained, and imperiled during his stint in office.

In assessing Nixon's legacy in matters of foreign policy and national security, it is imperative to remember that he inherited the Vietnam War—as well as social convulsions at home, in the streets, in government buildings, and on the nation's campuses, from Berkeley to Ann Arbor to Columbia. The war dominated the first Nixon term and affected so much of his behavior, even the unsavory and illegal acts that led to his downfall, that one must always see Nixon through the prism of the war in Vietnam. Given that Nixon inherited a divisive war, one must still evaluate his efforts to end that war. While pulling American troops from Southeast Asia, Nixon went on to extend, then end the war. The price for ending the war was a brutalized Vietnam and a devastated Cambodia. While it would be unfair and historically inaccurate to blame Nixon for the initiation of the Vietnam War, it is fair to criticize him for the secret bombing of Cambodia, and for his failure to end the carnage that overwhelmed America and Vietnam. Then too, there is justification for criticizing his conduct of the war—the tactics and strategies, both political and military—that failed the nation. While Nixon claimed that he brought the war to end in a respectable manner—"peace with honor"—there is nothing in the record to support such a characterization. Shortly after the United States withdrew its troops from the battlefields of Vietnam, brutal regimes assumed power in both Vietnam and Cambodia.

Nixon's War Power Legacy

President Nixon's bold claims of executive authority in war and foreign affairs, grounded in assertions of sweeping powers derived from the commander-in-chief clause and his standing as the nation's chief executive, were embraced by his successors. While Jimmy Carter came to office as the Anti-Nixon, vowing to demythologize the presidency, he too engaged in unilateral acts, including the failed hostage rescue mission in Iran.[18] Ronald Reagan intervened militarily in Lebanon, then invaded the nation of Grenada, in addition to ordering air strikes against Libya on his own claim of authority.[19] George H.W. Bush invaded Panama while Congress was out of session.[20] President Clinton likewise acted unilaterally in Somalia, Haiti, and in ordering air strikes in Bosnia, as well as Iraq.[21] And George W. Bush took claims of unilateral power full circle, back to Nixon's very own: "When the president does it, that means it is not illegal" approach.[22]

Both before and after 9-11, presidents, following the Truman-Johnson-Nixon model, advanced broad claims of independent foreign policy power, acted upon such claims, and further strengthened the precedent-setting force of unilateral action. They did this with little push back from Congress. The imperial presidency had become the new norm.[23]

The administration of George W. Bush presented a particularly vexing mixture of bold unilateral action, coupled with a legal defense of the president's actions that found no support in the Constitution, and defied the rule of law. Bush, through a series of memos produced by the Office of Legal Counsel (OLC), adduced unprecedented executive powers, including the notion of a presidential power to launch "preemptive" war. In a remarkable statement, he claimed that his actions were unreviewable by the judiciary.[24]

The excesses of the Bush administration, and the extravagant and constitutionally questionable attempts to justify those actions have been extensively chronicled elsewhere.[25] For our purposes what is most relevant is the eerie similarity between Nixon's imperial claims and President Bush's imperial actions. President Bush brought to fruition the Nixon dystopian constitutional dictatorship, writ large. And Bush's successor, Barack Obama, who during the 2008 presidential campaign railed against the excesses of Bush's unilateralism, nonetheless echoed some of Bush's legal claims, including the assertion of a unilateral executive war-making power.

Nixon's Constitutional Justifications for Presidential War-Making

Nixon's predecessors—Truman, Eisenhower, Kennedy, and Johnson—had, in various ways and by various means, plunged America into the war in Vietnam that he inherited. Nixon's inheritance, however, did not include a war in Cambodia; that was his initiative, his war. He inherited, as well, a host of legal and constitutional rationales supplied to justify "presidential war making." It is true, as we have observed, that he might have ended the war sooner, rather than later. It is also true that he might have dispensed with the impoverished legal defenses asserted on behalf of presidential wars. That he did not is a matter of record. In fact, his decision to continue the Vietnam War and to initiate the Cambodian war, was grounded on claims to authority that find no foundation in our constitutional architecture. In this, Nixon had both predecessors and imitators, for a succession of presidents, from Harry Truman's unilateral war-making in Korea in 1950, to Barack Obama's initiation of military strikes against Libya in March, 2011, have invoked similar legal and constitutional arguments to justify their actions.[26] President Nixon and his team of advisers proved eclectic and innovative in their legal defense; they discarded some familiar arguments, employed others rehearsed by predecessors, and invented some of their own.

President Nixon offered little in the way of a legal explanation, but what he did provide may be quickly summarized. The constitutional grant of executive power, Nixon claimed, carries with it the authority to initiate war. His predecessors, including Harry Truman in Korea and Lyndon Johnson in Vietnam, had invoked the Vesting Clause to justify their resort to unilateral executive war-making powers. The commander-in-chief clause, Nixon asserted, attributes to the president the power to invade foreign nations, the authority to initiate military hostilities against those nations whom he deems to represent a threat to U.S. security, and the power to determine tactics and strategies that he will in employ in his conduct of the war, all without congressional interference. Nixon's legal advisers, building on a memo written on behalf of President Johnson's assertion of executive power to wage war, cited some 155 "precedents"—alleged instances of unilateral presidential war-making that stretch back to the administrations of George Washington and John Adams.[27] On May 4, 1970, Assistant Attorney General (later, Chief Justice) William Rehnquist defended the constitutionality of Nixon's invasion of Cambodia: "The President's determination to authorize incursion into these Cambodian border areas is precisely the sort of tactical decision confided to the Commander-in-Chief in armed conflict."[28]

The very question raised in Rehnquist's assertion, indeed, the very issue raised by the Vietnam War, and in Korea before that, whether the president possessed the constitutional authority to initiate military hostilities on behalf of the American people, had been decided by the Supreme Court two centuries earlier. In fact, an 1806 circuit decision, written by Supreme Court justice, William Paterson, emphatically rejected the premise. Col. William S. Smith was alleged to have engaged in an effort to outfit an expedition in New York against the Spanish province of Caracas. He was indicted for violating a statute that prohibited military acts against a nation with which the United States was at peace.[29] Smith introduced an affidavit in which he claimed that the expedition "was begun, prepared, and set on foot with the knowledge and approbation of the president of the United States, and with the knowledge and approbation of the secretary of state of the United States."[30] Justice Paterson, riding circuit, wrote for the court:

> Supposing then that every syllable of the affidavit is true, of what avail can it be to the defendant on the present occasion?...Does it speak by way of justification? The president of the United States cannot control the statute, nor dispense with its execution, and still less can he authorize a person to do what the law forbids...Does he possess the power of making war? That power is vested exclusively in Congress....
>
> ...There is a manifest distinction between our going to war with a nation at peace, and a war made against us by an actual invasion, or a formal declaration. In the former case, it is the exclusive province of Congress to change a state of peace into a state of war.[31]

Justice Paterson's ruling reflected earlier Supreme Court decisions—in 1800, 1801, and 1804—which held that Congress, alone may initiate, that is, authorize military hostilities, broad or limited. The president, the Court consistently ruled, possessed no authority to order the use of force without prior congressional authorization.[32] These judicial decisions are the governing decisions for those constitutional provisions that involve the use of military force and commencement of war. The Supreme Court has never rendered a decision in favor of a unilateral presidential power to authorize military hostilities. This array of judicial rulings, it should be recalled, faithfully reflect the Constitution and the Framers' decision to vest the war power—the authority to initiate the use of military force—in the hands of Congress, not the president.

In their adoption of the war clause—"The Congress shall have power...to declare war...."—the framers of the Constitution changed an early draft that had granted to Congress the "power to make war" to a power to "declare war" out of a concern that the first draft might not permit the president to "repel sudden attacks."[33] To a man, delegates in the Convention preferred a congressional decision, rather than a unilateral determination by the executive, on an issue of grave importance to the nation, that of commencing military hostilities against a foreign foe. The framers understood that when a nation engages in military conflict, no one can anticipate the twists and turns that may occur, including those acts that might wreak devastation on a nation, including their own. In their view, American military force might not be employed without authorization from Congress which, itself, should be grounded on the most serious and solemn discussion and debate. The framers embraced republican principles, the essence of which was the cardinal principle of collective decision making, in both domestic and foreign affairs. From both their own experience and their vast reading of history, they had learned that kings, despots, and tyrants had, across the centuries, marched their people into war, often for less than meritorious reasons, including the executive's personal, political, and pecuniary interests. While they could not pretend that the location of the war power in Congress would assure wise decisions, they preferred to cast their lot with a solemn discussion and debate undertaken by representatives that spanned the nation, rather than vesting in one person the awesome power to take the nation to war.

James Wilson, second in importance only to James Madison as an architect of the Constitution, told delegates at the Pennsylvania Ratifying Convention: "This system will not hurry us into war; it is calculated to guard against it. It will not be in the power of a single man, or a single body of men, to involve us in such distress; for the important power of declaring war is vested in the legislature at large: this declaration must be made with the concurrence of the House of Representatives: from this circumstance we may draw a certain conclusion that nothing but our interest can draw us into war."[34] Similar assurance was provided in other state ratifying conventions. In North Carolina, James Iredell stated: "The President has not the power of declaring war by his own authority.... Those powers are vested in other hands. The power of declaring war is expressly given to Congress." And Charles Pinckney, like Wilson and Paterson, a delegate to the Constitutional Convention, told the South Carolina Ratifying Convention that "the President's powers did not permit him to declare war." Likewise, in New York, Chancellor R. R. Livingston responded to objections that the Continental Congress did not have the "same powers" as the proposed Congress. He explained that the two bodies shared "the very same" power including the power "of making war and peace.... They may involve us in war at their pleasure."[35]

It was not necessary for Congress to formally "declare" war before military force was commenced on behalf of the American people, but merely that Congress authorized it. As Chancellor James Kent of New York, one of the leading jurists of the Founding period explained, what "is essential is that some formal public act, proceeding directly from the competent source, should announce to the people at home their new relations and duties growing out of a state of war, and which should equally apprise neutral nations of this fact."[36] Kent was writing against a backdrop of international law presuppositions and established usage, which was thoroughly familiar to the framers and dated back as far as 1552; at law, "declare" was commensurate with "commence." As a consequence, Congress, for a variety of reasons, might dispense with a declaration of war. But the Constitution required congressional authorization and thus Congress might by resolution authorize the president to initiate military action. This teaching deprives presidents of laying claim to power to order military actions "short of war." Indeed, the president has no authority from any constitutional source to authorize hostilities.

The commander-in-chief clause, invoked by Nixon, grants to the president no authority to commence hostilities. If it did, then the Constitution would be vesting the power to authorize war in both Congress and the president, surely a prescription for chaos and disaster. Moreover, as we have seen, the Court ruled at the dawn of the republic that the president has no authority as commander-in-chief, to institute hostilities or to take the nation to war. The commander-in-chief clause grants to the president only the authority to repel an invasion of the United States. This represents an exception to congressional control of the war power because the framers had no wish to leave the country defenseless in the case of invasion. However presidential power to repel such an attack carried with it no authority to commence war. In Federalist 69, Alexander Hamilton sought to calm fears surrounding the commander-in-chief clause: "The President is to be commander-in-chief of the army and navy of the United States. In this respect his authority would be nominally the same with that of the king of Great Britain, but in substance much inferior to it. It would amount to nothing more than the supreme command and direction of the military and naval forces, as first General and Admiral of the Confederacy; while that of the British kings extends to the declaring of war and to the raising and regulating of fleets and armies,—all which, by the Constitution under consideration, would appertain to the Legislature."[37]

In sum, the president as commander-in-chief was to be "first General and Admiral" in the "direction of war when authorized or begun." All political authority remained in Congress. In fact, Congress retained the authority to issue instructions and directions to the president in the conduct of war. As Justice Paterson held in *United States v. Smith* in 1806, and as the Court, in an opinion by Chief Justice John Marshall had held in 1804 in *Little v. Barreme*, the president, in his capacity as commander-in-chief, is required to obey statutes enacted by Congress. While it is true, historically, that Congress tends to defer to presidential conduct of war, what that really means is that Congress, like the president, will defer to the generals and admirals who conduct it. But, at all events, Congress possesses the constitutional authority to impose instructions on the president; on more than one occasion, Congress has asserted that authority.[38]

President Nixon's legal rationales for his conduct of the Vietnam War, and his initiation of war in Cambodia, were unavailing. Like his predecessors since Harry Truman, he relied on constitutional claims and arguments which, under scrutiny, crumbled to dust. But his claims, nevertheless, have been advanced by his successors, Republicans and Democrats, conservatives and liberals alike. If it is true that Johnson and Nixon gave rise to the "Imperial Presidency," as Arthur Schlesinger contended, then it is clear that the claims and behavior of presidents since Nixon, have maintained the imperial presidency in every crucial respect.[39] The essence of such a presidency, Schlesinger explained, was the capture of war and foreign affairs powers. Since Nixon, every single president has claimed unilateral executive authority to wage war and to authorize military strikes. Moreover, presidents, have asserted expansive authority in the formulation, management, and conduct of American foreign relations. Presidents have been dismissive of a congressional role to the extent of excluding Congress, despite the fact that the Constitution vests in Congress the bulk of the nation's foreign affairs powers.[40] As a consequence, a string of presidents, stretching back 60 years, have been dismissive of the Constitution as well.

A catalogue of all of the examples of unilateral presidential acts that defy the text of the Constitution, the intentions of the Framers, and the understanding of those who ratified the Constitution, exceeds the scope of this chapter. Let us consider, however, a few illustrative examples. Presidential usurpation of the war power has become commonplace, exemplified by: Gerald Ford and his use of force in the Mayaguez incident; Jimmy Carter and his attempt to rescue hostages in Iran; Ronald Reagan and his invasion of Grenada and air strikes against Libya; George H.W. Bush and his use of the military to invade Panama for the purpose of capturing its dictator, General Manuel Noriega; Bill Clinton and his decision to launch missiles against Baghdad, combat operations in Somalia, air strikes in Bosnia, and the use of force in Afghanistan, Sudan, and Yugoslavia; George W. Bush and his military action against Afghanistan, and his war against Iraq, not to mention his claim of unilateral executive authority to engage in preemptive war. Finally, in sharp contrast to his declaration in December, 2007, while seeking the Democratic presidential nomination, that the president does not have unilateral authority to wage war, President Barack Obama, on March 19, 2011, ordered missile strikes against Libya.

In each of these episodes, U.S. presidents have invoked the commander-in-chief clause as constitutional justification for their military action. At times, most notably in the 2001 Authorization to Use Military Force (AUMF) that preceded the invasion of Afghanistan, and the 2003 Iraq War Resolution, Congress has seemingly legitimized this. However, those two statutes utterly failed to satisfy constitutional requirements of congressional authorization. In each situation, Congress failed to decide for war, as the Constitution commands, but instead allowed Bush to decide whether to use military force. In doing so, the legislature violated the delegation doctrine, which prohibits Congress from transferring to others its constitutional powers, such as the war power, lawmaking power, and appropriations power. The effort by Congress to provide some measure of support for the president, however lacking in constitutional justification, elicited no gratitude from the White House. In defiance of the founders' intent, Bush asserted that his commander-in-chief powers granted him authority to order the attacks on Afghanistan and Iraq.[41]

The rise of the imperial presidency, and its continued flight, is possible only because Congress has utterly failed to defend its constitutional prerogatives. Its abdication of the war power, as well as other foreign affairs powers, represents a grave threat to the republic. While presidents are apt to continue to aggrandize foreign affairs and national security powers, one wonders why members of Congress stand as idle spectators as the executives of both parties rampage across the constitutional landscape. An answer to this issue is beyond this chapter, of course, but it is sufficient to note that some of America's most influential statesmen over the past half century have expressed deep concern about the failure of Congress to defend its turf and halt executive aggrandizement of its powers. No less a personage than Senator Sam Ervin (D-NC), who confronted President Nixon's assault on the Constitution, questioned during 1973 hearings on the unchecked executive practice of impoundment "whether the Congress of the United States will remain a viable institution or whether the trend toward the executive use of legislative power is to continue unabated until we have arrived at a presidential form of government." While criticizing executive aggrandizement of legislative authority, he also found Congress culpable for the rise of presidential dominance: "The executive branch has been able to seize power so brazenly only because the Congress has lacked the courage and foresight to maintain its constitutional position."[42]

The executive domination feared by Ervin and characterized by some as "Presidential Government," is, in part, a legacy of Watergate and the Nixon presidency. Putative congressional efforts to stem the tide of presidential power, including assertions of unlimited powers by Nixon, have not succeeded. But the rise of unbridled executive power cannot be laid exclusively at the doorstep of the Nixon White House. While he unquestionably abused presidential authority and usurped congressional powers, he has not acted alone. Across the decades, he has kept company with presidents of both parties who have shared his expansive but constitutionally flawed conception of executive authority. But that's the point, precisely. Americans deserve presidents who will keep good company.

Notes

1. Andrew Rudalevige, *The New Imperial Presidency* (Ann Arbor: University of Michigan Press, 2005).
2. Jeffrey Kimball, *Nixon's Vietnam War* (Lawrence: University of Kansas Press, 2002).
3. H.R. Haldeman, files from Nixon Presidential Materials, National Archives, Alexandria, Virginia.

4. John D. Ehrlichman, files from Nixon Presidential Materials, National Archives, Alexandria, Virginia.

5. George C. Herring, *America's Longest War: The United States and Vietnam, 1950-1975* (New York: Wiley, 1979), 217–251.

6. Tad Szulc, *The Illusion of Peace: Foreign Policy in the Nixon Years* (New York: Viking, 1978), 150.

7. Nixon, *RN: the Memoirs* (New York: Grosset & Dunlap, 1978), 382.

8. The secret bombing of Cambodia was the basis of one of the impeachment charges against President Nixon. The article was voted down by a 26-12 margin.

9. Szulc, *The Illusion of Peace*, 54–55.

10. When the president spoke these words, American B-52s had been flying bombing missions over Cambodia for over 13 months.

11. Les Evans and Allen Myers, *Watergate and the Myth of American Democracy* (New York: Pathfinder, 1974).

12. Barbara Tuchman, *The March of Folly: From Troy to Vietnam* (New York: Harper and Row, 1986).

13. Nguyen Thien Hung and Jerrold L. Schecter, *The Palace File* (New York: Harper and Row, 1986).

14. Larry Berman, *No Peace, No Honor: Nixon, Kissinger, and Betrayal in Vietnam* (New York: Free Press, 2001).

15. David Gray Adler, "Court, Constitution and Foreign Affairs," in Adler and Larry N. George, eds., *The Constitution and the Conduct of American Foreign Policy* (Lawrence: University Press of Kansas, 1996), 19–56. See also, Michael A. Genovese, *The Supreme Court, the Constitution, and Presidential Power* (Lanham, MD.: University Press of America, 1980).

16. *Congressional Quarterly Almanac*, Washington, DC: *Congressional Quarterly*, (1973), 792.

17. For discussion of the War Powers Resolution, its origins and flaws, see Louis Fisher and David Gray Adler, "The War Powers Resolution: Time to Say Goodbye," *Political Science Quarterly*, 113 (Spring 1998): 1–20.

18. See: Louis Fisher, *Presidential War Power*, 2nd ed. (Lawrence: University Press of Kansas, 2004), 158–159.

19. Fisher. *Presidential War Power*, 160–165.

20. Fisher, *Presidential War Power*, 165–174.

21. Adler, "Clinton, the Constitution and the War Power" in David Gray Adler and Michael Genovese, *The Presidency and the Law: The Clinton Legacy* (Lawrence: University Press of Kansas, 2002), 19-57; Ryan C. Hendrickson, *The Clinton Wars The Constitution, Congress and War Power* (Nashville: Vanderbilt University Press, 2002).

22. See Fisher, *Presidential War Power,* Chapter 9; David Gray Adler, "The Law: George Bush as Commander in Chief: Toward the Nether World of American Constitutionalism," *Presidential Studies Quarterly*, 36 (September, 2006): 525-40 ; and James P. Pfiffner, *Power Play: The Bush Presidency and the Constitution* (Washington, DC: Brookings Institution Press, 2008).

23. Arthur Schlesinger, Jr., *The Imperial Presidency* (Boston: Houghton, Mifflin, 1973); David Gray Adler, "The President as King: The Usurpation of War and Foreign Affairs Powers in the Modern Age" in Michael A. Genovese and Lori Cox Han, eds., *The Presidency and the Challenge of Democracy* (New York: Palgrave MacMillan, 2006), 159–189; Michael A. Genovese, *Presidential*

Prerogative: Imperial Power in an Age of Terrorism (Stanford: Stanford University Press, 2011).

24. Karen J. Greenberg and Joshua L. Dratel, eds., *The Torture Papers: The Road to Abu Ghraib* (Cambridge: Cambridge University Press, 2005); John Yoo, *War By Other Means: An Insider's Account of the War on Terror* (New York: Atlantic Monthly Press, 2006). For discussion, see David Gray Adler, "Bush as Commander in Chief," 525, and "George Bush and the Abuse of History: The Constitution and Presidential Power in Foreign Affairs," *UCLA Journal of International Law and Foreign Affairs*, 12 (Spring 2007): 75–144.

25. See: Jack Goldsmith, *The Terror Presidency*, (New York: W. W. Norton, 2007); Pfiffner, *Power Play*; and Fisher, *Presidential War Power.*

26. A large and impressive literature has examined the constitutional governance of war making, including the assertions of presidential power to initiate military hostilities on behalf of the American people. See, for example, the seminal work of Francis D. Wormuth, "The Nixon Theory of the War Power: A Critique," *California Law Review*, 60 (May 1972): 623–703; and, later, Francis D. Wormuth and Edwin Firmage, *To Chain the Dogs of War: The War Power in History and Law* (Dallas: Southern Methodist University Press, 1986). See also: Louis Fisher's influential studies, *Presidential War Power* and *Military Tribunals and Presidential Power* (Lawrence: University Press of Kansas, 2005); and David Gray Adler, "The Constitution and Presidential Warmaking: The Enduring Debate," *Political Science Quarterly*, 103 (Spring 1988): 1–36. On March 19, 2011, President Obama ordered air strikes against Libya to prevent the government of Col. Muammar el–Qaddafi from killing dissidents and rebels who sought his removal from power. Obama invoked a variety of legal rationales, including authority as Commander in Chief. David D. Kirkpatrick, Steven Erlanger, and Elisabeth Bumiller, "U.S. Missiles Strike Libyan Air Defense Targets," *New York Times*, March 19, 2011, A-1.

27. Leonard Meeker, "The Legality of United States Participation in the Defense of Vietnam," 54 State Department Bulletin 474 (1966). Francis Wormuth examined and, it should be added, decimated this list of episodes, pointing out that most of the incidents which involved use of force by the United States had been ordered, not by presidents, but by various military officials. When presidents did authorize military hostilities, they did so by purporting to find authorization in statutes or treaties, but not constitutional provisions. See Wormuth, "The Nixon Theory of the War Power," 652–664; and *The Vietnam War: The President versus the Constitution*, (Santa Barbara CA: Center for the Study of Democratic Institutions, 1968). See, too, my discussion of the use of precedents in Adler, "Clinton, the Constitution and the War Power".

28. 6 Weekly Compilation of Presidential Documents, No. 18, at 597 (May 4, 1970).

29. Act of June 5, 1794, chapter 50, sec. 5, 1 Stat. 384.

30. *United States v. Smith*, 27 F. Cas. 1192, 1196-97 (No. 16342) (C.C.D.N.Y. 1806).

31. Id. At 1230.

32. See *Bas v. Tingy*, 4 U.S. (4 Dall.) 37 (1800); *Talbot v. Seeman*, 5 U.S. (1 Cranch) 1 (1801); *Little v. Barreme*, 6 U.S. (2 Cranch) 170 (1804). For discussion of these cases, and others, see: Adler, "Presidential Warmaking," 209–212; and Fisher, *Presidential War Power*, 25–26.

33. For a detailed review and analysis of the framers' discussions, see Adler, "Presidential War Making," 184–229; Fisher, *Presidential War Power*, 1–16.

34. Jonathan Elliot, *Debates in the Several State Conventions on the Adoption of the Federal Constitution*, 2nd ed., 4 vols. (Washington, DC: J. Elliot, 1836), 2:528.

35. Elliot, *Debates*, 4:107, 108, 287, and 2:278.

36. James Kent, *Commentaries on American Law*, 2nd ed., 4 vols. (Boston: Little, Brown, 1896), 1:55.

37. Federalist 69, in *The Federalist,* ed., Edward Mead Earle (New York: Modern Library Edition, 1937), 448.

38. For discussion of congressional control of the commander-in-chief, see Adler, "George Bush as Commander in Chief."

39. Arthur Schlesinger, Jr., *The Imperial Presidency* .

40. See Adler, "Court, Constitution and Foreign Affairs.".

41. For discussion, see Adler, "The President as King."

42. Quoted in Louis Fisher, *Congressional Abdication on War and Spending* (College Station, TX: Texas A&M University Press, 2000), 119.

Chapter Six

Richard Nixon, Reputation, and Watergate

Iwan W. Morgan

Reputation, reputation, reputation! O! I have lost my reputation, I have lost the immortal part of myself, and what remains is bestial.

William Shakespeare, *Othello*

The history books will write Richard Nixon in large letters.

President Nixon to his Cabinet, November 11, 1971[1]

Clare Booth Luce [told me in 1972] that each person in history can be summed up in one sentence.... She said, "You will be summed up, 'He went to China.'" Historians are more likely to lead with "He resigned the office."

Richard Nixon, 1990[2]

For Richard Nixon history was about the future not the past. When revealing to the Senate Select Committee on Presidential Campaign Activities (better known as the Ervin Committee) that his boss had routinely taped Oval Office conversations in secret, White House aide Alexander Butterfield remarked, "The President is very history-oriented and very history-conscious about the role he is going to play."[3] The recordings were mainly intended to provide source material for the writing of the presidential memoirs that Nixon hoped would shape his grandiose image for posterity. It was the supreme irony that their revelations of his misdeeds were the instrument of the downfall that would largely determine his place in history.

The disgraced Nixon did not fade away after resigning office to avoid impeachment. In 1977, he appeared in four television programs with David Frost, the first of which became the most watched political interview of all time with an estimated audience of 50 million. In May 1978, he published his 1,100 page memoirs that became an immediate bestseller and racked up hardback sales of 330,000 within six months. An outpouring of eight more books followed in the remaining 16 years of his life, several of which were also bestsellers. In between producing these tomes, Nixon was a regular presence in newsprint and on television. Testifying to this, a James Stevenson *New Yorker* cartoon from 1988 showed a psychiatrist reassuring an anxious client, "It's *not* your imagination. You *are* seeing Nixon everywhere."[4]

Nixon's media ubiquity was fundamental to his effort to redeem his place in history. On December 7, 1974, in the depth of post-resignation depression and still weak from a severe attack of phlebitis (and a life-threatening cardiovascular shock following surgery for this), he wrote in his diary, "I simply have to pull myself together and begin the long journey back."[5] What followed was a concerted postpresidential campaign without precedent in American history to shape remembrance of his achievements in office while downplaying his Watergate wrongdoings as misjudgments, rather than constitutional and criminal violations. As scholar Michael Schudson observed, "Metaphorically Nixon died when he resigned the presidency and he has been his own survivor, entrusted to preserve and promote the reputation of the Nixon who died."[6]

This chapter considers Nixon's bid for reputational resurrection and the extent of its success. It contends that far from fading with the passage of time, Watergate is the spot that will not out. Nixon may have achieved a greater degree of rehabilitation than had seemed possible when he resigned office, but his misdeeds rather than his achievements are still what define remembrance of him. He has remained a source of headline-making controversy in death almost as much as in life. Shortly before he died in 1994, he reportedly asked an aide, "Do you think interest in me is down?"[7] The answer to that question will always be no as long as Watergate engenders debate and dispute.

The Last Campaign

Reassured by Henry Kissinger shortly before his resignation that history would rank him a great president, Nixon responded, "That depends...on who writes the history." Taking a leaf from the playbook of one of his heroes, Winston Churchill, he became his own historian.[8] Nixon's self-depiction in his last campaign drew on his earlier incarnations as the American everyman risen through hard work, the lone battler against the institutional power of the liberal establishment, and the geopolitical maestro tirelessly advancing the nation's interests in the global arena.

No president in polling history had hitherto left office with lower popularity ratings than Nixon. Some two-thirds of Gallup survey respondents agreed that his resignation was warranted. So hostile was public opinion that Gerald Ford later admitted misjudgment of the national mood in so speedily pardoning a man whom many critics "wanted...drawn and quartered publicly."[9] In these circumstances Nixon began his quest for redemption by seeking to reconnect with the Middle Americans that had once been his bedrock support as president. Accordingly he set about presenting himself as still being one of them in terms of shared values and aspirations, Watergate notwithstanding.

This was not a new strategy for Nixon, who had advanced his career through emphasizing his representative origins in the lower middle class and his typically American dedication to the work ethic.[10] This was his shield against the pariah status that the so-called Eastern Establishment had tried to foist on him for denouncing foreign policy grandee Alger Hiss as a Communist spy in the late 1940s. It was his defense against the secret slush fund allegations that threatened his vice presidential candidacy on the Republican ticket in 1952. It was a common theme in friendly biographies that appeared before he ran for president against millionaire's son John F. Kennedy in 1960.[11] Finally, on becoming president, he linked himself to the silent majority of ordinary Americans when denouncing student anti-Vietnam protestors as a cosseted, privileged minority.

Building on themes already tested in the Frost interviews, Nixon's 1978 memoir was his most important reassertion of everyman status. Liberal reviewers such as John Kenneth Galbraith were aghast that such a "rascal" could still perceive himself "a deeply moral man" but they were not his target audience.[12] Nixon was intent on shaping how ordinary Americans would see him—not so much in the immediate aftermath of his downfall but in years to come. The memoir contained many lies, half-truths, and evasions that contradicted the historical record revealed in the secret Oval Office tapes and other sources. As memory of his misdeeds faded, however, Nixon anticipated that this tome would eventually become a definitive source for understanding his presidency and an essential tool of revisionism. As one historian astutely remarked, "For Richard M. Nixon and his band of followers it will be the ultimate Survivor's Kit."[13]

The memoir begins with a brief but telling sentence: "I was born in a house my father built." These nine words evinced its author's strong sense of family ties, his modest origins in the early twentieth-century equivalent of a log cabin, and his Horatio Alger-like rise from lowly status. Continuing this theme, the prepresidential portion of the book methodically presented Nixon as embodying the values that made America great. The influence of family, church, and school on his development, his dedication to the work ethic, and his common-man fearlessness in battling the odds to climb the political ladder were all highlighted to this end.[14]

Linking his presidency to his everyman roots, the Nixon's memoir depicted his domestic policy as limiting Washington's encroachments against local communities and making the federal government "more truly reflective of the rest of the country." Seeing himself as the embodiment of the nation, he portrayed his adversaries as its antithesis. In this scenario the Democrat-led Congress, the federal bureaucracy, the judiciary, and—above all—the elite media were the real power brokers who engineered his downfall because of his threat to their influence.[15]

Nevertheless, Nixon did not exonerate the public from some culpability for his fate. The Watergate portion of the book suggested that the moral corruption of Congress, the courts, and the media had spread to the populace, which had accepted the lies and exaggerations of his enemies as the truth. Nixon's explanation for this was that materialism and prosperity had made Americans complacent at the cost of "an underlying loss of will, an estrangement from traditional outlooks and attitudes." This jeremiad fitted the national sense of malaise amid the economic and international woes of the late 1970s.[16] As such, Nixon implicitly portrayed himself as the eternal exemplar rather than the betrayer of the nation's values, waiting for the rehabilitation that would symbolize America's renewal and the reaffirmation of its historic mission as the beacon of freedom in the world.

Since the American everyman could not be corrupt, Nixon tried to hide his Watergate misdeeds behind a web of lies, a continuation of the habitual mendacity that marked his entire career in politics.[17] At no stage did he admit to the gravity of his presidential wrongdoing. Even when accepting Ford's pardon, which implied commitment of a crime, he only issued a halfhearted statement of contrition for having been "wrong in not acting more decisively and forthrightly" over his aides' actions in the Watergate cover-up and making "mistakes and misjudgments" that might lead people to think that he had acted illegally.[18]

To avoid telling the truth about Watergate in his memoirs, Nixon resurrected his oft-used tactic of depicting himself as the adversary and ultimately the victim of the liberal establishment. Ignoring his own use of smear tactics that had scandalized opponents during his political rise, he had long insisted that the Hiss case left a "residue of hatred and hostility toward me" on the part of liberals and their media allies.[19] In terms of practicing the dark political arts, he deemed himself a saint in comparison to the all-powerful Kennedys. They had stolen the 1960 election through ballot box fraud, had sought to disgrace Nixon by ordering an audit of his tax returns in 1963, and engaged in other skullduggery without losing their halo of virtue. In general, Nixon portrayed himself as more sinned against than sinning when it came to dirty tricks. The political espionage operations of his White House were "tentative and feeble and amateurish" in comparison those of his Democratic predecessors.[20]

In the Frost interviews, Nixon came as close as he ever would to confessing that he did wrong, undoubtedly a strategic recognition of the need for some expression of regret in his first public statement since resignation in order for his comeback campaign to be taken seriously. As his eyes moistened, he told his interlocutor, "I let down the country. I let down our system of government and the dreams of all those young people that ought to get into government but think it's all too corrupt.... I let the American people down. And I have to carry that burden with me for the rest of my life." But what was he truly sorry for? This was left unclear in his 1977 television remarks but later statements would reveal his sense of very limited wrongdoing. Nixon considered himself guilty only of covering up run-of-the-mill political espionage that was all part of the rough-and-tumble of elections rather than high crimes and misdemeanors. In 1988, he declared on NBC's *Meet the Press* that the Watergate cover-up was "a great mistake" but claimed that the break-in itself "was a small thing...and break-ins have occurred in other campaigns as well."[21]

Nixon laid down clear requirements to guide the editorial staff that helped in the research and writing of his 1978 memoir: "We won't grovel; we won't confess; we won't do a *mea culpa* act; but we will be one hundred per cent accurate."[22] Living up to the first three dictates, as the volume did, made it impossible to uphold the remaining one. The memoir alternated between portraying Nixon as the unknowing victim of excessive actions by overzealous aides to cover up their connection to the infamous burglary and downplaying the importance of the cover-up. In the Watergate section that takes up the last third of the book, he is always the victim rather than the wrongdoer. In one typical passage, Nixon asserted of the Senate investigating committee that did much to reveal his culpability, "Historians will eventually conclude that even the serious issues raised and abuses revealed by Watergate did not justify such abuses of power as were committed by members of the Ervin Committee. With their prejudicial leaks, their double standards, and their grandstanding behavior, they only confirmed my feeling that this was a partisan attack, a determined effort to convert something minor into something major, and we had to fight back."[23]

Nixon's shameless posturing of innocence leaps out from many other pages. Watergate, he asserted, "mattered so much less than the things I did well." [973] Quoting his own remarks to aides in April 1973, he claimed that its place in history, "ten years from now...will be a few paragraphs. In fifty years it will be a footnote." [839] As proof that his enemies had blown things out of proportion to engineer his downfall, he reproduced the alleged remarks of *Washington Post* publisher Kathryn Graham in the 1972 presidential campaign: "I hate [Nixon] and I'm going to do everything I can to beat him."[895] In line with this, he dismissed the House Judiciary Committee's approval of impeachment proceedings as a partisan fraud: "The votes [of the Democratic members] were in even before the witnesses had been heard or a defense had been made."[1041]

Nixon later seized on the Reagan White House's embroilment in the Iran-contra scandal in 1986–1987 to support his claims that congressional investigations of supposed presidential wrongdoing were the stuff of partisan skullduggery. This involved a triangle of illegal secret actions—selling arms to Iran in return for the release of western hostages held in Lebanon and the diversion of the proceeds to the U.S.-backed Contra rebels in Nicaragua. Reagan avoided the threat of impeachment with some ease because there was no "smoking gun" evidence that he had directed operations and key aides initially accepted liability for the wrongdoing. Nevertheless, the episode gave Nixon the opportunity to gloat. On the one hand, he sneered at "overstaffing and duplication" in the various investigations of the affair, drawing a contrast with the small-scale operation that succeeded in exposing Alger Hiss because "we were on the right side." In addition, he defended presidential secrecy in foreign policy, now under renewed attack from Congress and the media, by citing his China initiative as proof that covert diplomacy was sometimes essential. Missing from these ruminations, of course, was any acknowledgement that the Reagan scandal reaffirmed Watergate's lesson of the imperial presidency's tendency to flout the law.[24]

The further away Watergate became in time, the more Nixon downplayed its importance. This strategy reached its apogee with the opening of the Richard M. Nixon Library and Birthplace in July 1990. Financed from private pledges of $27 million (including a $2 million contribution from Nixon), it was administered by the Nixon Foundation, an organization composed of Nixon's aides, supporters, and friends. This privately funded and operated establishment did not have to observe the historical standards required of other presidential libraries administered by the National Archives and Records Administration (NARA). Dubbed the "liebrary" by some critics, it was a shrine to Nixon the world statesman, man-of-peace, and great president. The Watergate section, which was located in an uninviting dark tunnel with unending blocks of small-text panels, effectively portrayed Nixon's downfall as a coup perpetrated by his liberal enemies. Bob Bostock, the Nixon aide responsible for developing the exhibit, intended that "people walk away from it shaking their heads, wondering how the nation ever let such a great president get away from them." The appreciative former president pronounced his work "brilliant."[25]

In parallel with his library's manipulation of history, Nixon marked its opening by publishing a final memoir that dismissed Watergate in a few sentences as "one part wrongdoing, one part blundering, and one part political vendetta." While admitting that he should have set "a higher standard for the conduct of the people who participated in my campaign and administration," he insisted on being guilty only of playing by "the rules of politics as I found them. Not taking a higher road than my predecessors and my adversaries was my central mistake."[26] In other words, his behavior was the norm in the amoral political arena, but his exceptional purpose in doing wrong was to acquire the power necessary to do good, particularly in the field of international affairs.

Projecting himself as a great foreign policy president, with the corollary promise of serving the nation as a wise elder statesman once rehabilitated, was the third element in Nixon's comeback strategy.[27] Without doubt he had shown himself capable of thinking on a grand scale in international affairs while evolving from a militant anticommunist in the early Cold War to architect of détente with the Communist powers in the 1970s. This was the policy domain on which he had based his presidential ambitions. All three of his campaigns for the White House had presented him as uniquely equipped to lead the nation in a dangerous world. Seemingly confirming his claims on this score, his first term had culminated in 1972 in the dazzling success of triangular diplomacy that forged nuclear arms limitation agreement with the Soviet Union and a new accord with the hitherto hostile People's Republic of China.

Nixon launched his redemption campaign just when the United States appeared in Cold War retreat. The loss to communism of South Vietnam, Cambodia, and Laos in 1975 was followed over the next five years by the Soviet invasion of Afghanistan, further U.S. reverses in the third world—notably the Horn of Africa, and Central America, and the national humiliation of the Iranian hostage crisis. Seizing on this catalog of woes, Nixon followed his memoirs with a best-selling critique of American decline under Jimmy Carter. In a highly selective retelling of history, *The Real War* put his foreign policy record in best light, blamed a Democratic Congress for abandoning his commitment to use air power in defense of South Vietnam against renewed communist assault, and insisted that he never conceived of détente as entente. The admonition at its start that America "appears so lost in uncertainty or paralyzed by propriety that it is either unable or unwilling to act" chimed with Ronald Reagan's critique of national malaise in the 1980 presidential election. Indeed his speechwriters lifted passages from Nixon's book for unattributed insertion into his campaign addresses. As payback, Reagan let himself be photographed holding a copy of *The Real War* after entering the White House.[28]

Further books appeared at regular intervals to reinforce Nixon's image as a foreign policy sage. Having decried Carter's failure to be tough with the Soviets, he counseled Reagan in *Real Peace* to emulate his policy of hard headed détente instead of making the world more dangerous through unremitting hostility to Moscow. Published in 1985, on the tenth anniversary of the fall of Saigon, *No More Vietnams*, upheld America's involvement in the war as a just cause and again defended the 1973 terms he negotiated with the communists as ensuring a peace with honor that the Democratic Congress had squandered. Urging the nation to renew its commitments to defend freedom across the globe, Nixon declared the lesson from Vietnam was not that America should not try again but that "we should not *fail* again." In similar vein, *1999: Victory without War* reviewed America's *Fin-de-siècle* prospects of bringing about "a new dawn for all those who cherish freedom in the world."[29]

Well as they did in sales, Nixon's books did not gain him renewed entrée to the corridors of power. They were too enmeshed with defense of his legacy to offer a fresh perspective on the new challenges facing America. Though consulted in confidence by his three Republican successors, there is no evidence that he actually influenced their foreign policy. By the end of his life, moreover, scholars were moving away from initially favorable assessment of his presidential record in international affairs. The new orthodoxy evinced more skeptical evaluation of his contribution to eventual Cold War victory, denied that his Vietnam policy laid the basis for peace with honor, and decried his fixation on great power politics to the neglect of better relations with developing nations. Paradoxically, Nixon revisionism moved in the other direction on domestic policy to laud him as the pre-Reagan "last liberal" for his civil rights, environmental, and social welfare reforms in particular.[30]

In essence, Nixon's foreign policy writings attracted interest more for their source than as a blueprint for the way ahead. Nevertheless, this sufficed to rehabilitate him as a world affairs savant with the once hated media. In 1980, Nixon left his post-Watergate exile in San Clemente, California to live in New York City and later New Jersey, where he had better access to influential journalists. A steady stream of reporters and columnists received invitations to visit his new home, almost all of whom ended up paying homage to his geopolitical expertise. Having accused Nixon in 1974 of "charting himself a course straight into the sloughs of history," Hugh Sidey of *Time* typically reassessed him ten years later as "a strategic genius."[31]

Such admiration begot Nixon new opportunities to hold forth on foreign policy in newspaper columns and television appearances. The highlights included *New York Times* op-eds, a videotaped memoir with a tame interviewer (former aide Frank Gannon) that reportedly earned him one million dollars and aired on two CBS programs in 1984, and a long *Time* interview on the nuclear arms race on the fortieth anniversary of the Hiroshima atomic bombing. On April 21, 1986, he received a standing ovation for a mesmerizing overview of the international scene at an Associated Press luncheon. This performance so impressed Kathryn Graham that his old nemesis arranged for him to be interviewed for *Newsweek*, part of the *Washington Post* group. Nixon's insistence on a cover appearance paid handsome dividends. His smiling visage on the magazine's glossy front next to the headline "He's Back: The Rehabilitation of Richard Nixon" was widely hailed as evidence that he had become a respected elder statesman.[32]

Rehabilitation did not mean reconstruction of reputation, however. Despite the hype, the *Newsweek* piece cast an unforgiving lens on Watergate, even while celebrating Nixon's foreign policy expertise. Many of the laudatory articles that appeared in other outlets were also framed in terms of his efforts to substitute memory of his wrongdoing with awareness of his diplomatic triumphs. As a result, one historian has noted, "Watergate and the flight from it remained central, if submerged, themes of Nixon's late career."[33]

Reinforcing this was Nixon's utility for journalism as the memorial of its finest hour.[34] Watergate had made the investigative reporter a folk hero, but this proved a mixed blessing. Over the next 20 years, some critics claimed that the press's tendency to see itself as the guardian of political morality often worked against the best interests of American democracy. Such an outlook could lead to "feeding frenzies" of bandwagon investigative reporting that failed to distinguish between serious malpractice in high places and human peccadilloes. Nixon's high profile offered a contrasting validation for journalistic pursuit of public officials because he embodied the substantive wrongdoing that could go unexposed without a vigilant press. Even if the media was no longer kicking him around, his constant presence in it arguably reinforced memory of his misdeeds. Reflecting this, Gallup polls over the course of his attempted comeback generally recorded higher support for the view that his resignation was necessary (75 percent in June 1982, 71 percent in May 1986, and 70 percent in June 1992) than had been the case in its immediate aftermath.[35]

Slick Willie and Trick E. Dick

Far from signaling the end of the battle over his reputation, Nixon's death on April 22, 1994, only marked a new stage in it. His funeral, attended by President Bill Clinton and the four living former presidents—Gerald Ford, Jimmy Carter, Ronald Reagan, and George H.W. Bush—became a public celebration of his life and statesmanship. Clinton's eulogy appeared to put an official imprimatur on his campaign for redemption: "May the day of judging President Nixon on anything less than his entire life and career come to a close." To give history a nudge in this direction, Nixon had selected a line from his first inaugural address as his headstone epitaph: "The greatest honor history can bestow is the title of peacemaker." Satirizing this, *Los Angeles Times* cartoonist Paul Conrad, who had featured in Nixon's enemies list, drew a gravestone suggesting his eternal mendacity: "Here lies Richard M. Nixon." For the first and only time since his resignation, however, Nixon had a positive approval rating in a public opinion poll assessing his presidency immediately after his funeral. That this outlook did not last was indirectly thanks in part to Bill Clinton.[36]

Clinton had served in George McGovern's 1972 presidential campaign and his wife had worked on the House Judiciary Committee's impeachment inquiry legal staff in 1973–1974. Accordingly he had cause to dislike Nixon, but was willing to let bygones be bygones. Respecting his onetime adversary as a geopolitical thinker and fellow comeback artist, Clinton consulted him on postcommunist Russia.[37] This arguably gave Nixon in the last year of his life somewhat greater foreign policy influence with a Democratic White House than with recent GOP ones. However, Clinton's second-term impeachment scandal did much to revitalize memory of the significance of his misdeeds.

As *Washington Post* journalist Peter Baker observed, the partisan adversaries in the 1998–1999 impeachment imbroglio interpreted Watergate to their "own favor, embracing its lessons when they were useful and dismissing them when they were not." This was a far harder task for the Republicans than the Democrats. The impeachment articles against Clinton featured perjury in his grand jury testimony concerning his relationship with White House intern Monica Lewinsky and obstruction of justice by encouraging a witness to lie, concealing evidence, and trying to prevent truthful testimony. The Democratic riposte from the likes of Representative John Conyers of Michigan, a member of the House Judiciary Committee when it recommended articles of impeachment against Nixon and when it did so against Clinton, was in effect: "It isn't Watergate." Republicans, in contrast, appropriated Watergate whistleblower John Dean's famous remark about a cancer growing on the presidency (in his March 21, 1973, Oval Office conversation with Nixon) to argue the renewed need for moral cleansing of the office through impeachment.[38] However, this strategy only made Clinton's misconduct look puny and personal next to Nixon's. As the famed Watergate reporter Bob Woodward commented, "There was no conspiracy.... There were no orders...to lie or to obstruct justice.... The cover-up was Clinton's lonely effort to save face and embarrassment."[39]

Conservative pundits also used Watergate as a frame of reference to demand Clinton's impeachment. They deemed the forty-second president the embodiment of the 1960s values that had eroded America's moral strength. Former Nixon aide Pat Buchanan had already rung the alarm bell of national emergency in his 1992 campaign for president in prophesying that the United States faced "a cultural war as critical to the kind of nation we shall be as the Cold War was. This war is for the soul of America."[40] Claiming that Nixon was only responsible for hiding the misconduct of his subordinates, which she still considered sufficient to merit impeachment, conservative lawyer Ann Coulter declared in her best-selling *High Crimes and Misdemeanors* that Clinton had lied and obstructed justice to hide his own wrongdoing. The likes of former Reagan Secretary of Education William Bennett and British conservative intellectual Paul Johnson also produced variations on the same theme that Monicagate, as right-wingers called it, was worse than Watergate.[41] Ultimately, however, these commentators manifested an almost surreal determination not to recognize the obvious difference between the two cases of presidential wrongdoing: Nixon had covered up abuses of power, while Clinton had covered up illicit sex. Deplorable though the latter's conduct certainly was, it did not, in the words of one scholar, "constitute the same level of threat to the polity as Watergate."[42]

Most Americans showed limited interest in the scandal because they viewed Clinton's misconduct as more private than public. Even after his admission in a national address of an inappropriate relationship with Lewinsky had given the lie to his previous denials, a PEW survey found that his job rating ran at 66 percent approval and 29 percent disapproval. Meanwhile, opinion of him as a person was equally divided at 48 percent approval and disapproval. There was relatively little change in popular attitudes as the scandal moved to its denouement. Following the Senate vote of acquittal in January 1999, one poll found 64 percent of respondents in support of the verdict and 35 percent favoring impeachment. Scandal weariness was more evident than anger in the public mood. Reflecting this, the House Judiciary Committee hearings on whether to recommend impeachment attracted a small television audience in contrast to the 35 million that had daily watched the six days of its 1974 Watergate hearings. Moreover, media criticism of Clinton's conduct failed to fire popular outrage because its coverage dealt with sex more than the broader meaning of the scandal.[43]

After his acquittal by the Senate, Clinton granted an interview to CBS anchorman Dan Rather, who had clashed with Nixon in Watergate-era press conferences.[44] Challenged that his impeachment would do much to define his historical reputation, the president's response clearly marked his difference from Nixon. Firstly, he depicted the outcome as proof that "the Constitution works" because the two-thirds Senate majority required for a guilty verdict had thwarted a partisan-motivated impeachment. He also ascribed the not guilty verdict to the will of the American people "who almost always get it right if you give them enough time to think through things and really work on things." Finally, he predicted that his place in history would be as the president who thwarted efforts to use a constitutional and legal process for political ends: "I am honored that something indefensible was pursued and I had the opportunity to defend the Constitution."[45]

Twenty-First Century Watergate Wars

At one juncture it seemed that George W. Bush's constitutionally dubious assertions of presidential authority would downplay Watergate's enormity in historical memory. These precipitated a host of tracts about the dangers of a new imperial presidency that Arthur Schlesinger, Jr. adjudged "more grandiose" than the Nixon version.[46] Paralleling this largely academic critique, a "worse than Watergate" argument now held that the Bush administration had misled the American people about Saddam Hussein's possession of Weapons of Mass Destruction (WMD) to justify invading Iraq in 2003. According to Princeton professor and *New York Times* columnist Paul Krugman, the "selling of the [Iraq] war" on the basis of false information constituted "arguably the worst scandal in American political history." John Dean, once an actor in the Watergate drama and now enjoying a new career as a political commentator, similarly charged that the Bush administration had far exceeded anything attempted by Nixon if it had manipulated intelligence to justify the invasion of Iraq. Other pundits drew a comparison between White House leaking of Valerie Plame's identity as a CIA official in retaliation for her husband's public comments expressing doubts about the Iraqi nuclear threat and the Nixon administration's efforts to discredit *Pentagon Papers* whistleblower Daniel Ellsberg.[47]

Nixon loyalists were uncomfortable with the condemnation of Bush because it still impugned their man. Accordingly, some drew parallels between opposition to the Iraq and Vietnam wars. Pepperdine University fellow and onetime Nixon aide Stanley Herschensohn asserted that the 1973 peace settlement achieved America's war aims because it guaranteed the existence of South Vietnam. Echoing his old boss in *The Real War* and *No More Vietnams*, he blamed the U.S. Congress for snatching defeat from the jaws of victory in refusing to use air power against the communist offensive of 1975. In television interviews to market the book, Herschensohn excoriated the American left (among whom he included Democrats, university professors, and antiwar activists) for wanting the United States to be seen as the loser in the conflict. He also replicated the tone of Nixon's memoir jeremiad to warn that if the United States retreated from global engagement, "civilization as a whole would decline.... we are the only nation in the world that has the power and will to spend our lives for the liberty of strangers."[48]

Although Bush had lower approval ratings than Nixon when he left office, the "worse than Watergate" critique did not become the new measure of his imperial presidency. In part, this was because his expansive claims of power were too great to be understood through reference to the past. Moreover, Bush did not get a comeuppance in the manner of Nixon. There was no "smoking gun" evidence to prove high crimes and misdemeanors on his part. The House Judiciary Committee under the chairmanship of John Conyers produced recommendations for reining in the imperial presidency but there was not to be a third involvement in a presidential impeachment for the Michigan congressman.[49]

Meanwhile renewed controversy over Nixon's secret tapes showed that Watergate continued to have a life of its very own. In February 2009, the *New York Times* ran a front-page report under the headline, "John Dean's Role at Issue in Nixon Tapes Feud." This harked back to reporters Len Colodny and Robert Gettlin's 1991 best-selling book, *Silent Coup: The Removal of a President.* They contended that White House counsel John Dean had ordered the Watergate break-in to get hold of a Democratic National Committee official's little black book holding the names of high-priced call girls, among whom was mistakenly listed his fiancée, and had then orchestrated the cover-up that embroiled Nixon. Dean subsequently sued the authors and publisher St Martin's Press, settling for an undisclosed but reputedly huge sum.[50]

Stanley Kutler's publication in 1997 of edited transcripts of cover-up recordings in *Abuse of Power: The New Nixon Tapes* seemingly reaffirmed presidential guilt. This eminent Watergate historian had fought a four-year lawsuit alongside the Public Citizen organization to compel National Archives release of 201 hours of recordings that the Nixon estate sought to block.[51] However, Colodny claimed that there were serious omissions in Kutler's editing, allegations that won the support of historian Peter Klingman. Working together, they assembled the available tapes in their own archive and established *The Nixon Era Center* website. Their case gained little publicity for over a decade, but did undergo substantial modification. In 2002, after reviewing all the Watergate tapes subpoenaed in his lawsuit with Dean, Colodny became convinced that Nixon was equally culpable of involvement in the Watergate cover-up. According to this new scenario, based on statements in the March 13–20, 1973, tapes, Nixon tried to set up Dean to take the fall, only to have the latter turn the tables on him. In Colodny's estimate, Nixon could probably have saved his presidency by claiming to have discovered White House staff involvement in plotting the break-in, but ensured its demise through taking charge of concealing wrongdoing that he had nothing to do with.[52]

Unable to hook media interest in the new theory, Klingman submitted a paper on it to the *American Historical Review*, a tract that also questioned the objective professionalism of Kutler's transcripts. It was this bid for academic validation that attracted the attention of the *New York Times*, but scholarly response to its article was broadly critical for lending legitimacy to unjustified attacks on Kutler. The *American Historical Review* subsequently rejected the Klingman essay for publication, partly because it did not consider itself the right outlet for this exposé and partly for the egregious allegations against a distinguished scholar.[53] Nevertheless, this did not constitute a judgment on the accuracy of the Colodny-Klingman revisionism. Controversy over the tapes will never be resolved so long as scholars have to rely on edited versions instead of having full access to every word (and each pause, grunt, and stutter) of their entire content. As Joan Hoff, author of an important scholarly work of Nixon revisionism, observed, "What this dispute...really demonstrates is the need for an authoritative set of transcriptions which the government should have undertaken years ago."[54]

Before long, another Watergate donnybrook had grabbed the headlines. In 2007, the NARA took control of the Richard M. Nixon Presidential Library and Birthplace, which was renamed the Richard M. Nixon Presidential Library and Museum. This prefaced the transfer by July 2010 of 42 million pages of presidential papers and over four thousand hours of tapes from the National Archives at College Park, Maryland, to the Yorba Linda facility that already held Nixon's pre- and postpresidential papers. This development promised to end the access problems to documentary and electronic sources that had dogged historical study of the Nixon presidency. To facilitate his campaign to be his own historian, Nixon had fought to limit release of his presidential records, a battle continued by his estate after his death. New library director Timothy Naftali promised, "The hallmark of this new institution will be true acceptance and love for history—the good, the bad, and the ugly." Delivering this goal with regard to Watergate, a condition of the NARA takeover, landed him in dispute with Nixon supporters.[55]

Nixon Foundation consultant and former Nixon administration aide Geoff Shephard delivered a preemptive defense of loyalist orthodoxy in 2008. In *The Secret Plot to Make Ted Kennedy President: Inside the Real Watergate Conspiracy*, he asserted that Kennedy clan Democrats engaged in the real abuse of power in hijacking the scandal with the aim of getting their man into the White House in 1976. Naftali's plan for new Watergate exhibition contradicted virtually every element of this case. Invoking its advisory rights pertaining to museum attractions, the Nixon Foundation stalled the scheduled opening for nine months. Organization president Ronald Walker presented its detailed objections in a 158-page memorandum to NARA. These included the excessively negative image of Nixon that contrasted with how other libraries lionized their presidents, the lack of context detailing the political intelligence activities of other presidents, and the distortions of the section entitled "Dirty Tricks and Political Espionage," whose removal was demanded.[56]

The Watergate exhibit finally opened in April 2011 to the general approbation of Nixon scholars. Instead of its predecessor's evasions and dense
text, it featured interactive video displays of participants, witnesses, and
observers commenting on Watergate in 131 interviews with a combined
time of 40 hours. In detailing Nixon's abuse of power, the exhibit begins
the Watergate story with the 1971 break-in to the Los Angeles office of the
psychiatrist treating Pentagon Papers leaker Daniel Ellsberg. It ends not
with Nixon's resignation and pardon but with Watergate's legislative legacy.
Included in this section are: the Privacy Act of 1974 limiting the authority
of government agencies to pass on private information to each other and
guaranteeing individuals' rights to access government files on them; the
Presidential Materials and Preservation Acts of 1974 and 1978 prohibiting destruction of presidential records; the Federal Election Campaign Act
amendment of 1974 establishing new regulations for election contributions;
and the Ethics in Government Act of 1978 that established the special prosecutor's office.[57]

Naftali's hope that the exhibit dispute was "the last fight over
Watergate" appeared overly optimistic. The Nixon Foundation did not
seem ready to bury the hatchet—other than in him. A disgruntled Bob
Bostock sarcastically asked, "Isn't there an Alger Hiss library somewhere
he would like to be director of?" However, loyalist charges of bias carried
little weight. While other presidential libraries promote their subject's
reputation, Nixon's has to be different because he was the only president
to resign rather than face impeachment. His administration's increasingly
available records have invalidated claims that he was the victim of partisan conspiracy. According to public historian Benjamin Hufbauer, a presidential library goes through three phases in its life: first, founding and
initial development (largely controlled by the president and his supporters); second, the organization and opening of its archives for scholarly use
(largely controlled by NARA); and, finally, a period of maturity when it
must reinvent itself to remain relevant. The Nixon library has belatedly
entered its second stage that will not end until the release of undisclosed
files and tapes is as complete as possible.[58]

Conclusion

The early twenty-first century disputes over Watergate underline the difficulty of rescuing Nixon's reputation from its obloquy. There was certainly
more to him than Watergate and the other aspects of his career deserve
full historical analysis and assessment. It is remarkable, for example, that
there is still no definitive biography of him. Nevertheless, recognition of
Nixon's many accomplishments does not mean that his misdeeds can ever
be discounted.

The new Watergate exhibit at the Nixon library offers a timely warning
of the dangers of further abuse of power by those in high places. Some of

the firewalls erected to prevent another Watergate have been eroded (such as campaign finance controls) or removed (such as the special prosecutor provision). With government in the twenty-first century much larger and more complex than in Nixon's day, it can more easily control information and enforce secrecy. Moreover, the security climate that is the legacy of 9/11 terrorist attacks on New York and Washington facilitates even more grandiose assertions of presidential power than was the case in the Cold War.

As is the case in other democracies, U.S. history does not contradict the ethos that power tends to corrupt, but Watergate offered some reassurance about the self-correcting mechanisms of the Constitution. Timothy Naftali dubbed it "the ultimate stress test" for the nation. The crisis seemingly affirmed Alexis de Tocqueville's optimistic mid-nineteenth century judgment that America's greatness "lies not in being more enlightened than any other nation, but rather in her ability to repair her faults."[59] If this is the case, vigilance against a repeat of the abuse of power that lay at the heart of Watergate is constantly necessary. For that reason, Richard Nixon's place in history is likely to be as the touchstone for presidential wrongdoing for the foreseeable future.

Notes

1. H. R. Haldeman, *The Haldeman Diaries: Inside the Nixon White House* (New York: Putnam, 1994), 374.
2. "Interview: Paying the Price," *Time*, April 2, 1990, 46.
3. Quoted in Stanley I. Kutler, ed., *Abuse of Power: The New Nixon Tapes* (New York: Touchstone, 1997), xiv.
4. The cartoon is reproduced and analyzed in Daniel Frick, *Reinventing Richard Nixon: A Cultural History of an American Obsession* (Lawrence: University Press of Kansas, 2008), 227, 229. It can also be viewed at *The New Yorker* cartoonbank.com.
5. Quoted in Jonathan Aitken, *Nixon: A Life* (London: Weidenfeld & Nicolson, 1993), 535.
6. Michael Schudson, *Watergate in American Memory: How We Remember, Forget, and Reconstruct the Past* (New York: Basic Books, 1992), 187.
7. Monica Crowley, *Nixon in Winter* (New York: Random House, 1998), 308.
8. Richard Nixon, *RN: The Memoirs* (New York: Grosset and Dunlap, 1978), 1084. See also his Frost interview remarks quoted in Joan Hoff, *Nixon Reconsidered* (New York: Basic Books, 1994), 341.
9. George Gallup, Jr., "'Watergate' Twenty Years Later," in *The Gallup Poll: Public Opinion 1992* (Wilmington, DE: Scholarly Resources, 1993), 105; Gerald Ford, *A Time to Heal: The Autobiography of Gerald R. Ford* (New York: Harper, 1979), 178.
10. For discussion, see Stephen Ambrose, *Nixon: The Education of a Politician 1913–62* (New York: Simon & Schuster, 1987); and Iwan Morgan, *Nixon* (London: Arnold, 2002), esp. Chapter 2.
11. See, for example: Earl Mazo, *Nixon: A Personal and Political Portrait* (New York: Harper, 1959); and Ralph de Toledano, *Nixon*, 2nd ed. (New York: Duell,

Sloan & Pearce, 1960). These studies also conflated Nixon's family history with that of the United States, a theme more extensively emphasized later in Edwin Hoyt, *The Nixons: An American Family* (New York: Random House, 1972).

12. John Kenneth Galbraith, "The Good Old Days," *New York Review of Books*, June 29, 1978, 3. For similar critiques, see Richard Rovere, "Richard the Bold," *New Yorker*, June 19, 1978, 96–97; John Osborne, "White House Watch: R. Nixon, His Book," *New Republic*, May 27, 1978, 9; and Daniel Schorr, "Nixon: Wrestling with Himself," *Progressive*, August 1978, 41.

13. James MacGregor Burns, " A Final Appeal to History," *New York Times Book Review*, June 11, 1978, 54.

14. Nixon, *RN*, 3–30 (quotation p. 3)

15. Nixon, *RN*, 351, 762, 770.

16. Nixon, *RN*, 762–763 (quotation), 889, 1033; Frick, *Reinventing Richard Nixon*, 64–76. For discussion of the late 1970s popular mood, see Bruce Schulman, *The 1970s: The Great Shift in American Culture, Society, and Politics* (New York: Simon & Schuster, 2001); and Dominic Sandbrook, *Mad as Hell: The Crisis of the 1970s and the Rise of the American Right* (London: Allen Lane, 2011).

17. Hoff, *Nixon Reconsidered*, 3. See also Morgan, *Nixon*, 26–29.

18. Stanley Kutler, ed., *Watergate: The Fall of Richard M. Nixon* (St James, NY: Brandywine Press, 1996), 213.

19. Richard Nixon, *Six Crises* (Garden City, NY: Doubleday, 1962), 69.

20. Nixon, *Six* Crises, 393, 399, 413–415; Nixon, *RN*, 628–629, 641, 675–676 [quotation].

21. David Frost, *"I Gave them a Sword:" Behind the Scenes of the Nixon Interviews* (London: Macmillan, 1978), 270; Stephen Ambrose, *Nixon: Ruin and Recovery 1973–1990* (New York: Simon & Schuster, 1991), 566.

22. Aitken, *Nixon*, 538.

23. Nixon, *RN*, 896.

24. Richard Nixon, *In the Arena: A Memoir of Victory, Defeat and Renewal* (New York: Simon & Schuster, 1990), 276–277, 331–332. For analysis of how the Reagan White House's scandal management drew lessons from Watergate, see Robert Busby, *Reagan and the Iran-Contra Affair: The Politics of Presidential Recovery* (New York: Palgrave, 1997).

25. Jon Wiener, "Inside the Nixon Liebrary," *Nation*, September 1990, 242–245; Frick, *Reinventing Richard Nixon*, 182–198; Bostock quoted in Christopher Goffard, "A New Take on Watergate at Nixon Library," *Los Angeles Times*, April 1, 2011, www.LATimes.com/news/local/. For the historical significance of presidential libraries in general, see Benjamin Hufbauer, *Presidential Temples: How Memorials and Libraries Shape Public Memory* (Lawrence: University Press of Kansas, 2005).

26. Nixon, *In the Arena*, 40–41.

27. For good discussion of this, see: Ambrose, *Nixon: Ruin and Recovery, 1973–1990*, 538–80; and David Greenberg, *Nixon's Shadow: The History of an Image* (New York: Norton, 2003). Stephen Ambrose also charts Nixon's foreign policy interest in the first two volumes of his biography: *The Education of a Politician 1913–62* and *The Triumph of a Politician, 1962–72* (New York: Simon & Schuster, 1989)

28. Richard Nixon, *The Real War* (New York: Warner, 1980), 3 [quotation], 96–125, 279–306; Peter Carroll, *It Seemed Like Nothing Happened: The*

Tragedy and Promise of America in the 1970s (New York: Holt, Rinehart & Winston, 1982), 343.

29. Richard Nixon, *Real Peace* (New York: Warner, 1984); Richard Nixon, *No More Vietnams* (New York: Arbor House, 1984), 237; Richard Nixon, *1999: Victory without War* (New York: Simon & Schuster, 1988), 321.

30. See Hoff, *Nixon Reconsidered*; and Melvin Small, *The Presidency of Richard Nixon* (Lawrence: University Press of Kansas, 1999). Foreign policy critiques include: William P. Bundy, *A Tangled Web: The Making of Foreign Policy in the Nixon Presidency* (New York: Hill & Wang, 1998); Jeffrey P. Kimball, *Nixon's Vietnam War* (Lawrence: University Press of Kansas, 1998); and Larry Berman, *No Peace, No Honor: Nixon, Kissinger, and Betrayal in Vietnam* (New York: Free Press, 2001); J. Brooks Flippen, *Nixon and the Environment* (Albuquerque: University of New Mexico Press, 2000); and Dean Kotlowski, *Nixon's Civil Rights: Politics, Principle, and Policy* (Cambridge, MA: Harvard University Press, 2001) exemplify domestic reassessment..

31. Robert Sam Anson, *Exile: The Unquiet Oblivion of Richard Nixon* (New York: Simon & Schuster, 1984), 235.

32. Larry Martz, "The Road Back," and "Interview: The Sage of Saddle River," *Newsweek*, May 19, 1986, 26–33.

33. Greenberg, *Nixon's Shadow*, 303. See also, Schudson, *Watergate in American Memory*, 193; and Thomas J. Johnson, *The Rehabilitation of Richard Nixon: The Media's Effect on Collective Memory* (New York: Garland, 1995), 6.

34. For insightful discussion, see Mark Feldstein, "The Myth of the Media's Role in Watergate," *History News Network*, August 30, 2004, http://hnn.us/articles/6813.html.

35. Schudson, *Watergate in American Memory*, 103–126; Larry Sabato, *Feeding Frenzy: How Attack Journalism has Transformed American Politics* (New York: Free Press, 1991); James Fallows, *Breaking the News: How the Media Undermine American Democracy* (New York: Vintage, 1996); Gallup, "'Watergate' Twenty Years Later," 105.

36. For Nixon's funeral and editorial commentary on his legacy, see Greenberg, *Nixon's Shadow*, 340–344.

37. Marvin Kalb, *The Nixon Memo: Political Respectability, Russia and the Press* (Chicago: University of Chicago Press, 1994), 144–159; Crowley, *Nixon in Winter*, 127–129.

38. Peter Baker, *The Breach: Inside the Impeachment and Trial of William J. Clinton* (New York: Berkley, 2001), 134–135, 121, 343. Party strategies are also discussed in Nicol C. Rae and Colton C. Campbell, *Impeaching Clinton: Partisan Strife on Capitol Hill* (Lawrence: University Press of Kansas, 2004). For Nixon's charges of excessive partisanship against Conyers in 1974, see *RN*, 990.

39. Bob Woodward, *Shadow: Five Presidents and the Legacy of Watergate* (New York: Simon & Schuster, 1999), 515.

40. James T. Patterson, *The Restless Giant: America from Watergate to Bush v. Gore* (New York: Oxford University Press, 2005), 251–252.

41. Ann H. Coulter, *High Crimes and Misdemeanors: The Case against Bill Clinton* (Washington, DC: Regnery, 1998); William J. Bennett, *The Death of Outrage: Bill Clinton and the Assault on American Ideals* (New York: Free Press, 1998); and Paul Johnson, *A History of the American People* (New York: Perennial, 1999), 917–923, 951–961.

42. James Pfiffner, *The Character Factor: How We Judge America's Presidents* (College Station TX: Texas A & M University Press, 2004), chapter 6 (quotation p. 139). See also Rick Shenkman, "Remember Watergate?" *History News Network*, July 7, 2003, http://hnn.us/articles/1553.html.

43. This discussion is based on Robert Busby, *Defending the American Presidency: Clinton and the Lewinsky Scandal* (New York: Palgrave, 2001), 170–214.

44. For Rather and Nixon, see Greenberg, *Nixon's Shadow*, 173–176.

45. "Interview with Dan Rather of CBS News," March 31, 1999, John Woolley and Gerhard Peters, *The American Presidency Project* (Santa Barbara: University of California, www.presidency.ucsb.edu).

46. John Nichols, "Arthur Schlesinger v. the Imperial Presidency," *Nation*, March 1, 2007; Andrew Rudalevige, *The New Imperial Presidency: Renewing Presidential Power after Watergate* (Ann Arbor: University of Michigan Press, 2006); Charlie Savage, *Takeover: The Return of the Imperial Presidency and the Subversion of American Democracy* (Boston: Little, Brown, 2007); James P. Pfiffner, *Power Play: The Bush Presidency and the Constitution* (Washington, DC: Brookings Institution Press, 2008).

47. Paul Krugman, "Standard Operating Procedure," *New York Times*, June 3, 2003; John W. Dean, *Worse than Watergate: The Secret Presidency of George W. Bush* (Boston: Little, Brown, 2004); Chris Matthews comments on "Plamegate" on MSNBC's "Hardball," September 30, 2003.

48. Stanley Herschensohn, *An American Amnesia: How the U.S. Congress Forced the Surrender of South Vietnam and Cambodia* (New York: Beaufort Press, 2010); and comments in Dennis Prager interview, "Professor Bruce Herschensohn on Amnesia," December 23, 2010, *Ellis Washington Report*, http://www.elliswashingtonreport.com/.

49. House Committee on the Judiciary Majority Staff Report to Chairman John C. Conyers, Jr., *Reining in the Imperial Presidency: Lessons and Recommendations Relating to the Presidency of George W. Bush* (Washington, DC: Government Printing Office, 2009).

50. Patricia Cohen, "John Dean's Role at Issue in Nixon Tapes Feud," *New York Times*, February 1, 2009; Len Colodny and Robert Gettlin, *Silent Coup: The Removal of a President* (New York: St. Martin's Press, 1991) [the publisher stopped selling the book after the court case but it can be read on http://www.silentcoup.com]. John Dean's Watergate memoir, originally published in 1976 was re-issued with an afterword that trashed attempts at Nixon revisionism. See *Blind Ambition: The End of the Story* (New York: Polimedia, 2009).

51. Kutler, *Abuse of Power*. He had previously written what is broadly considered the best academic study of Watergate, *The Wars of Watergate: The Last Crisis of Richard Nixon* (New York: Norton, 1990).

52. Rick Shenkman, "The Watergate Transcript Controversy: The Story Behind the Story," *History News Network*, February 5, 2009, http://hnn.us/articles/61160.html; Len Colodny, "Hidden History: The Day Nixon Lost His Presidency," *The Nixon Era Times*, undated, http://www.watergate.com/stories/watergate.asp.

53. For a statement of this thesis posted on his Nixon Era Center website, see Peter D. Klingman, "What Did The President Know and When Did He Know It? Redefining Richard Nixon's Guilt and John Dean's Role in the Watergate Cover-Up," http://www.watergate.com/stories/watergate.asp; Robert A. Schneider (*AHR* editor), "'The Nixon Tapes,' an Author, and the *American*

Historical Review," *History News Network*, February 9, 2009, http://hnn.us/articles/61694.html; Clark Hoyt, "They Still Have the Nixon Tapes to Kick Around," *New York Times*, February 21, 2009.

54. Joan Hoff, email to HNN, undated, reproduced in *HNN Hot Topics: The Watergate Transcript Controversy*, February 4, 2009, http://hnn.us/articles/61197. For Hoff's more extensive assessment of the tapes issue, including detailed criticism of Kutler's *Abuse of Power* editing, see Joan Hoff, "Why the Nixon Tapes Pose Problems for Scholars, John Dean, and the President," *The Nixon Era Times*, http://www.watergate.com/stories/watergate.asp.

55. Joan Hoff, "Researcher's Nightmare: Studying the Nixon Presidency," *Presidential Studies Quarterly*, 26 (Winter, 1996), 259–275; James Worsham, "Nixon's Library Now a Part of NARA: California Facility Will Hold All Documents and Tapes from a Half-Century Career in Politics," *Prologue*, 39 (Fall, 2007), www.archives.gov/publications/prologue/2007/fall/nixon-lib.html; Gillian Flaccus, "Federal Archivists Take Control of Nixon Library," *Washington Post*, July 12, 2007.

56. Geoff Shephard, *The Secret Plot to Make Ted Kennedy President: Inside the Real Watergate Conspiracy* (New York: Sentinel, 2008); Adam Nagourney, "Watergate Becomes a Sore Point at Nixon Library," *New York Times*, August 6, 2010; Guy Adams, "Nixon's backers make last stand over Watergate," *The Independent*, August 14, 2010, http://www.indepndent.co.uk. The full text of the Nixon Foundation letter can be accessed through a link [Nixon stalwarts' 158-page critique] in Goffard, "A New Take on Watergate at Nixon Library."

57. Karin Tanabe, "Nixon library re-examines scandal," *Politico*, April 1, 2011, http://dyn.politico/com/click; Jon Wiener, "At the new Watergate Gallery, the truth finally wins out," *Los Angeles Times*, April 5, 2011; Robert Johnson, "The Nixon Library's Watergate Exhibit," *History News Network*, April 11, 2011, http://hnn.us.blogs/entries/138399.html. For a critical view by the wife of the Nixon Foundation chair, see Anne Walker, "The New Watergate," *The New Nixon Blog*, April 5, 2011, http://blog.nixonfoundation.org/2011/04/the–new–watergate.

58. Goffard, "A New Take on Nixon at the Watergate Library;" Maarja Krusten, "What Role Should a Presidential Library Play?" *History News Network*, May 3, 2010, http://hnn.us/articles/125934.html; Hufbauer, *Presidential Temples*.

59. Naftali quoted in Wiener, "At the new Watergate Gallery, the truth finally wins out;" de Tocqueville quoted in Lexington, "Two Cheers for America," *Economist*, September 19, 2009.

Chapter Seven

The Ripple Effect of Scandal and Reform: The Historical Impact of Watergate-Era Campaign Finance Regulation and Its Progeny

Victoria A. Farrar-Myers

Looking into the future on October 15, 1974, the day on which President Gerald Ford signed major amendments to the Federal Election Campaign Act (FECA) into law, one might have many questions about the world of campaign finance in the twenty-first century. How did we get from the Senate Watergate Committee uncovering numerous instances of corporations making illegal campaign contributions to President Nixon's reelections efforts, to allowing corporations to pay for advertisements advocating the election or defeat of candidates for federal office? How did we get from allegations that the Justice Department settled a lawsuit with International Telephone and Telegraph Corporation (ITT) in exchange for ITT's promise to pay for part of the 1972 Republican National Convention to a system in which corporations openly provide large portions of funding for both major parties' national conventions? How did we get from an era in which a president was impeached in part for failing "to take care that the laws were faithfully executed…concerning other unlawful activities including…the campaign financing practices of the Committee to Re-elect the President"[1] to one in which presidential candidates of both parties routinely opt out of the system established out of the reforms generated during the previous era?

When President Ford signed the FECA amendments into law, he proclaimed, "the times demand this legislation."[2] In the nearly 40 years since the June 17, 1972, break-in in the Democratic headquarters at the Watergate Hotel that provided the impetus behind the legislation, though, the times have changed. What may have seemed unfathomable in 1974—corporate campaign spending and presidential candidates eschewing "free money" in their quests for the White House—have become par for the course. Perhaps more surprising to someone from 1974 would be that the landscape of twenty-first century campaign finance developed, not contrary to or despite the Watergate-era reforms, but because of these reforms. The primary focus of the Watergate-era campaign finance reform advocates to root out corruption and the appearance of corruption associated with campaign contributions to candidates begat the legal framework, judicial decisions, and campaign finance practices that define the post-Watergate world of campaign finance. This system is the legacy of the times that demanded the campaign finance legislation that Ford signed into law in 1974.

This chapter begins with an examination of the Watergate-era campaign finance reforms, focusing on what reform proponents were trying to accomplish with the FECA amendments and why, and what issues did they know they were not sufficiently addressing. From there, it will explore the changes in the campaign finance system in the post-Watergate era in the courts and in practice, with an emphasis of how the underlying objectives of the Watergate reforms have shaped actions and outcomes since the 1970s. The chapter will then conclude addressing some of the implications of the Watergate era's legacy for campaign finance and American democratic theory.

Watergate and the Objective of Campaign Finance Reforms

It its official, commissioned report to the Senate Watergate Committee, a panel of the National Academy of Public Administration (NAPA) condensed the challenges of addressing the "considerable expense" involved in "bring[ing] contested policies and contrasting candidacies before the electorate" to this primary issue: "How can the funds essential to inform the entire electorate be raised and spent without recourse to past abuses and without victors heavily beholden to any special interest?".[3] The campaign finance abuses of the Nixon administration and Nixon's Committee to Reelect the President (CRP) were still fresh in the minds of the members of Congress and the public as the Watergate hearings and related congressional action on campaign finance proceeded. In fact, during the on-floor debate in Congress on the FECA amendments, members in both chambers expressed concern about the public perception about why Congress was taking so long to produce campaign finance legislation.[4]

In addition to the illegal corporate contributions and the possible connection between the Justice Department's settlement with ITT and ITT's pledge of money for the 1972 Republican convention discussed above, the campaign finance abuses that those associated with Nixon's reelection effort committed or were alleged to have committed included the following:

- the use of a secret slush fund of undeclared campaign contributions;
- the selling of ambassadorships in exchange for large contributions; and
- the president's use of control over milk price supports as a means for obtaining contributions from the Associated Milk Producers.

As campaign finance reform critic John Samples noted, most of the Watergate-related campaign finance abuses were either already illegal prior to the 1974 FECA amendments, or at least would have been illegal if sufficient evidence were available to prove the alleged abuses.[5] Where the problem rested for those seeking to change the campaign finance reform system was not the actual corruption that was already prohibited or could easily be prohibited with episodic revisions to existing campaign finance reform laws.[6] Instead, the fundamental issue that needed to be addressed was the systemic problems associated with the appearance of corruption. The Senate Watergate Committee acknowledged as much in discussing its recommendation that a statutory limit must be preset on the amount contributed by an individual to a presidential campaign: "The basic purpose of a limit on contributions from any one source is to minimize the potential influence or appearance of impropriety which might result from large contributions."[7]

The 1974 FECA amendments were geared to reduce corruption and the appearance of corruption by limiting the financial influence of moneyed "fat cats" through limits on contributions and expenditures, disclosure, offering funding alternatives for presidential candidates, and providing for independent enforcement of campaign financing laws. They included provisions that addressed the following areas:

(1) **limits on direct contributions**: from individuals, PACs, and party committees;
(2) **spending limits for political parties expenditures on behalf of federal candidates**: so-called coordinated expenditures;
(3) **candidate spending limits**: for House, Senate, and presidential candidates, which replaced the media expenditure ceilings in the 1971 FECA;
(4) **limits on independent expenditures**: for expenditures by individuals or interest groups made independently of a candidate's campaign to advocate the election or defeat of a federal candidate;
(5) **the Federal Election Commission**: the FEC was created to implement and enforce the federal campaign finance laws;
(6) **new disclosure and reporting rules**: requiring quarterly contributions and spending reports from candidates, with such reports made publicly available; and
(7) **amending the presidential election public funding system**: to allow major party presidential nominees to receive public funds up to a preset spending limit provided they do not accept any additional private money and to establish a voluntary system of public matching funds in presidential primary campaigns.[8]

These provisions supplemented or enhanced the existing campaign finance system, which had already included public funding of presidential elections, bans on contributions by corporations and labor unions, disclosure

requirements during primary and general elections, limits on media advertising, and limits on self-financing.

One notable provision that was omitted from the 1974 FECA amendments was public financing for congressional elections. Early versions
of the legislation that would ultimately result in the FECA amendments
included public financing provisions. As Senator Ted Kennedy argued,
"Just as Watergate and private campaign contributions have mired the
executive branch in its present quicksand of corruption, so, I am convinced, the present low estate of Congress is the result of the ingrained
corruption and appearance of corruption that our system of private financing of congressional elections has produced."[9] Opponents of the public
financing proposal, including some prominent supporters of campaign
finance reform generally, voted down this alternative. Among the reasons
given in opposition to public financing for congressional elections were
that public financing would favor the reelection of incumbents,[10] would
result in an unnecessary burden on the public treasury,[11] and would discourage contributions by small donors at a time when such participation
should be encouraged.[12]

One problem that often plagues reform-oriented legislation is the
unintended consequences that may result.[13] Looking back at congressional debate and Watergate hearings related to campaign finance, though,
one sees the roots of what many would subsequently consider one of the
biggest threats in the campaign finance system—namely, independent
expenditures of third parties. This issue was not lost on those involved
in these debates. The official, commissioned report prepared by a panel
of the NAPA noted, almost in passing, that the approximately $400 mil-
lion spent by political parties and candidates in 1972 did not include
"spontaneous and unauthorized expenditures by interested individuals
and organizations, acting outside the standard framework."[14] Senator
Howard Baker (R-TN) argued at one point that "support [for candi-
dates] should only come from individual human beings who can vote.
Corporations cannot vote. Common Cause cannot vote. Chambers of
Commerce cannot vote. Why should they contribute?"[15] Representative
Joel Broyhill (R-VA) offered an amendment that would deny tax-exempt
status to organizations if they endorse or oppose candidates "publicly or
with open or covert campaign contributions."[16]

Each of the above statements indicates some level of concern with the
political activity of outside groups and their independent spending and
activities. Underlying these concerns is a key question of what rights should
organizations be given within the campaign finance arena. Congress, however, was not able to focus on this question, instead emphasizing the more
fundamental issue at the time of controlling contributions to candidates.
Nevertheless, Congress did attempt to tackle the issue by seeking to limit
independent expenditures to $1,000. In the most directed exchange on this
topic, Representative Bill Frenzel (D-MN), the floor manager for the legislation, and Representative William Armstrong (R-CO) proved to be almost

prophetic in their insights:

> *Frenzel*: "...We decided we should let an individual spend $1,000 to defeat or to elect the candidate, which amount would not be spent through the particular candidate's campaign committee or through the candidate personally. What we are doing, I think, in a short phrase, is to allow every individual a thousand dollars' worth of free speech."
>
> *Armstrong*: "Mr. Chairman, the gentleman from Minnesota has come quickly to the heart of my concern. We are talking about other persons, not candidates or their committees. The thing I do not understand, and I wish we could have some explanation, is how we can limit the right of free speech to $1,000 worth. The first amendment says we may not abridge free speech; we may not curtail; we may not diminish; we may not shorten. Is that not exactly what we are doing by this amendment?"
>
> *Frenzel*: "...The gentleman is correct. We are at least modifying or containing the right of free speech exactly as the Supreme Court said, that one can shout 'Fire' anywhere he wanted to except in a closed building. We are saying that a person can have $1,000 worth of free speech to elect a candidate or defeat him. We chose $1,000 because that was the limit we put on individual contributions to the committees. We said there ought to be a limit which would be similar for independent expenditures. The constitutionality may be doubtful, but if so, then the individual limitation is also doubtful."
>
> *Armstrong*: "...But let me make it clear my concern is not primarily legalistic, but simply to draw attention of the Members to the fact that we are tampering in a very unfortunate way with free-speech rights, not of candidates or their supporters, but other persons, persons who may be entirely unrelated to the candidates, who may be citizens' groups...."

Armstrong concluded later in this debate, "I think they are making a terrible mistake which will be ultimately invalidated by the courts."[17] As will be seen below, the Supreme Court did in fact invalidate dollar limits on independent expenditures, and one of the recurring themes in any discussion of the post-Watergate world of campaign finance involves what, if any, restrictions or conditions can and/or should be placed on outside groups' independent expenditures.

For some, like Representative Armstrong, the 1974 FECA amendments went too far in trying to change the campaign finance system. For others, particularly proponents of public financing for congressional elections, the legislation did not go far enough. What was abundantly clear, though, is what the amendments were in response to, namely Watergate. Senator Claiborne Pell (D-RI) contended, "We may not eradicate all future Watergates, but certainly we will discourage the perpetuation of a climate in which power is abused by the clever at the expense of the unwary."[18] As President Ford noted, the times demanded legislation that would discourage the possibility of future Watergates, and in the context of campaign finance that demand meant dissipating the influence or perceived influence associated with large contributions to candidates. In the words of Representative Dante Fascell (D-FL), "Understandably, speculation and charges of undue influence and of 'buying' candidates have gone hand in hand with the growing size of individual contributions. It is indeed difficult to make a convincing case that the contributor who gave $50,000 or $100,000 or even $1 million has not or cannot wield undue influence at some point with an elected official. And the Watergate related scandals...have substantiated the charges and convinced the American people that their suspicions were warranted."[19]

The Judiciary's Impact on Watergate's Legacy for Campaign Finance

If Watergate is one part of the foundation for the campaign finance system in the twenty-first century, the other significant portion is the Supreme Court's decision in *Buckley v. Valeo*, 424 U.S. 1 (1976). The *Buckley* decision has had a profound effect on the world of campaign finance and reform politics generally for over 35 years. Most directly, the Supreme Court struck down the spending limitations in the FECA amendments for both candidates and independent expenditures alike, but upheld other key provisions such as the limitations on contributions and disclosure requirements. More broadly, *Buckley* and the set of campaign finance-related Supreme Court cases decided in its wake established a paradigm for reform politics "grounded in the prevention of both actual corruption and the appearance of corruption."[20]

For the purposes of the discussion here, *Buckley*'s effect on Watergate's legacy for campaign finance is two-fold. First, it validated the fundamental premise underlying the 1974 FECA amendments, namely (in the Supreme Court's words) "the prevention of corruption and the appearance of corruption spawned by the real or imagined coercive influence of large financial contributions," as being a "constitutionally sufficient justification" for upholding the limits on contributions to candidates and other provisions that survived judicial challenge.[21] Second, by distinguishing between contributions and expenditures in its decision, the Court concluded that the potentially corrosive influence of money in politics that arises in the context of direct contributions to candidates did not pose the same level of threat in expenditures made independently of a candidate. On this latter issue, the *Buckley* judgment ruled, "Unlike contributions, such independent expenditures may well provide little assistance to the candidate's campaign and indeed may prove counterproductive. The absence of prearrangement and coordination of an expenditure with the candidate or his agent not only undermines the value of the expenditure to the candidate, but also alleviates the danger that expenditures will be given as a quid pro quo for improper commitments from the candidate."[22]

In the words of a subsequent Court decision, while "corruption [is] understood not only as quid pro quo arrangements, but also as undue influence on an office-holder's judgment, and the appearance of such influence,"[23] none of those elements are deemed to be as present and dangerous enough in the context of independent expenditures to warrant the FECA amendments' limitation on independent expenditures. Indeed, Representative Armstrong's concerns about limiting people to $1,000 worth of free speech were also validated by the Supreme Court.

Throughout the years following *Buckley*, the Supreme Court would regularly return to the issue of campaign finance regulation to address the competing values of free speech and having an undistorted representational relationship between the governing and the governed.[24] The Court has seemingly alternated between pro-regulation and a pro-free speech positions. Such swings, though, have often been driven on whether the issue at hand involved contributions or electioneering activities akin to contributions, on the one hand, and limitations on expenditures that fall outside the bounds of permissible restrictions, on the other hand. In continuing the dichotomy, the Court has used the *Buckley* paradigm to assess the constitutionality of certain restrictions, despite calls from both pro- and antiregulation camps at times to overturn *Buckley*.

For example, in 2002, Congress passed the Bipartisan Campaign Reform Act (BCRA), better known as the McCain-Feingold Act after its chief sponsors—Senator John McCain (R-AR) and Russell Feingold (D-WI). Signed into law without any public fanfare by President George W. Bush, its constitutionality came under immediate challenge in a law suit filed by Senator Mitch McConnell (R-KY). The case quickly made it to the Supreme Court due to a requirement in the legislation to expedite judicial review of its provisions. In *McConnell v. Federal Election Commission*, 540 U.S. 93 (2003), the Supreme Court upheld BCRA's primary provisions banning soft money in federal elections and regulating "sham issue advertisements."[25] Although soft money involved contributions to political parties rather than contributions to candidates directly, the Court cited evidence that "connects soft money manipulation of the legislative calendar"[26] to support the proposition that "[j]ust as troubling to a functioning democracy...is the danger that officeholders will decide issues...according to the wishes of those who have made large financial contributions valued by the officeholder."[27] In adopting this position, the Court expressly based its decision on a premise that was implied in *Buckley*: a systemic conception of "corruption in the political arena" could be an equally sufficient basis for regulating contributions as concerns about an individualistic quid-pro-quo conception of corruption.[28]

One matter that the *McConnell* decision highlighted centers on the tension between the increasingly complex system of federal and state campaign finance regulations as well as the creative ways political activists, corporations and unions, and other contributors were finding to evade constraint by those regulations (in other words, the "spontaneous and unauthorized expenditures by interested individuals and organizations, acting outside the standard framework" that the NAPA referenced in its Watergate-era report). In many ways the lines between contributions and independent expenditures were getting blurred such that judicial analysis could not simply place the issue at hand in one category or another and decide accordingly. Following the *McConnell* decision, the Court utilized a "balancing of interests" approach to conclude, for example, that contribution limits could be set too low as to be constitutionally impermissible (*Randall v. Sorrell*, 548 U.S. 230 (2006)) and that BCRA's regulation of advertisements of the functional equivalent of express advocacy were permissible but only under a strict, as-applied test (*Wisconsin Right to Life v. Federal Election Commission*, 551 U. S. 449 (2007)).

In *Citizens United v. Federal Election Commission*, 558 U.S. ___(2010), the issue of independent expenditures was squarely at the center of the case; specifically, BCRA's ban on corporate independent expenditures for electioneering advertisements. The Supreme Court's decision generated a great deal of news coverage as it overruled Court precedent, struck down portions of BCRA as well as the 1947 Taft-Hartley Labor Act banning campaign independent expenditures by corporations and labor unions in elections, reversed a century of public policy ever since the Tillman Act of 1907 prohibited corporations from making financial contributions in elections for any political office, and greatly expanded the pot of money that could be spent in and around elections. The newsworthiness of the case reached its apex when President Barack Obama, in his 2010 State of the Union address, criticized the Court's decision. "With all due deference to separation of powers," he declared, " last week the Supreme Court reversed a century of law that I believe will open the floodgates for special interests—including foreign corporations—to spend without limit in our elections." In reaction to this assertion, Justice Samuel Alito, who was present in the audience, mouthed the words "not true."[29]

From a public policy perspective, *Citizens United* generated a great deal of debate about the complex role of money in elections. From a judicial analysis point of view, though, the Court's decision was very straightforward. Involved was an outright ban on certain types of independent expenditures, and the primary basis supporting the ban was the Court's decision in *Austin v. Michigan Chamber of Commerce*, 494 U.S. 652 (1990). In *Austin*, the Supreme Court upheld a Michigan state ban on corporate independent expenditures based on the government's interest in preventing "the corrosive and distorting effects of immense aggregations of wealth that are accumulated with the help of the corporate form and that have little or no correlation to the public's support for the corporation's political ideas."[30] The *Citizens United* Court noted that *Austin*'s antidistortion interest allowed the Court to bypass the rationales in *Buckley* and the subsequent decision in *First National Bank of Boston v. Bellotti*, 435 U. S. 765 (1978) that struck down bans on independent expenditures and the principle that "the Government lacks the power to ban corporations from speaking" respectively.[31] The Court "return[ed] to the principle established in *Buckley* and *Bellotti* that the Government may not suppress political speech on the basis of the speaker's corporate identity"[32] and struck down *Austin* and its reliance on the antidistortion principle. Implicitly distinguishing the "appearance of influence or access" from the appearance of corruption, the Court concluded that the former "will not cause the electorate to lose faith in our democracy."[33] As further support that a corporation's independent expenditure in and of itself would not distort the relationship between the governing and the governed, the Court reasoned that the "fact that a corporation, or any other speaker, is willing to spend money to try to persuade voters presupposes that the *people have the ultimate influence* over elected officials."[34]

The campaign finance system that has developed since the Watergate era and has been molded by judicial decisions is shaped by numerous dichotomies: contributions versus independent expenditures; government regulations versus free speech; concerns about the "coercive influence" of money versus a system that permits types of potentially unlimited spending. This system and these dichotomies can trace their roots to what Congress was trying to accomplish during its post-Watergate attempts to rein in the campaign finance abuses of the Watergate era. Recall that Congress's primary focus during 1974 was on preventing the corruption of elected officials resulting from large financial contributions. Through all the Supreme Court cases, from *Buckley* through *Citizens United*, that concern has been fundamentally upheld.

Where the Supreme Court has restricted Congress's attempts to regulate campaign spending has been in the area that Congress paid the least attention to in 1974: independent expenditures made outside the system of contributions to candidates and political parties. While Congress included the limitations on independent expenditures in the FECA amendments, members saw the shortcomings in its efforts in this area. They recognized that what Congress sought to do would not fully address independent actions outside the system and was of questionable constitutionality. Nevertheless, Congress forged on with an admittedly imperfect bill designed to appeal to the public's appetite for some form of campaign finance regulation. It is hard to say what the result would have been if Congress had paid attention to the concerns that were raised at the time. Legislators may or may not have developed a method for regulating independent expenditures that would have stood up to the strict scrutiny of a First Amendment challenge. However their failure to do so meant that the Supreme Court was faced with deciding the constitutionality of the FECA amendment provisions on this score in *Buckley*. The resulting decision and subsequent jurisprudence has made it more and more difficult to ever conceive of a permissible system of independent expenditure regulation.

Campaign Finance in the Post-Watergate Era

The most prominent feature of campaign finance in the post-Watergate era is the increase in the flow of money in and around elections. Figure 7.1, for example, reflects the mean expenditure for a major party House and Senate candidate for each election from 1974–2010. The growth in expenditures has been phenomenal over that time period. In 1974, the average House candidate spent $53,384 in the primary and general election and the average Senate candidate spent $437,482; in 2010, the corresponding totals were $1,130,559 and $6,340,912 respectively. The increase can be seen even taking inflation into account as the 2010 values equate to $255,607 and $1,433,608 respectively in 1974 dollars. In other words, when adjusting for inflation, the average 2010 House candidate is spending 4.78 times, and the average Senate candidate is spending 3.28 time what their 1974 counterparts expended.

The increased financial activity is not limited to candidates alone. Outside groups have followed a similar upward trend in contributions or expenditures (see figure 7.2). PACs have increased the level of contributions to congressional candidates over the period from 1990 to 2010, supplying nearly three times as much in actual dollars and 1.68 times in inflation-adjusted dollars to congressional candidates in 2010 than they did 20 years before. Similarly, outside group spending, through independent expenditures, electioneering communications, and other communication costs, has increased

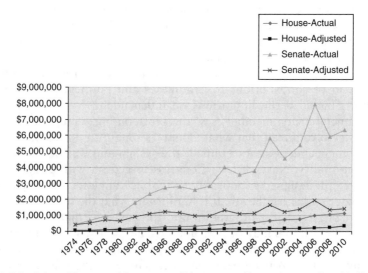

Figure 7.1 Mean House and Senate candidate expenditures in actual and inflation-adjusted dollars, 1974–2010.

Source: Actual dollar expenditure data available from The Campaign Finance Institute at http://www .cfinst.org/pdf/vital/VitalStats_t2.pdf (last visited on February 27, 2011). Inflation-adjusted data calculated by the author using the Bureau of Labor Statistics CPI Inflation Calculator, available at http://www .bls.gov/data/inflation_calculator.htm (last visited on February 27, 2011).

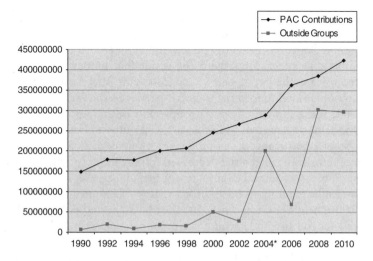

Figure 7.2 PAC Contributions and outside group spending in Congressional Elections, 1990–2010.

Source: PAC Contribution data for 1990-2008 are available through the Campaign Finance Institute at http://www.cfinst.org/pdf/vital/VitalStats_t10.pdf (last visited on February 27, 2011). PAC data for 2010 and Outside Groups data based on data available through www.OpenSecrets.org (last visited on February 27, 2011).

* *Note:* 2004 was the first election cycle operating under BCRA's increased disclosure requirements and soft money ban.

throughout the 20-year period. In evaluating figure 7.2 with respect to outside groups, two separate periods should be considered. The first runs from 1990 to 2002, in which outside groups showed a slight increase in spending during this period. The large growth shown in 2004 cannot be attributed solely to increase spending by outside groups. Rather, the 2004 election was the first conducted under BCRA, which meant outside groups (1) could no longer contribute undisclosed soft money to political parties, and (2) faced greater disclosure requirements for their own expenditures. Even after taking BCRA into account, however, the level of outside group spending in the 2008 and 2010 elections (approximately $300 million each election) significantly outdistances the approximately $200 million and $69 million spent in 2004 and 2006 respectively.

One of the end results of the campaign finance system that has developed in Congress and through the courts since Watergate is that money is being pushed into the category of independent expenditures by outside groups. Money in politics, like nature, abhors a vacuum. If one outlet for contributing or spending money is closed off, the money and those looking to spend it to influence the outcome of the election will find new and alternative ways to do so. Consider the primary forces that have shaped how the campaign finance system has developed, and what vacuum they have left. With the 1974 FECA amendments, Congress wanted to limit the corruption or appearance of corruption of elected officials through contributions to candidates. The legislation directly addressed this issue but its failure to do the same with regard to independent expenditures proved a significant area of weakness. The Supreme Court has generally upheld limits on contributions, but struck down limits on expenditures, with the result that money has increasingly gravitated toward the latter. Later, Congress with BCRA eliminated undisclosed amounts flowing into the political parties in the form of soft money. As a result, those individuals and groups who in the past contributed soft money to the parties needed to find a different outlet for their funds.[35]

The other significant development in campaign financing since the Watergate reforms has been the decreased importance of public funding for the most viable presidential candidates. When George W. Bush decided not to accept public funding in his bid for the Republican presidential nomination in 2000, he was taking a risk. In effect he eschewed guaranteed money for the chance to raise and spend more money than the amount to which he would be limited if he accepted public financing. The gamble paid off as he far outraised any challenger in either party; in fact the $91,331,951 in individual contributions that Bush accumulated was approximately the same aggregate amount, including public funds, as raised either by Democrats Al Gore and Bill Bradley together or all his Republican opponents combined.[36]

Prior to Bush's fund-raising success in 2000, receiving public funding was an integral part to any presidential candidate's fundraising and electoral strategy. Since 2000, however, accepting public financing has become a sign of weakness and a campaign that may not be viable. Figure 7.3 shows the percentage of funds received from public funding as part of a candidate's overall receipts for the top five fundraisers in either party for each election cycle from 1996 to 2008. The top five fundraisers in 1996 (Bill Clinton, Bob Dole, Phil Gramm, Pat Buchanan, and Lamar Alexander) derived on average about 30 percent of their campaign funds from public financing. In 2004, the

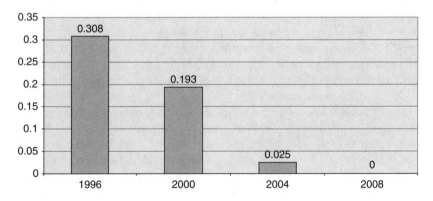

Figure 7.3 Top presidential candidates' percentage of primary campaign funds from public financing, 1996–2008.

Source: Compiled by author from data available through the Federal Election Commission's website at www. fec.gov (last visited on February 27, 2011).

top three fundraisers (Bush, John Kerry, and Howard Dean) did not accept public financing, driving the average received from public financing for the top five candidates down to 2.5 percent. In 2008, none of the top fundraisers (the top five of Barack Obama, Hillary Clinton, John McCain, Mitt Romney, and Rudi Giuliani, plus Ron Paul) elected to receive public financing.

The future relevance of the public financing system faced its greatest challenge in 2008 when Democratic presidential candidate Barack Obama elected to forego $84.1 million in public funding during the general election cycle and rely on individual contributions alone. The end result is that he raised approximately $230 million from September 1, 2008, through the election, or nearly 2.75 times more than what McCain received in public funding for the general election campaign. One of the most significant aspects about Obama's model for fundraising was that a majority of the contributions to his primary and general election campaign came from donors whose aggregated contributions equaled $1,000 or less, with nearly a third of the contributions coming from donors whose total contributions were $200 or less. In other words, Obama established fundraising records by drawing significantly on small donors. By comparison, John McCain (60 percent) and Hillary Clinton (56 percent) in 2008, and George W. Bush (60 percent) and John Kerry (56 percent) in 2004, each received a majority of the individual contributions from those who gave $1,000 or more.[37]

To its supporters, the public finance system is "a post-Watergate initiative hailed for decades as the best way to rid politics of the corrupting influence of money."[38] They consequently fear that the early twenty-first century trend toward opting out of it "places an unyielding demand on the candidates to raise huge amounts of private contributions and to use individual 'bundlers' [i.e., a person who aggregates contributions from other donors] to provide six-and-seven figure total amounts for their campaigns. The big-money donors of the Watergate-era presidential election will be big-money bundlers in the 2008 presidential election."[39] From its advocates' perspective, therefore, the end of the public financing system's effectiveness would mark the end of the Watergate-era's reform legacy for presidential campaign finance.

Such a viewpoint does have merit, but it is also possible that the decision of the most viable candidates to opt out of the public financing system may be consistent with and extend the Watergate legacy for presidential campaign finance. Raising hundreds of millions of dollars from individual donors who can give no more to any candidate than $2,300 per election cycle in 2008 (a Watergate-era reform whose monetary limit was increased for inflation under BCRA) forces candidates to appeal to a broader audience and to seek funds from as many people as possible. This appeal, in turn, promotes greater participation among the electorate in the political process and dilutes the effect that any one contributor or even a bundler could have.

Based on rough estimates, Barack Obama had over 1,500,000 individuals contribute to his presidential campaign during the Democratic primaries and John McCain had over 500,000 separate contributors.[40] With so many contributors helping build a campaign with the resulting funds raised being so large, one may be hard pressed to show how one contributor or even a bundler who raised $1,000,000 based on 500 contributions of $2,000 could have that much of a singular corrosive effect that would corrupt the candidate. Even with the substantial campaign finance disclosures required from presidential candidates (another Watergate-era reform) and the continually sustained limits on individual contributions, candidates have proven highly successful at building a broad-based fundraising campaign—and have done so without being a burden on the public treasury.

Indeed, this model of presidential campaign financing may be the ultimate end result of the Watergate era: a system in which a presidential candidate can be so successful at raising funds from so many varied sources and increasing participation that he or she cannot be corrupted by any individual or set of large contributions. Interestingly, one member of Congress during the Watergate era foresaw this possibility; he was none other than Senator James Buckley (Conservative Party–NY), the lead plaintiff in *Buckley v. Valeo* whose arguments against public financing of congressional campaigns still fits today in the context of presidential candidates opting out of the public funding system:

> More important than the specifics of S. 3044 or any other specific bill, however, is the assumption that private financing is an evil to be avoided at all costs. I am afraid, I have to reject that basic assumption. A candidate for public office is currently forced to compete for money from thousands—or in the case of Presidential candidates—millions of potential contributors. Viable candidates rarely have trouble raising the funds needed to run a credible campaign and, in fact, their ability to raise money is one very good gauge of their popular support.... [P]otential candidates must essentially compete for private support, and to attract that support they have to address themselves to issues of major importance to the people who will be contributing to their campaigns and voting for them on election day. Public financing might allow candidates to ignore these issues, fuzz their stands, and run campaigns in which intelligent debate on important matters is subordinated to a 'Madison Avenue' approach to the voters.... The need to compete for campaign dollars forces candidates to address many issues and I consider this vital to the maintenance of a sound democratic system.[41]

To paraphrase Buckley's words, a presidential candidate who is not dependent on public financing must appeal to a broader constituency who will contribute to *and* vote for that candidate, and building such broad-based support is healthy for the American political system.

The Ripple of Watergate: The Focus on Cause and Effect

If one drops a coin in a fountain holding still water, it creates a ripple in the water; starting from the point of impact, small waves emanate outward such that when they get further away they may look very different from the initial waves, but are the result of the initial impact just the same. Such is the case of campaign finance regulation, where the ripple of Watergate and the subsequent reforms it generated still shape the system in place today. The world of campaign finance may appear vastly different than the one envisioned during the crafting of the FECA amendments in 1974, but it very much is the result of the campaign finance abuses that arose during the Senate's Watergate investigation.

Certainly, critics can point to many areas of concern about the big-money nature of the current campaign finance system. The Watergate-era reforms have done little to rein in the amount of money spent on elections, which was one of the side benefits regulation sponsors hoped to achieve in the 1970s. In fact, as shown above, candidates are raising and spending substantially more on elections than during the 1970s, and changes in laws and the impact of judicial decisions have forced more money into independent expenditures outside the control or influence of candidates or parties. The need to raise large amounts of money each election cycle may deter initially unknown or underfunded candidates from seeking office or establishing their viability early enough to sustain a challenge against an incumbent or other more established candidate. One might even question the social utility of spending hundreds of millions of dollars on elections—either in public funding or private donations—year after year when other problems beckon.

Further, as noted above, not all behavior clearly falls in the category of permissible independent expenditures and behavior that might warrant additional attempts at regulation. For example, even though independent expenditures are by definition not coordinated with the parties or a candidate, strategic behavior can possibly blur the line separating coordination and independence. In the case of the 2010 campaign for the Texas 17th District House of Representatives race between incumbent Democrat Chet Edwards and Republican challenger Bill Flores, outside groups' independent expenditures played an important role. While these expenditures remained independent, actions by the Flores campaign and the Republican Party led to strategic decisions by conservative outside groups, and vice versa. The outside groups ran ads that mirrored the Flores campaign's message and rhetoric against Edwards. Similarly, when the outside groups chose to run these ads in the last week of the campaign, the National Republican Campaign Committee canceled $75,000 worth of advertisements it planned to run in the district and diverted these funds to other races. While no one involved in the Edwards-Flores race did anything improper, this example highlights that independent expenditures could easily slip into what might be called "structurally independent but functionally coordinated" expenses.[42]

When a critic looks at the system of big money in elections, one might conclude that the lessons from Watergate died many years ago, and the corrosive effect of big money has taken control. Such a viewpoint, however, does not take into account the primary objectives of Watergate-era reforms and what, in some ways, might be deemed their outstanding accomplishments. They were successful in their principal aim of tackling corruption caused by large contributions. The FECA amendments borne out of the Watergate scandal and subsequent legislation that built on them produced a campaign finance system that includes, at its core: constitutionally permissible limits on contributions; increased disclosure and reporting requirements of candidates, parties, and those running electioneering advertisements; and an enforcement mechanism to investigate and punish violations.

Candidate reliance on big money in the twenty-first century is substantively different from candidates relying on large contributions during the Watergate era. The former requires continuously diligent engagement with fund-raising, while the latter gave rise to the corruption and campaign finance abuses associated with the Nixon-era scandal.. This difference also highlights a fundamental distinction that can be found in the ripples of the campaign finance fountain: cause and effect. Specifically, much of the debate surrounding campaign finance reform efforts since Watergate have been premised on addressing the corrosive *effects* in the American political system *caused* by the presence of big money in elections.

Cast differently, this premise equates to the question of how to cure the "mischiefs of big money," which is just a variation of James Madison's famous exposition in Federalist No. 10 of how to cure the "mischiefs of faction." The principal political theorist of the Constitution noted that one approach to the problem would be to remove the causes of faction by destroying the liberty that nourishes factions. However, he warned that such a remedy would be worse than the disease since liberty was essential to political life, a tenet cited by the Supreme Court in its *Citizens United* decision.[43] Because "the causes of factions cannot be removed," Madison reasoned that "relief is only to be sought in the means of controlling its effects," which he considered one of the benefits to the federal Constitution devised by the Founders. [44]

Applying Madison's logic to the issue of campaign finance, the more that any given reform effort has tended toward trying to remove the presence of big money in elections, the more likely that such regulation would be deemed to be impermissible by the Supreme Court. The more that any given reform effort focused on controlling the effects of big money in elections, specifically by preventing corruption or the appearance of corruption, the more likely that the Court would sustain the regulation against constitutional challenge. In other words, removing money in politics and the related freedom of speech associated with the expenditure of money creates a remedy worse than the disease.[45]

Underlying this focus on cause and effect is a belief that money in politics is not itself an evil, but rather that it is the effect of the presence of money that should be of concern. To bring this analysis to a head, one need only to distinguish between the Supreme Court's decision in *McConnell* with its *Citizens United* judgment overruling *Austin*. In *Citizens United*, the Court criticized the antidistortion premise on which *Austin* rested, but that criticism was leveled at the fact that the *Austin* judgment sustained a regulation by seeking to remove the accumulation of wealth by corporations as a potential cause of corruption in the political system. *McConnell*, however, broadened the scope of corruption to incorporate a systemic conception of corruption, but its analysis was grounded in evidence on the distortive effects of money in campaigns on legislative outcomes. In short, just because a person, even a corporation, has money and spends it in the context of campaigns, that is not corruption. If, as a result of that spending, the legislative process and more importantly the representational relationship between the governing and the governed is distorted, that is the type of behavior and speech that can be regulated.

The *Citizens United* Court addressed this issue directly as it tried to reconcile its decision with the prior, seemingly contradictory decision in *McConnell*:

> Ingratiation and access, in any event, are not corruption. The BCRA record establishes that certain donations to political parties, called "soft money," were made to gain access to elected officials. This case, however, is about independent expenditures, not soft money. When Congress finds that a problem exists, we must give that finding due deference; but Congress may not choose an unconstitutional remedy. *If elected officials succumb to improper influences from independent expenditures; if they surrender their best judgment; and if they put expediency before principle, then surely there is cause for concern.* We must give weight to attempts by Congress to seek to dispel either the appearance or the reality of these influences. The remedies enacted by law, however, must comply with the First Amendment; and, it is our law and our tradition that more speech, not less, is the governing rule. An outright ban on corporate political speech during the critical preelection period is not a permissible remedy. Here Congress has created categorical bans on speech that are asymmetrical to preventing quid pro quo corruption.[46]

In other words, the *McConnell* Court acknowledged that Congress had sufficiently identified and documented an improper effect resulting from money in politics, and BCRA's remedy was narrowly tailored enough to controlling that effect to be sustained against a First Amendment challenge. In *Citizens'* Council, the Court's dicta (as italicized above) implies that even otherwise permissible independent expenditure could be regulated, if its effects were to distort the representational relationship between the governing and the governed. Absent an explicit need to control these effects, though, the Supreme Court will not permit campaign finance regulation that seeks to attack the mere presence of money in politics. Ultimately in looking at the historical impact of the Watergate-era campaign finance regulation and its progeny, we see the core tenets of the system have been and likely will continue to be a strong mitigating factor in controlling the potential corruption of individual politicians. The hopes, however, of the Watergate-era and subsequent reformers to control "big money" in elections will continue to remain bounded by the limits of free speech that have come to shape the debate over campaign finance regulation.

Notes

1. Articles of Impeachment Adopted by the Committee on the Judiciary, July 27, 1974, visited March 2, 2011, http://watergate.info/impeachment/impeachment-articles.shtml.
2. Gerald R. Ford, "Statements on the Federal Election Campaign Act Amendments of 1974," October 15, 1974, in John T. Woolley and Gerhard Peters, *The American Presidency Project* (Santa Barbara: University of California), /www.presidency.ucsb.edu.
3. Frederick C. Mosher et al. , *Watergate: Implications for Responsible Government* (New York: Basic Books, 1974), 88.
4. For example, Representative Frank Thompson (D-NJ) proclaimed, "[W]e are answering to an honest and much–needed response from the American public for meaningful election reform. That is the essence of this legislation." *Congressional Record*, August 7, 1974, 27230.
5. John Sample, *The Fallacy of Campaign Finance Reform* (Chicago: University of Chicago Press, 2006).
6. See Sample, *The Fallacy of Campaign Finance Reform*, 218.
7. Senate Watergate Committee, "The Final Report of the Select Committee on Presidential Campaign Activities United States Senate," 1974, 570.
8. Summary of 1974 FECA Amendments taken from Victoria Farrar-Myers, *Encyclopedia of the American Presidency*, Michael A. Genovese, ed., (New York: Facts on File, 2004).
9. *Congressional Record*, March 28, 1974, 8772
10. For example, Senator Howard Baker (R-TN) claimed that public financing in congressional elections would create a "distinct advantage on behalf of the incumbents, and diminishes the chance for new and aggressive, intelligent and worthwhile challengers." *Congressional Record*, March 28, 1974, 8771.
11. Senator James Allen (D-AL) contended that "I do not believe it is right for Members of Congress to provide that the taxpayers, through the public Treasury, should pay for their election campaigns." *Congressional Record*, March 28, 1974, 8771.
12. Rep. Joel Broyhill (R-VA) stated that "The cure for 'Fat-cat' contributions, as they are called, is not by discouraging more contributors to political campaigns, but inviting more in, by giving them an incentive to participate." *Congressional Record*, August 8, 1974, 27466.
13. See, for example, Steven M. Gillon, *That's Not What We Meant To Do: Reform and Its Unintended Consequences in Twentieth-Century America* (New York: W.W. Norton & Company, 2000).
14. Frederick C. Mosher et al., *Watergate: Implications for Responsible Government* (New York: Basic Books, 1974), 89.
15. Senator Howard Baker (R-TN), *Congressional Record*, March 28, 1974, 8772.
16. Representative Joel Broyhill (R-VA), *Congressional Record*, August 8, 1974, 27466.
17. *Congressional Record*, August 7, 1974, 27229–27230.
18. *Congressional Record*, March 26, 1974, 8184.
19. *Congressional Record*, August 9, 1974, 27472.
20. Victoria A. Farrar-Myers, "Money for Nothing?: The Politics of Reform, Actual Corruption, and the Appearance of Corruption" in Michael A. Genovese and

Victoria A. Farrar-Myers, eds., *Corruption and American Politics* (Amherst, NY: Cambria Press, 2010) 309–310.

21. *Buckley v. Valeo*, 424 U.S. 1, 25 (1976).

22. Buckley, 424 U.S. at 47.

23. *Federal Election Commission v. Colorado Republican Federal Campaign Committee*, 533 U.S. 431, 441 (2001).

24. For an analysis of how these and other competing values have played out in various aspects of the political arena, see Victoria A. Farrar-Myers and Diana Dwyre, *Limits & Loopholes: The Quest for Money, Free Speech, and Fair Elections* (Washington, DC: CQ Press, 2008).

25. "Soft money" was unregulated money raised by the political parties supposedly for party-building activities, but that often was used for election-related purposes. "Sham issue ads" were advertisements that technically did not expressly advocate for the election or defeat of a particular candidate, but were intended to influence an election.

26. *McConnell v. Federal Election Commission*, 540 U.S. 93, 150 (2003).

27. McConnell, 540 U.S. at 153.

28. *Austin v. Michigan Chamber of Commerce*, 494 U.S. 652, 660 (1990); quoted in part in McConnell, 540 U.S. at 205.

29. Alan Silverleib "Gloves Come off after Obama Rips Supreme Court Ruling," January 28, 2010, visited February 26, 2011, http://www.cnn.com/2010/POLITICS/01/28/alito.obama.sotu/index.html?iref=allsearch.

30. *Austin*, 494 U.S. at 660.

31. *Citizens United v. Federal Election Commission*, 558 U.S. ____ (2010) (slip opinion p. 31).

32. *Citizens United*, 558 U.S. at 50 (slip opinion).

33. *Citizens United*, 558 U.S. at 44 (slip opinion).

34. *Citizens United*, 558 U.S. at 44 (slip opinion; emphasis added).

35. As campaign finance website, opensecrets.org notes, "Beginning with the 2004 election cycle, the Bipartisan Campaign Reform Act of 2002 (BCRA) eliminated the unlimited contributions to national political parties that were known as soft money. Before the prohibition, corporations, labor unions and wealthy individuals made most of these contributions.... After BCRA, many of these contributors started giving similarly large amounts of money to advocacy groups such as 527s." Available at http://www.opensecrets.org/bigpicture/softtop.php?cycle=2008 (last visited on March 2, 2011). Groups like 527s or 501(c)(3) are tax-exempt advocacy groups designed to actively campaign in an election.

36. This statement excludes the $42,330,000 in contributions and loans that Steve Forbes made to his own campaign for the Republican nomination.

37. All data regarding small donors were derived from Anthony J. Carrado, Michael J. Malbin, Thomas E. Mann, and Norman J. Ornstein, *Reform in an Age of Networked Campaigns: How to Foster Citizen Participation through Small Donors and Volunteers*, 2010, visited February 28, 2011 http://www.cfinst.org/books_reports/Reform-in-an-Age-of-Networked-Campaigns.pdf .

38. Common Cause, "Presidential Public Financing," visited on February 28, 2011 http://www.commoncause.org/site/pp.asp?c=dkLNK1MQIwG&b=4773833.

39. Campaign Legal Center et al., "Letter to Senator Hillary Clinton," February 20, 2008, visited on February 28, 2011, http://www.commoncause.org/site/apps/nlnet/content2.aspx?c=dkLNK1MQIwG&b=4773617&ct=5064115.

40. These estimates were calculated based on data available in Carrado et al. In their report, Carrado et al. present data for the total dollars each candidate raised during the 2008 presidential primary system grouped by contributors who donates $200 or less, $201–$999, and $1,000 or more. If one assumes that the average contribution within each grouping is $100, $500, and $1,500 respectively, dividing the total fund raised by a candidate within each group by the assumed average contribution amount for that group will yield an estimated number of contributors. The basis for this analysis is drawn from Victoria A. Farrar-Myers, "Donors, Dollars and Momentum: Waging a Viable Campaign for the White House," in Meena Bose, ed., *From Votes to Victory: Winning and Governing the White House in the Twenty-First Century*, (College Station: Texas A&M University Press, 2011).

41. *Congressional Record*, June 26, 1974, 21371 (Speech by Senator James Buckley to New York Republican Volunteers inserted into the Congressional Record by Representative William L. Dickinson (R-AL); internal paragraph breaks omitted).

42. For a more in-depth examination of the Texas 17th district race, see Victoria A. Farrar-Myers and Daniel Davis Sledge, "The Perfect Storm: Edwards vs. Flores in Texas's Seventeenth Congressional District," in Randall E. Adkins and David A. Dulio, eds., *Cases in Congressional Campaigns: Riding the Wave*, (New York: Routledge, 2011).

43. Citizens United, 558 U.S. at 39 (slip opinion). Madison also discussed that a second method to remove the cause of faction would be to given everyone the same interests, but concluded that such method would be both impractical and unwise.

44. Federalist No. 10. visited on March 2, 2011, http://thomas.loc.gov/home/hist-dox/fed_10.html.

45. For a discussion of "The 'Mischiefs of Faction' and Campaign Finance," see Farrar-Myers and Dwyre, *Limits and Loopholes*, 3–8.

46. *Citizens United* 558 U.S. at 45 (slip opinion; emphasis added; internal quotations and citations omitted).

Chapter Eight

Nixon, Watergate, and the Attempt to Sway Public Opinion

Todd Belt

Introduction

Richard Nixon never had a particularly good relationship with the press during his long political career. Upon parting the electoral scene after his 1962 California gubernatorial defeat by Pat Brown, he famously admonished the press that they would not "have Nixon to kick around anymore." But his subsequent comment about the coverage he received during the campaign is very telling: "[the press] have a right and a responsibility, and if they're against a candidate, give him the shaft, but also recognize if they give him the shaft, put one lonely reporter on the campaign who will report what the candidate says now and then."[1] These comments were supposed to be his last press conference in a career marked by a particularly conflictual relationship with the press. But Nixon resumed his battles with the press as he reentered the political fray to campaign for the presidency in 1968. His five and a half years in office were marked by a continuance of the combative relationship, culminating in his all out war with the press over the Watergate affair.

Nixon's poor relationship with the press made it difficult for him to use them to sway public opinion in his favor. He knew his messages were being filtered by the press, and was frustrated by his inability to speak through them. Nixon felt that he didn't get the credit he deserved for many successful policies. Following the 1970 midterm elections, Nixon wrote the following to his chief of staff, H .R. Haldeman: "In the final analysis, elections are not won or lost by programs. They are won or lost on how these programs are presented to the country, and how all the political and public relations considerations are handled."[2] Nixon knew that he needed to regain the upper-hand in the PR battle.

As time wore on, Nixon became even more furious about bad press spreading as a result of leaks emanating from his administration. In addition to the leaks, Nixon was frustrated by an apparent lack of cohesion in messages coming from his two main conduits to the press, Communications Director Herb Klein and Press Secretary Ron Ziegler, though they were both ostensibly under the direction of White House Chief of Staff H.R. Haldeman.[3] Following Nixon's reflections on the midterm elections, the liberals of his cabinet were assigned to talk about issues of poverty and civil rights and to interact with Senators on these issues, thus creating the façade of accommodation and bipartisanship for public consumption.[4] But Nixon's crafty ways of dealing with the public through the press were short-lived, as he and his administration took on what was widely described as a "bunker" mentality during the Watergate scandal. This study examines the nature and effectiveness of Nixon's public opinion battles during this time period, and whether this approach had utility for subsequent presidents.

Explaining Nixon's Attempts at Influencing Public Opinion

During Watergate, Nixon used five means of getting his message out through the press. The first two were the most prominent: *televised speeches* and *news conferences*. In addition to these, Nixon used strategically timed releases of written statements. The fourth method was twice-daily press briefings handled by Press Secretary Ronald Ziegler. The last was news leaks to trusted reporters, but this was the least used method because of the president's near-universal distrust of journalists.

When examining the rate of Nixon's speeches and news conferences before and after the Watergate story broke on June 18, 1972, a peculiar asymmetry emerges. In the 42 months prior to Watergate, Nixon gave 16 major speeches, not including campaign speeches, inaugurals or State of the Union addresses. This put him at a rate of about one every three months, or 0.38 per month (see Table 8.1). During Watergate, Nixon's rate of speeches dropped to less than half that, at 0.15 per month ($F(1, 66) = 4.11, p < .05$). This significant clamming-up on the part of the president certainly makes sense during a time of duress. However, what is less explicable is the trend in the rate of news conferences.

Table 8.1   Richard Nixon's Speeches and News Conferences

	Speeches per month	News Conferences per month	F
January 1969–June 1972 (42 months)	0.38	0.15	4.11*
June 1972–August 1974 (26 months)	0.60	0.54	0.65

Note: *$p < .05$, Speeches to US Audience. Does not include Inaugural or State of the Union Addresses, campaign or convention speeches. Data Source: Renka, 2010.

Both during and after Watergate, Nixon maintained roughly the same rate of press conferences, at a little over one every other month (0.60 per month before Watergate, 0.54 during, $F(1, 66) = 0.065$, n.s.). He did not hide from the press, he went directly to them. What is puzzling is that presidents have vastly more control over content and presentation during a speech than a news conference. In delivering a speech, the president is carefully scripted, can choose his venue of delivery, can control the topic addressed, and can do all these things undisturbed. By contrast, in a news conference the president has little control over what is asked of him, save the reporters he chooses to call on. Subjects may be brought up in the least favorable light by the way questions are worded. And though many questions are anticipated and answers prescripted, unanticipated questions can make the president look rattled and out of control. News conferences place presidents at a much greater disadvantage than do speeches. So, why did Nixon opt to get his message out regarding Watergate through news conferences rather than speeches?

Based on historical record and the exigencies of the office, there are three hypotheses that can be drawn to answer this question. Certainly these three hypotheses are not mutually exclusive—it could be one, two, or all three of the hypotheses working together to produce the asymmetry between speeches and newscasts. They all may be right, or one may be more right than others. As this chapter examines Nixon's public relations decisions over the course of the crisis, these three hypotheses will be kept in mind:

Psychological Hypothesis

One of Nixon's fatal flaws was his trust in his own ability to think on the fly. Nixon was smart, and he knew it. He loved to engage in verbal sparring with his opponents, and he was good at it. This came from early in his political career, and was crystallized in his 1959 visit to Moscow and his verbal sparring with Khrushchev over the course of it, especially in what became widely publicized as the "Kitchen Debate."[5] He thought he was at his best in these situations and relished them. This hypothesis proposes that Nixon's confidence in this regard is what caused him to favor news conferences over speeches during the Watergate scandal. Moreover, Nixon's combative nature as an "active-negative" personality implies that he derives a great deal of pleasure and personal validation in going toe-to-toe with political opponents and coming out on top.[6] In this sense, news conferences were personal tests that he couldn't resist. To borrow a quote from *Lawrence of Arabia*, he did so "because it pleases [him]."

Structural Hypothesis

The press expects that news conferences are to be periodically scheduled events. By contrast, speeches are unscheduled and are not constantly demanded by the White House Press Corps. News conferences have developed into expected rituals of democratic governance, whereby the public can ask questions of leaders through newspeople.[7] News conferences are held in high value by the press, and the Press Secretary feels the heat when they are not held as frequently as the press corps would like. In turn, the Press Secretary lobbies the president to hold them more frequently.[8] Forgoing news conferences agitates the press, making for a more hostile experience the next time one comes around. Lastly, if Nixon were to avoid press conferences, it would give the *appearance* that he had something to hide. If Nixon wanted to avoid the public eye during Watergate, it would have been easier for him to limit his number of speeches than to delay news conferences.

Strategic Hypothesis

During Watergate, the Nixon administration was engulfed in uncertainty. Nixon knew that the battle for public opinion would be fought through the media, whom he considered enemies. He had to get inside the head of his enemy. He needed to know what the press knew. He knew that reporters had leads but were looking for verification in order to run their stories. Allowing them to question him would reveal what they knew so that he could draw up effective means of counterattack.

Watergate as a Case Study

Watergate is a uniquely singular event in American history, but it is also a fascinating case study. At no other time in American political history have the public been so engaged with the press, their opinions measured, and the ramifications of their opinions been so decisive. With the president and Congress increasingly locked into confrontation as the Watergate revelations unfolded, both sides knew the consequences of losing the public opinion battle —legislators for their prospects for holding their seats in the upcoming 1974 midterm elections, and Nixon for his political life.

The ability of strategies to influence public opinion is mediated by the public's attentiveness. Much research has failed to find media effects on public opinion simply because the public, for the most part, is not particularly attentive to political events.[9] Even more difficult is the fact that the politically attentive public is highly partisan. Attempts to influence partisans largely result in strengthening already held positions rather than attitude change.[10] During the Watergate hearings, a poll found that 85 percent of Americans had watched at least part of the coverage. The hearings were first shown simultaneously by all three major networks, then covered on a rotating basis among the networks.[11] The major networks provided real-time coverage during the day, and PBS aired tape-delayed broadcasts in the evening.[12] Coverage of the hearings began on May 9, 1974, and lasted until Nixon's resignation, compiling 319 hours of television.[13] Considering that the public was highly attentive to Watergate, the scandal provides a unique case for analysis.

As noted above, the primary purpose of this chapter is to evaluate Nixon's decision making at key points in the Watergate battle for public opinion, bringing to light his methods of persuasion. In doing so, the subsidiary question of Nixon's decision to use news conferences instead of speeches will be addressed. As with any empirical case study, multiple sources of evidence will be evaluated.

The Context: Public Opinion and Watergate

In 1972, Nixon was reelected in one of the greatest landslide victories in presidential electoral history. In the Electoral College, Nixon lost only Massachusetts and Washington, DC to his opponent, Senator George McGovern, for a final crushing tally of 520 to 17 electoral votes.[14] Nixon garnered 60.7 percent of the popular vote to 37.5 percent for McGovern.[15] Considering how lopsided the contest turned out to be, observers continue to wonder why Nixon felt the need to resort to his old ways of cheating and dirty tricks—which would ultimately undo his presidency.

Following the election, Nixon received a boost in his popularity, peaking at 66 percent approval in January 1973 with his second inauguration (see Figure 8.1). This was his highest point of popularity, even higher than at his first inauguration. Nixon bottomed out in December 1973 at 22 percent approval, the lowest on record for any president, matched only by Truman's low in his second term. Nixon's approval hovered in the 20s for all of 1974, and was at 24 percent when he left office in August.

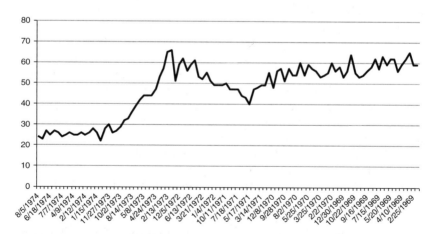

Figure 8.1   Richard Nixon job approval over time.

Source: Gallup.

This begs the question: Did Nixon even care about public opinion? The answer is he didn't just care, he was obsessed with it. Nixon thought that if public opinion turned against him, it would override his mandate from his reelection.[16] Nixon considered public opinion to be a danger to his policies and ultimately to himself, rather than a tool of power. As Watergate unfolded, Nixon saw the impeachment battle as a "race for public support."[17] He went so far as to refer to it as his "The Last Campaign" in his memoirs.[18]

Nixon was buoyed by the knowledge that he would be engaging a Democratic Congress with opinion polls even lower than his own.[19] He also knew that if congressional Republicans sided with impeachment they could be perceived as "self-interested and disloyal" by their constituents as their midterm election grew closer.[20] Indeed, many members of the House were hesitant to act against Nixon until public opinion favored the move. Considering these factors, Nixon noted that the danger of being impeached came "from the public's being conditioned to the idea that I was going to be impeached."[21] Nixon resigned when the result of this battle was no longer in doubt. Let's look at how he chose to fight it.

Pre-Watergate Nixon

Nixon's decision making during Watergate was affected by the organizational structure he created as president and those he chose to fill critical positions. The Office of Communications was created by Nixon to permit the general planning of the president's message as well as to reach out to news outlets based outside of Washington, DC, a group that Nixon believed to be less hostile to himself than the DC insiders.[22] The Communications Director, Herbert Klein, was placed in between White House Chief of Staff H. R. Haldeman (on top) and the Press Secretary (below).[23] Klein's background was in the newspaper business, but he also took time out to assist Nixon in various campaigns, and became an assistant to Vice-President Nixon in 1956. [24]

Nixon felt that he had lost the 1960 election to Kennedy because of style rather than substance, so he knew the importance of PR.[25] He appointed the young Ronald Ziegler, whose experience was in advertising and public relations, as his Press Secretary. Ziegler gave twice-daily press briefings, and was known for sidestepping issues with complex and hard to follow explanations, earning him the nickname "Zigzag."[26] H. R. Haldeman also had a background in advertising, and it was his job to coordinate the work of the Press Secretary and Communications Director.

Nixon took great interest in being deeply involved in his own speech-writing. And by all accounts, he was good at it. His rhetorical flourishes ranged from fiery in his speech on the Alger Hiss affair, to folksy and homespun as in his "Checkers" speech.[27]

Nixon's traditional public style was to stay on the offense. This largely stems from his "active-negative" personality, described as having compulsive traits, including a preoccupation with failure and success.[28] It is not surprising that Nixon had always placed winning the public-opinion battle as central to his endeavors. Moreover, this outlook caused him to see the press as an impediment rather than a conduit in the quest for popular support.

From the very beginning of his presidency, Nixon considered the press to be his adversary in an ongoing war.[29] He was just as convinced that the press felt the same way about him. Nixon purposely screened certain reporters out of his information loop.[30] For Nixon, the game was "to manipulate and attack, not to inform or establish a mutually respectful give and take."[31]

One of Nixon's liabilities was that he always suffered from the problem of being less than telegenic. He seemingly never had a suit that fit properly. His disheveled appearance juxtaposed with that of the polished John F. Kennedy in the 1960 debates left an indelible mark on Americans.[32] He simply never came across well on television. This limited what he could accomplish through the medium.

There is another contrast that can be struck between Nixon and Kennedy. Nixon was born into a lower-middle-class family and was in essence a self-made man. His accomplishments were the result of his own hard work and study. Nixon abhorred everything the Kennedys stood for—born into wealth and privilege, attending Ivy League schools, and their general East Coast upper-class snobbery. Nixon's connections to the common man came through in his speeches and news conferences. He upheld the common farmer or tradesman as the virtuous soul of the American people.[33] It wasn't just good speechwriting, Nixon was a true believer.

Soon after Nixon took office, his administration launched "Operation Sandwedge." This program involved collecting intelligence and looking for dirt on political opponents, notably leading Democrats such as Senators Edward Kennedy (MA), Edmund Muskie (ME), and Hubert Humphrey (MN), and House Speaker Carl Albert (OK).[34] The White House also used the Internal Revenue Service (IRS) to conduct audits of organizations opposed to Nixon's policies.[35] Nixon vastly expanded the CIA's program of spying on leftist groups, known as "Operation Chaos."[36] The administration ordered an operation to obtain and divulge embarrassing information on Daniel Ellsberg, the whistleblower who leaked the *Pentagon Papers*.[37] Dirty tricks were a pattern and practice of the Nixon administration.

From 1969 through mid-1970, wiretaps on government officials and members of the press expanded with every leak that was made public. A plan to further broaden domestic surveillance, known as the Huston Plan, finally met resistance from FBI Director J. Edgar Hoover and was abandoned. Hoover warned that it was a matter of when rather than if the public became aware of illegal wiretaps and break-ins.[38] He knew that Nixon had already gone too far.

Finally, Nixon's expansive view of presidential power was evident in his first term. When the *Pentagon Papers* were leaked in June, 1971, Nixon felt that it was within his purview as president to prevent their publication. His reasoning was that although he was never mentioned in the papers, allowing secrets to be published would create a precedent for future actions that could imperil national security. Privately, he worried that any such precedent could make it difficult to protect his own secrets.[39] Though the Supreme Court sided against Nixon, he never strayed from his personal belief that he had the power to use the national security rationale to conceal documents from the public.

Key Decisions from the Bunker

During Watergate, the Nixon administration was widely described as having taken a "bunker" mentality. In this sense, anyone outside the bunker, including the press, was an enemy to be fought. So, during the two-plus years Watergate wore on, the Nixon administration stayed tight lipped publically while pursuing several backdoor tactics of influence. There were two main aspects to the bunker mentality—the first was to keep secrets in order not to give the enemy any ammunition; the second was to stay on attack.

Nixon's distrust of others was legendary. The bunker mentality came with Nixon as he took office. Beginning in 1969, his administration began wiretapping reporters and those within the administration suspected of being disloyal.[40] The phones of four reporters and 13 government officials were tapped. One of the staff members was Nixon's own speechwriter, William Safire, who was surveilled for his loose lips rather than questions of his loyalty.[41] Nixon's paranoia became full public knowledge when his "enemies list" was later exposed.[42]

Breaking Story: Keep it Secret, Keep it Safe

Though the Watergate story broke on June 17, 1972, it failed to become an issue in Nixon's reelection campaign. Nixon's avoidance of the issue at the outset proved highly successful considering his landslide victory. What reason was there to change this strategy? None. So the president adopted a defensive posture of stonewalling information while plugging leaks internally. In July, 1971, Nixon authorized top aide John Ehrlichman to establish a White House investigative unit that became known as the "Plumbers," whose task was to plug the news leaks emanating from his administration. Although soon disbanded after its involvement in the break-in into the Los Angeles offices of Daniel Ellsberg's psychiatrist, the formation of this group was an indication of the president's mindset.. He demanded complete control of information released to the public through the press. Nixon wanted to shut off the hose, but the Plumbers weren't the solution, they became the problem.

Haldeman noted that within three days of the Watergate break in on June 17, 1972, Nixon wanted a "PR offensive to top this [*sic*]."[43] The president's first instinct was to cover-up the mess of illegal operations associated with the White House that went back to the activities of the Plumbers and beyond. Gordon Strachan, an aide to H.R. Haldeman, destroyed files in his boss's office, including information gleaned from wiretaps on the Democratic National Committee (DNC).[44] Ehrlichman ordered White House counsel John Dean to spirit Watergate conspirator and former Plumber E. Howard Hunt away to another country, but later rescinded the order.[45] Considering the physical moving of potentially damaging individuals out of the country was a level of PR not generally practiced.

Another Watergate conspirator and former Plumber G. Gordon Liddy was willing to take the fall for the botched break-in by telling investigators that he acted contrary to the orders of his superiors that he return money from the campaign slush fund once they discovered that it was being used for illegal surveillance.[46] Nixon was impressed by Liddy's loyalty, calling him a "true believer," and promising "We'll take care of him...we'll wait a discreet interval and pardon him."[47]

John Dean was deeply involved in the cover-up as well. Shortly after the Watergate break-in, he gave Acting FBI Director L. Patrick Gray two files ostensibly from Howard Hunt's office, warning him that the files were "political dynamite" and "should never see the light of day."[48] Gray consequently burned the files rather than make them available to the FBI's own investigation of the Watergate affair.[49]

Nixon was aware that if the Watergate burglars testified about their White House connections, it would open the floodgates to revelations of larger operations rather beyond the "third-rate burglary." Accordingly they received hush money from the Committee to Reelect the President's slush fund.[50] One of the defendants, James McCord was promised funds if he pleaded guilty and refused to say anything. He was then threatened by White House security operative Jack Caulfield who told him "your life is no good in this country if you don't cooperate."[51] Dean would later testify that Nixon had prior knowledge about the hush money payments and knew about clemency deals being offered to certain Watergate defendants.[52]

The Nixon administration tried to use Dean as a scapegoat. Dean testified that Nixon attempted to have him sign a resignation letter that included a confession that Dean had directed the cover-up, and that Nixon knew nothing about it.[53]

The elements of Nixon's attempts to control the flow of information included destroying files, moving people out of the country, setting up fall guys, threats, and hush money. This wide-ranging cover-up would ultimately fail. Had Nixon not been involved in the cover-up and so worried about the public reaction, he may have saved his presidency. His actions in this regard gave rise to the long-enduring phrase that "the cover-up is worse than the crime."

Volley: The Saturday Night Massacre

On October 12, 1972, the US Court of Appeals judgment upholding Special Prosecutor Archibald Cox's subpoena of the Watergate tapes opened a new front in the battle in the public opinion war. After some stonewalling, the president offered a week later to transcribe the tapes and have the transcription verified by John E. Stennis, the Democratic Senator from Mississippi, but Cox would not countenance this.[54]

In response, Nixon went on the offensive publicly, issuing a statement that all parties but Cox had accepted the spirit of the Court of Appeals decision, to make it look as if the Special Prosecutor the one holding up the process. Moreover, the Nixon administration timed the release for 8:15pm EDT on the Friday-night ahead of the Veteran's Day holiday in an attempt to win the propaganda battle. If this ploy worked as planned, the president's adversary would have to wait until Tuesday to get out his response, making it harder to get the public on his side.[55] The plan looked good on paper: there would be no evening news until the following Monday, which was a holiday, and the morning newspapers would not publish reactions until their Sunday editions as deadlines had already passed for the Saturday issues; moreover, many people were away for the long holiday weekend, and most government offices were closed for the Monday holiday.

Not to be outdone, Cox hastily scheduled a news conference on October 20 at which he came off like a country lawyer instead of unreasonable, as Nixon had hoped.[56] Two networks carried the event live and ABC provided bulletins on it during a football game. In the end, Nixon's attempt to reduce the number of people exposed to the news over the weekend was a flop that prompted an even greater miscalculation on his part. In what became known as the "Saturday Night Massacre," the president ordered the firing of Cox, causing Attorney General Elliot Richardson and Deputy Attorney General William Ruckelshaus to resign in protest. The offices of the attorney general, deputy attorney general, and special prosecutor were occupied and sealed off by the FBI. It played on TV like a Latin American *coup d'état*. The office takeover happened even before the official order had arrived.

At this point, Nixon began his diversionary tactic by saying that the Watergate difficulties in America could be a temptation to those in the international arena to strike while America was vulnerable and distracted. Thus, focusing on Watergate would empower our enemies. Nixon contended that Cox had been engaged in a "fishing operation,"[57] discrediting and trivializing his investigation.

Over the preceding summer, a majority of Americans had already become convinced of Nixon's culpability in the scandal, even before congressional hearings were to take place (see Figure 8.2).[58] The public was primed and reacted swiftly to the Saturday Night Massacre. Three million messages were sent to Washington in the form of telegrams and phone calls.[59] Both Gallup and NBC polls found that support for impeachment jumped 15 points, to about 45 percent. Political elites felt the heat from public opinion, with most Democrats telling a *Congressional Quarterly* survey that they felt pressure to bring impeachment proceedings.[60]

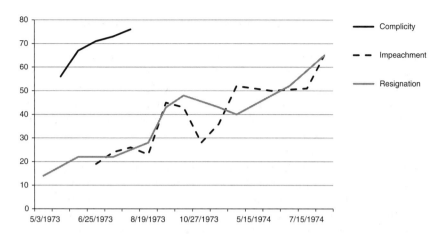

Figure 8.2 Public opinion: Nixon complicity, impeachment and resignation.
Source: Gallup, Harris and ORC. See Lang and Lang, 1980 for discussion of data and methods.

On October 23, Nixon agreed to surrender the tapes. Alexander Haig spoke on behalf of the president, indicating that it was Nixon's desire to promote national unity, and that he would be vindicated by the tapes.[61] Haig's message framed the issue as a partisan one, rather than a legal one. Nixon would return to this type of issue framing several times throughout the scandal.

On October 25, Nixon put the US military on high alert. His stated reason was to dissuade the Soviets from becoming involved in the situation in the Middle East during a ceasefire. Some in the media speculated that this was a diversionary tactic used by Nixon to take the public's eye off Watergate. Some in the White House Press Corps joked that "a crisis a day keeps impeachment away."[62]

On October 26, Nixon finally held a press conference that had been twice postponed. The press conference was heavy on foreign policy—Nixon's strong suit. Following the press conference, Gallup found that support for impeachment declined to 28 percent (see again Figure 8.2). In this press conference, Nixon singled out CBS for implying that it was "a blown-up exercise, not a real crisis."[63] He chose a formidable target for attack, as a poll in November found CBS's Walter Cronkite to be the most trusted source of news. Nixon was second to last in the poll only to his disgraced ex-Vice President Spiro Agnew.[64]

Coordinated charges of news bias emanated from the White House. CBS was forced to defend its coverage publicly. Administration officials were particularly perturbed by language such as *"coup d'état"* and "Saturday Night Massacre", as well as "The Mysterious Alert."[65] During a very long press briefing on October 25, 1972, Ziegler singled out the *Washington Post* for a prolonged attack and accused its executive editor, Ben Bradlee of being a political opponent of the president.[66] For a time, it looked like

Nixon had a strategy in place to turn the tide. All he needed to do was turn over the tapes.

But, a week after agreeing to turn over the nine subpoenaed tapes, word came out that two did not exist. The fact that tapes were missing made it look like Nixon had something to hide. An ABC poll showed that two-thirds of Americans thought that Nixon's story that the tapes never existed was unbelievable.[67] Against a shifting tide of public opinion, and *Time*, the *National Review*, and *ABC News* editorialized that Nixon had lost his moral authority and should step down or be removed.[68]

On November 7, 1973, the president ended a speech on energy policy declaring "I have no intention whatever of walking away from the job I was elected to do. As long as I am physically able, I am going to continue to work 16 to 18 hours a day for the cause of a real peace abroad, and for the cause of prosperity without inflation and without war at home."[69] Nixon had dug in his heels. While his timed release of the Stennis Compromise and his firing of top officials backfired, Nixon's tactics of stonewalling, partisan framing, diversionary use of the commander-in-chief powers, and his attack on the messenger with claims of news bias helped to slow his skid in the polls. Nonetheless, he was still losing ground, prompting the development of a new White House strategy in the battle for public opinion.

Going Public with Operation Candor

"Operation Candor" (a catch phrase coined by *Newsweek*) was the White House counteroffensive launched in November, 1973, and ended when the transcripts of the tapes were released on April 30, 1974.[70] It was supposed to turn around public opinion from the dual PR disasters of the Saturday Night Massacre and the missing tapes episode by meeting the administration's problems head-on.[71] Operation Candor was both an elite and mass opinion strategy. First, it involved the president holding face-to-face small-group meetings with every Republican member of Congress and many Democratic members, with food and drink served to lessen the tension.[72] Several legislators asked the president to take questions on the floor of congress, but Nixon could not abide looking like a defendant.[73] Instead, he went on the road, beginning in the South, to hold news conferences in front of supportive audiences with friendly congresspersons to lend support.[74] Strategically, the idea made sense, but its execution was catastrophic.

On November 17, while in Florida, Nixon made a mistake that would haunt him forever. Replying to questions about his personal finances, he replied that "People have got to know whether or not their President is a crook. Well, I am not a crook. I've earned everything I've got."[75] There were 400 Associated Press managing editors in attendance. Nixon's comment was etched into history, irrespective of the context of the actual question asked of him. If Nixon had to tell people that he was not a crook, then what exactly was he? Did saying he wasn't one when his veracity was increasingly in doubt do more to suggest the opposite of what he intended?

Disasters continued. When meeting with Republican governors on November 20, Nixon was asked if there would be any more "bombshells" coming from his administration. When Nixon assured them that there would be no more, headlines read "No More Bombshells."[76] But there was a bombshell—the next day news came out of the 18½ minute gap of missing material on one of the tapes that Nixon had turned over. The material in the 18½ minutes was blocked by a "shrill buzz."[77] The president's secretary, Rose Mary Woods, took the blame for accidentally causing it, though many found her claim dubious when trying to reenact her purported "stretch" that caused the erasure. At the time of the turnover of the tapes, polls suggested that Americans by a two-to-one margin believed that Nixon had altered the recordings. After the story of the 18½ minute gap broke, that number increased to three-to-one, including over half of the Republicans sampled.[78] Nixon's plan to go over the heads of the Washington establishment to appeal directly to the people proved an abject failure. The poorly executed strategy of "going public"—appealing to the people directly so that they could then put pressure on their representatives to do the president's bidding—put him in an even deeper hole.[79] The outcome meant that it was time for desperate measures.

Hail Mary Pass: The Edited Transcripts

Each time the Nixon tried to portray Watergate in partisan terms, it worked, but only briefly.[80] By the beginning of 1974, he was down to two cards he had left to play—his State of the Union address and how to turn over the subpoenaed tapes. Nixon used his State of the Union address in 1974 to emphasize that he would not resign and that all investigations should be called off: "I believe the time has come to bring that investigation and the other investigations of this matter to an end. One year of Watergate is enough."[81] His call went unheeded.

The House Judiciary Committee ordered the president to turn over 42 more tapes by the end of April. Nixon gave a speech on April 29 asserting that he would only turn over edited transcripts of the tapes in which "everything that is relevant is included—the rough as well as the smooth."[82] He further stated that the Chair and Ranking Minority member of the House Judiciary Committee would be invited to the White House to verify the transcripts. Nixon underscored that the 1,200 pages were "private" conversations and intimated to the audience that he was opening up his private life for public scrutiny. His speech implied that his reluctance had nothing to do with criminality, but rather, with personal embarrassment. Nixon showed a number of "envelopes" (actually binders) ostensibly containing transcripts of the tapes. The binders were an image of a hefty amount of work, indicating Nixon's willingness to comply. It was later revealed that half of the binders were merely stage props that contained blank pages,[83]

Political scientist Richard Neustadt observed that "the ultimate custodian of Nixon's power came to be his tapes."[84] They provided the smoking gun that not only could be used against him in the impeachment hearings, but would solidify his culpability in the eyes of the public. Ultimately, the House Judiciary Committee demanded that Nixon turn over the tapes, and the Supreme Court sided against Nixon and his claims of executive privilege. The battle for public opinion was over and the impeachment proceedings were unstoppable. Nixon's efforts at vindication during his presidency were over, but they would continue into his post-presidency.

Correcting the Record: Efforts Post-Presidency

After leaving the presidency and spending a few years in exile, Nixon wanted to clear his name for the historians. In his famous televised interviews with David Frost in 1977, Nixon again asserted his innocence by saying: "When the President does it, that means it's not illegal."[85] In the interview, he referred to the political activities that culminated in his resignation, not criminality.[86] The interviews were a hit, with the first interview reaching 50 million viewers.[87] After the interviews, Gallup found that 44 percent of the viewing audience felt more sympathetic to Nixon, compared to 28 percent who felt less so.[88]

The next stage in Nixon's attempted comeback was the publication of his memoirs in 1978. Despite racking up best-selling sales, it had little immediate effect in resurrecting his reputation, but it was another shot in the PR battle. Nixon followed it up with increasingly prestigious public appearances that mainly consolidated his reputation as a foreign policy guru and published a host of other book that portrayed him as an elder-statesman sage. His presidential library in Yorba Linda, California, which opened in 1990 and was entirely funded from private sources in contrast to other presidential libraries, was the ultimate embodiment of the way he wanted to be remembered—it was heavy on his foreign policy success, offered a dash of domestic achievement, and obscured remembrance of Watergate.

Evaluating the Hypotheses

Evaluating Nixon's efforts to influence public opinion influence reveals a broad range of tactics. They run the gamut from cover-up, redirection, assertions of media bias, payoffs, and threats. Why did he choose to engage the press largely through news conferences rather than speeches in order to do these things?

There is some historical evidence to support the psychological hypothesis. In grade school, Nixon earned a reputation for liking to argue about anything.[89] By the time he reached college, he was a champion debater, winning 27 straight contests and tutoring his teammates on the fly.[90] He owed his first electoral victory (a race for congress) to a series of five debates that he was counseled against by his advisors—he was up against a strong and entrenched Democrat.[91] When he attained the presidency, Nixon was concerned about his administration looking too cautious, and demanded action from his Cabinet from their very first meeting.[92] News conferences allowed the president to look engaged and activist to a greater degree than speeches do.[93] They also enabled him to address many different areas of accomplishment at once, whereas speeches generally focus on one or a limited number of topics.[94]

Comparison of news conferences and speeches given by other presidents lends support to the structural hypothesis. Beginning with Truman, only one president held news conferences less than twice per month—Kennedy, and his rate was at 1.9 per month (see Table 8.2). Nixon's rate of news conferences was three times slower than his nearest predecessor, at 0.6 in his first term and 0.5 in his second. He simply couldn't give any fewer than he was already giving. He couldn't ignore the press any longer. This evidence undercuts the psychological hypothesis, which would have predicted that Nixon would give more, rather than fewer press conferences than his predecessors. It also undermines the strategic hypothesis—in the time of uncertainty, Nixon would be expected to increase the number of press conferences in order to gain more insights from reporters. Moreover, Nixon attempted to keep the news conferences on the topic of foreign policy and away from Watergate. He wasn't probing the press for information.

Also in contrast to the psychological hypothesis, speeches were Nixon's preferred manner of speaking to the public. Nixon give a major speech roughly once every two months, compared to three month intervals for his modern predecessors.[95]

Table 8.2 Presidential News Conferences

	News Conferences Total	*News Conferences per month*
Truman	160	3.3
Eisenhower (First Term)	99	2.1
Eisenhower (Second Term)	94	2.0
Kennedy	65	1.9
Johnson	132	2.1
Nixon (First Term)	30	0.6
Nixon (Second Term)	9	0.5

Data Source: King and Ragsdale, 1988. See also Kumar, 2007.

Lastly, Nixon was often accused of being a compulsive liar. He lied to his closest aides and even to his own family.[96] Since deception was the name of the game for Nixon, it would hardly make sense to opt for press conferences over speeches. He could be too easily caught in his lies when the press had the opportunity to interrogate him. Speeches would be safer. This undercuts the psychological hypothesis, and we are left with the structural hypothesis as the best explanation.

Conclusion: The Legacy

Nixon's tactics may have shifted slightly around the edges over the course of the Watergate scandal, but there seems to be more consistency than change. Certainly, Operation Candor was a unique and clever strategy, but it was the only time when Nixon broke with his standard operating procedure. Nixon didn't adapt as situations changed, he dug in his heels and stonewalled investigators at every turn. He covered things up and asserted his innocence to the bitter end, and beyond. But even in retirement, Nixon's preferred tactic was redirection. He wanted the focus of discussion to always remain on his strong suit, and then to move on. As political psychologist James D. Barber comments on Nixon's rhetorical style:

> In speech after speech, he urged the public to forget this Watergate nonsense and march on into the future. This was a trick that had worked so well in the past that it had become Nixon's habitual way to wind up a crisis before plunging into a new one. All the way back to the Checkers speech, Nixon had succeeded not by giving us new facts but by giving us new explanations, not by acting but by redefining the meaning of acts.[97]

Some of Nixon's strategies were copied by his successors but such instances were rare because of his ultimate failure. The timing of the release of his statement on the Stennis Compromise to coincide with a relative news blackout was later followed by other presidents, including George H.W. Bush's Christmas Eve pardon of the Iran-contra felons. This tactic is much less effective today given the 24-hour news cycle and the internet medium. But Nixon's Operation Candor tactic of speaking to friendly crowds has endured. Foregoing the Washington establishment press and doing interviews with smaller local news outlets was a major strategy in George W. Bush's 2004 reelection campaign.

During Watergate, television sped up the process of information distribution. Political elites became aware of situations at the same time as the general public. In conjunction with increased media coverage of polls, this made them more prone to react to public opinion than shape it. While television coverage democratized the political process and significantly informed public opinion on a daily basis during Watergate, it gave leaders less time to react to events and to craft responses. The ramping up of the news cycle during Watergate foreshadowed greater increases in the speed of interaction among the press, elites, and the public as 24-hour cable news and internet news sources developed.

President Nixon's attempts to sway public opinion during and after the Watergate scandal have had a profound effect on the practice of politics in America. It was a foretaste of the so-called permanent campaign to win popular support for presidents and their policy. Paradoxically, however, Nixon's successors have not learned the lesson from his experience that "the cover-up is worse than the crime." A second effect of Nixon's cover-up is the decline in Americans' trust in government. While this began with the Vietnam War, Watergate exacerbated the problem. In 1974, the number of people who agreed with the statement that government is "run for the benefit of a few big interests" rose by 20 percent. A similar spike was seen in the number of people who answered "only some of the time" to the question "How much of the time do you think you can trust the government to do what is right?"[98] While trust in government has increased at certain times since Nixon's resignation, it has never come close to matching its pre-Watergate level.

For better and worse, Nixon's specific Watergate PR strategies have been mimicked by his successors. As noted earlier, the "timed news drop" technique used ahead of the "Saturday Night Massacre" was used to shield attention from the Iran-contra pardons issues by George H.W. Bush. Subsequent presidents have continued make use of this technique when issuing pardons, often waiting until the last days of their presidencies when public and press attention is focused on the incoming president and his inauguration. The "eleventh hour" timing of decisions has been extended to executive orders to executive-branch agencies in order to hide decisions that would have otherwise proved politically intractable earlier in the president's term, such as Bill Clinton's lowering of the safety threshold for the content of arsenic in drinking water.

Nixon's strategy of focusing on foreign policy and "doing the work of the people" has remained a time-tested presidential PR strategy for dealing with scandal. When the president reiterates that he is focused on doing the work of the people, he is distinguishing between the importance of his work and the work of his adversaries, which by implication is framed as a waste of time and the public's money. Foreign policy remains the president's strong suit, and using it to deflect attention away from other issues is still a winning strategy. Whether the president *intentionally* uses military force to divert attention from scandals remains unproven, though coincidences abound, such as Clinton's cruise missile attack on Iraq during the Monica Lewinsky scandal and George W. Bush's "Orange Alerts."

Other techniques seem best avoided. Though having different legal merits, claims of executive privilege by the Bill Clinton and George W. Bush administrations rang hollow with the public as they rhetorically summoned the ghost of Watergate. And if presidents are still using the techniques of hush-money payments or moving people out of the country, they have successfully kept it from the public view.

Lastly, Nixon's PR strategies have resulted in institutional changes to American politics. The Ethics in Government Act of 1978 established independent counsels that could not be fired by the president. Rightly or wrongly, these independent counsels have become a political tool for the out-party and have dogged every president from Jimmy Carter onward.[99] Nixon's evasion and stonewalling spawned a resurgent Congress, wresting its lost power away from the executive branch. Lastly, the importance of truth-telling through leaks and prosecutorial plea bargains remain an important check on the aggrandizement of executive power.

Notes

1. Garry Wills, *Nixon Agonistes: The Crisis of the Self-Made Man* (New York: Houghton Mifflin, 1970).
2. Walter Pincus, "More Insights from Nixon the Political Scientist," *Washington Post*, January 26, 2010, http://www.washingtonpost.com/wp-dyn/content/article/2010/01/25/AR2010012503632.html.
3. Lewis W. Liebovich, *Richard Nixon, Watergate, and the Press: A Historical Retrospective* (Westport, CT: Praeger, 2003); Pincus, "More Insights from Nixon the Political Scientist."
4. Pincus, "More Insights from Nixon the Political Scientist."
5. Richard Nixon, *RN: The Memoirs of Richard Nixon* (New York: Grosset & Dunlap, 1978).
6. James David Barber, *The Presidential Character: Predicting Performance in the White House*, 4th ed. (Upper Saddle River, NJ: Prentice-Hall, 1992).
7. Martha Joynt Kumar, *Managing the President's Message: The White House Communications Operation* (Baltimore, MD: Johns Hopkins University Press, 2007).
8. Kumar, *Managing the President's Message.*
9. John Zaller, *The Nature and Origins of Mass Opinion* (New York: Cambridge University Press, 1992).
10. Stephen Ansolabehere and Shanto Iyengar, *Going Negative: How Political Advertisements Shrink & Polarize the Electorate* (New York: Free Press, 1995).
11. RAND, *Watergate and Television: An Economic Analysis.* (Santa Monica, CA: RAND Corporation, 1975).
12. Michael J. Robinson, "The Impact of the Televised Watergate Hearings" *Journal of Communication* 24:2 (1974): 17–30; Analysis of the audiences for the live versus tape-delayed audiences indicate that the tape-delayed audience was more politically active, James E. Fletcher, "Commercial versus Public Television Audiences: Public Activities and the Watergate Hearings." *Communication Quarterly* 25:4 (1977): 13–66.
13. Ronald Garay, "Watergate." *The Museum of Broadcast Communications* (2010) http://www.museum.tv/eotvsection.php?entrycode=watergate.
14. Libertarian candidate John Hospers received one electoral vote from Roger MacBride, a faithless elector from Virginia.
15. See: uselectionatlas.org.

16. Gladys Engel Lang and Kurt Lang, *The Battle for Public Opinion: The President, the Press, and the Polls During Watergate* (New York: Columbia University Press, 1983).

17. Gladys Engel Lang and Kurt Lang, "Polling on Watergate: The Battle for Public Opinion," *The Public Opinion Quarterly* 44:4 (1980): 530–547.

18. Nixon, *RN*, 971.

19. Nixon, *RN*.

20. Nixon, *RN*, 972.

21. Nixon, *RN*, 972.

22. Kumar, *Managing the President's Message*.

23. Woody Klein, *All the Presidents' Spokesmen: Spinning the News—White House Press Secretaries From Franklin D. Roosevelt to George W. Bush* (Westport, CT: Praeger, 2008).

24. Patricia Sullivan, "Obituary: Herbert G. Klein, 91, White House Director Of Communications During Watergate," *The New York Times*, July 4, 2009, http://www.washingtonpost.com/wp-dyn/content/article/2009/07/02/AR2009070203390.html.

25. Klein, *All the Presidents' Spokesmen*.

26. Klein, *All the Presidents' Spokesmen*.

27. Roderick Hart, *Verbal Style and the Presidency: A Computer-based Analysis* (Orlando, FL: Academic Press Inc., 1984)

28. Barber, *The Presidential Character*.

29. Liebovich, *Richard Nixon, Watergate, and the Press*.

30. Liebovich, *Richard Nixon, Watergate, and the Press*.

31. Liebovich, *Richard Nixon, Watergate, and the Press*, 3.

32. Sullivan, "Obituary: Herbert G. Klein."

33. See: Hart, *Verbal Style and the Presidency*.

34. John M. Orman, *Presidential Secrecy and Deception: Beyond the Power to Persuade* (Westport, CT: Greenwood Press, 1980).

35. Stanly I. Kutler, *The Wars of Watergate: The Last Crisis of Richard Nixon* (New York: Knopf, 1990).

36. J. Anthony Lukas, *Nightmare: The Underside of the Nixon Years* (New York: Penguin, 1988).

37. Kutler, *The Wars of Watergate*.

38. Richard Reeves, *President Nixon: Alone in the White House* (New York: Simon & Schuster, 2001).

39. Kutler, *The Wars of Watergate*.

40. Carl Bernstein and Bob Woodward, *All the President's Men* (New York: Simon & Schuster, 1974).

41. Pincus, "More Insights from Nixon the Political Scientist."

42. Kutler, *The Wars of Watergate*.

43. Cite in: Lukas, *Nightmare*.

44. Lukas, *Nightmare*.

45. "The Hearings: Dean's Case against the President," *Time*. July 9, 1973, http://www.time.com/time/printout/0,8816,907488,00.html

46. Reeves, *President Nixon*.

47. Reeves, *President Nixon*, 512.

48. Fred Emery, *Watergate: The Corruption of American Politics and the Fall of Richard Nixon* (New York: Touchstone, 1994).

49. Reeves, *President Nixon*.

50. Kutler, *The Wars of Watergate.*

51. Bernstein and Woodward, *All the President's Men*, 318.

52. Kutler, *The Wars of Watergate.*

53. Kutler, *The Wars of Watergate.*

54. Tian-jia Dong, *Understanding Power through Watergate: The Washington Collective Power Dynamics* (Lanham, MD: University Press of America, 2005).

55. Lang and Lang, *The Battle for Public Opinion.*

56. Lang and Lang, *The Battle for Public Opinion.*

57. Nixon, *RN*, 933.

58. Lang and Lang, *The Battle for Public Opinion*, 91.

59. Lang and Lang, *The Battle for Public Opinion.*

60. Lang and Lang, *The Battle for Public Opinion.*

61. Lang and Lang, *The Battle for Public Opinion.*

62. Lang and Lang, *The Battle for Public Opinion*, 107.

63. Richard M. Nixon, *News Conference,* October 26, 1973, Transcripts from *The Presidency Project.* http://www.presidency.ucsb.edu.

64. Lang and Lang, *The Battle for Public Opinion.*

65. Lang and Lang, *The Battle for Public Opinion*, 111.

66. Barry Sussman, *The Great Cover-up: Nixon and the Scandal of Watergate* (New York: Thomas Y. Crowell Company, 1974).

67. Lang and Lang, *The Battle for Public Opinion.*

68. Lang and Lang, *The Battle for Public Opinion.*

69. "Address to the Nation About Policies To Deal With the Energy Shortages," November 7, 1973, John T. Woolley and Gerhard Peters, *American Presidency Project [APP]* (Santa Barbara, CA: University of California)/www.presidency .ucsb.edu.

70. Lang and Lang, *The Battle for Public Opinion.*

71. Lukas, *Nightmare.*

72. Lukas, *Nightmare.*

73. Lang and Lang, *The Battle for Public Opinion.*

74. Lang and Lang, *The Battle for Public Opinion.*

75. Carroll Kilpatrick, "Nixon Tells Editors, 'I'm Not a Crook,' " *Washington Post*, November 18, 1973. A01, http://www.washingtonpost.com/wp-srv/ national/longterm/watergate/articles/111873-1.htm.

76. Lang and Lang, *The Battle for Public Opinion*, 120.

77. Lukas, *Nightmare*, 456.

78. Lang and Lang, *The Battle for Public Opinion.*

79. Samuel Kernell, *Going Public: New Strategies Of Presidential Leadership,* 4th ed, (Washington, DC: Congressional Quarterly Press, 2006).

80. Lang and Lang, *The Battle for Public Opinion.*

81. Richard M. Nixon, "State of the Union Address, ". January 30, 1974, *APP.*

82. "Speech on the Release of the Watergate Tapes," April 29, 1974, *APP.*

83. Lang and Lang, *The Battle for Public Opinion.*

84. Richard E. Neustadt, *Presidential Power and the Modern Presidents: The Politics of Leadership from Roosevelt to Reagan* (New York: Free Press, 1990), 212.

85. David Frost, *Frost/Nixon: Behind the Scenes of the Nixon Interviews* (New York: HarperCollins, 2007).

86. Kutler, *The Wars of Watergate*, 614.

87. Michael Schudson, *Watergate in American Memory: How We Remember, Forget, and Reconstruct the Past* (New York: Basic Books, 1992).
88. Kutler, *The Wars of Watergate.*
89. Barber, *The Presidential Character.*
90. Barber, *The Presidential Character.*
91. Barber, *The Presidential Character.*
92. William W. Lammers, and Michael A. Genovese, *The Presidency and Domestic Policy* (Washington DC: Congressional Quarterly Press, 2000).
93. Kumar, *Managing the President's Message.*
94. Kumar, *Managing the President's Message.*
95. Gary King and Lyn Ragsdale, *The Elusive Executive: Discovering Statistical Patterns in the Presidency* (Washington DC: Congressional Quarterly Press, 1988).
96. Barber, *The Presidential Character.*
97. Barber, *The Presidential Character*, 159.
98. Barbara A. Bardes and Robert W. Oldendick, *Public Opinion: Measuring the American Mind* 2nd ed, (Belmont, CA: Thomson Wadsworth, 2003).
99. See Bob Woodward, *Shadow: Five Presidents and the Legacy of Watergate* (New York: Touchstone, 2000).

Chapter Nine

The Cinematic Watergate: From All the President's Men to Frost/Nixon

Kingsley Marshall

Richard Nixon is frequently represented in Hollywood movies as the embodiment of presidential villainy, the polar opposite of filmmakers' conventional representations of Abraham Lincoln, Franklin D. Roosevelt, and John F. Kennedy as heroic leaders.[1] He provides a convenient metaphor for the shortcomings, inauthenticity, and antidemocratic tendencies of America's political establishment.[2] Despite this, very few made-for-cinema films have explored his Watergate downfall in purportedly realistic fashion. This chapter examines how these movies contribute to remembrance and understanding of one of the key events in American history. In its assessment, they have reinforced the image of Watergate as a scandal pertaining to Nixon, with a subtheme of the media's fundamental role in exposing presidential wrongdoing, rather than a systemic crisis of the imperial presidency.

Hollywood's emphasis on the symbolic Nixon is entirely understandable because the search for the 'real' one is so frustrating. As scholar Mark Feeney remarked, he had "a unique capacity among U.S. presidents for constructing narratives around himself as he presented for public inspection all those 'new Nixons.'"[3] A man of many masks, he "still casts a shadow upon our age" in the estimation of historian David Greenberg because of the different images he inspired in life and death among different groups. Nevertheless, the meanings imparted to Nixon were "contested and ever-changing" over time.[4] As cultural analyst Daniel Frick remarked, "When we fight about Nixon, we are fighting about the meaning of America. And that is a struggle that never ends."[5]

All the President's Men: The Journalist as Watergate Hero

The first cinematic representation of Watergate, *All the President's Men* (1976), exemplified the shortcomings of film as an agency of remembrance of it. This is based on the book of the same title by *Washington Post* journalists Carl Bernstein and Bob Woodward, which became the fastest selling hardcover title in U.S. history after its publication in May 1974, three months before Nixon quit office.[6] The film, featuring top stars Dustin Hoffman and Robert Redford in the lead roles, went on to become the fifth largest grossing movie of 1976. Nixon only features through occasional use of newsreel footage rather than dramatic depiction by an actor, but audiences of the time would have constantly felt his presence in the movie's depiction of the journalistic investigation of Watergate. With intentional symbolism, it was the first film that Jimmy Carter, who had won election as president on a promise never to lie to the American people, watched in the White House movie theatre two days after taking office.[7]

The origins of the film were seeded in the 1972 presidential election campaign when Robert Redford first made contact with the reporters following publication of their initial newspaper stories suggesting a White House connection with the Watergate break-in. The actor, who also produced the movie, secured the film option on the story immediately after Simon and Schuster awarded Bernstein and Woodward a book contract in the spring of 1973. As Woodward acknowledged, however, Redford's influence on the project from conception was "a factor in getting us to write the book we wrote." It was at his suggestion that the *Washington Post* duo framed the instant history of their investigation in terms of how they had got information rather than what they had discovered. In Redford's assessment, Watergate-weary readers and filmgoers were more likely to be interested in this approach.[8] In other words, profit-making priorities ensured that entertainment trumped examination of what Watergate truly constituted.

True to the book, the movie is almost a police procedural film that features reporters instead of cops. Billed as "The Most Devastating Detective Story of the Century," it focused on the nuts and bolts of investigative journalism—a world of cold calls, denials, late night meetings, and the slow grind of getting and pursuing leads. In one of its most famous scenes, the two reporters trawl for hours through book order stubs in the Library of Congress vainly seeking evidence of White House plans for a dirty tricks campaign against Senator Edward Kennedy (D-MA). Other than scenes of Bernstein and Woodward hunting out sources and the latter's garage basement meetings with his Deep Throat informant, the principal locus of the movie is the *Washington Post* newsroom.

The essentially action-less story plays as a paean to the dogged determination of two lowly beat journalists in exposing White House links with the Watergate burglars and the backing they received from the newspaper's famous editor, Ben Bradlee (played by Jason Robards in a best supporting actor Oscar-winning performance). In the estimate of Deborah Knight and George McKnight, the film followed a "detection" rather than a detective narrative, with a mystery that required "hermeneutical investigation, one that promised rather than delivered explanation." This is at once the strength of the movie as entertainment and its weakness as history because it traded on reliance of the audience's basic memory of Watergate without explaining its significance. Critical of its "nagging hollowness," Mark Feeney dubbed it "a political film devoid of issues of ideology, a marvel of sustained tension in which no true dramatic resolution occurs."[9]

Director Alan J. Pakula and scriptwriter William Goldman maintain audience interest in a story whose ending is universally known by concocting it as a David versus Goliath contest. The fictional political conspiracy movies of the 1970s, like David Miller's *Executive Action* (1973), Pakula's own *The Parallax View* (1974), and Francis Ford Coppola's *The Conversation* (1974), almost universally offered a bleak view of the capacity of powerful and hidden elites to subvert American democracy. In contrast, even though *All the President's Men* is regarded by some as "the centerpiece of the conspiracy subgenre" that dominates noir films, the good little guys win out in its optimistic scenario. As Pakula put it, the movie was "a kind of contemporary myth," which affirmed the "American belief that a person or small group can with perseverance and hard work and obsessiveness take on a far more powerful impersonal body and win—if they have truth on their side."[10]

However the Watergate truth being exposed in the movie is a very partial one. It relates initially to the White House's connection with the Watergate burglars and its efforts to cover this up. In the course of the investigation, Bernstein and Woodward stumble upon the involvement of the Committee to Re-elect the President (CREEP), a body with links to the upper echelons of the White House, in financing illegal campaign activities and political espionage against Nixon administration opponents. This resulted from Deep Throat's advice to "follow the money," which became one of the quintessential phrases associated with Watergate. Showing the power of film to turn myth into popular truth, the most famous leaker in history never actually spoke these words, which scriptwriter Goldman put in his mouth for dramatic effect.[11]

Other than that, there are only vague allusions to the administration's use of the intelligence agencies and other government bodies for illegal political activities. In the most significant scene pertaining to this, Deep Throat warns Woodward that the journalists' investigation is putting their lives in danger. This was another fictional construct to link the movie in the mind of audiences with the paranoid conspiracy thrillers then in cinematic vogue. In general, however, the whistle-blower's appearances in the film do more to titillate audience interest in trying to guess his actual identity, which remained hidden for another 20 years. In 2005, Mark Felt, associate director of the FBI at the time of Watergate, revealed that he was Deep Throat, so bringing to an end the tide of speculation that tended to distract attention from the broader significance of Watergate. As one journalist commented when the secret came out, "For many Americans under 40, this is the most potent distillation of the complicated brew that was Watergate. Students who lack the time or interest to follow each element of the scandal's slow unravelling in comprehensive history books can quickly digest the vivid relationship of a nervous elder guiding a relentless reporter."[12]

It was Pakula's direction of *The Parallax View* that persuaded Redford to hire him, but some critics had panned the earlier movie for its fantastical flourishes. Some decried its exemplification of "the empty-headed fence straddling approach to controversial issues that has made Hollywood's political movies such a joke."[13] As a result, Pakula was careful not to over stylize the Bernstein-Woodward film, preferring an approach that was "totally un-self-conscious…an immediate experience, trying to say what it was like at the time." The *Washington Post* newsroom was recreated on the Warner Bros. back lot in Burbank in meticulous detail that included shipping tons of assorted papers and trash from the real one to dress the bins and desks of the set. Pakula traded on a sense of realism that lent the picture immediacy, but a *Time* magazine reviewer thought this emphasis on authenticity could be self-defeating in turning "national trauma into a mere movie."[14]

All the President's Men says virtually nothing about the constitutional violations of the imperial presidency as detailed by Arthur M. Schlesinger, Jr. in his 1973 book. It is mainly concerned with the obstruction-of-justice cover-up pertaining to the Watergate break-in rather than abuse-of-power matters. Hence there is no reference to Nixon's secret bombing and later invasion of Cambodia without congressional authorization, presidential impoundment of funds appropriated by Congress, and the administrative presidency project to marginalize other branches of government.[15] As testimony to its tendency to portray Watergate through the prism of investigative reporting, the movie's sole reference to it as constitutional crisis is framed in light of justifying the Bernstein-Woodward sharp practice in getting sources to speak against their will and surreptitiously obtaining documentary information about CREEP. In excusing their transgressions, Ben Bradlee comments sardonically, "There's nothing riding on this except the First Amendment to the Constitution, freedom of the press, and maybe the future of the country."

The movie's heroic representation of the press opens with a symbolic demonstration not only of the power but also the purity of the written word. This features a close-up of a reporter's bond paper, its whiteness contrasting with the darkness of the burglarized Democratic National Committee (DNC) offices in the next scene. The shot is held for 18 seconds before a typewriter keystroke breaks the silence like a cannon volley. The film similarly ends with a series of close-up of major Watergate stories, with dates through to Nixon's August 9, 1974, resignation, being printed out on a teletype machine against the sound background of real cannon-fire from a fading shot of his second inauguration. Lighting reinforces the message of the media's steadfastness throughout the movie. As he had done in previous Pakula movies, *Klute* (1971) and *The Parallax View*, cinematographer Gordon Willis contrasted the darker corners that held information from well-lit places where government secrets were exposed. To this end, the *Washington Post* newsroom is always bathed in fluorescent light to show, in Pakula's words, "the total accessibility of everyone [there]…compared to the inaccessibility of the President."[16] Such devices suggest that *All the President's Men* had begun a "movement toward hope" in conspiracy cinema.[17]

In focusing on one element of the Watergate imbroglio, *All the President's Men* overstates the significance of journalism in general (there is passing reference to stories broken by the *New York Times* and *Los Angeles Times*) and the *Washington Post* in particular in exposing White House criminality. Though courageous and determined in pursuit of their story, Bernstein and Woodward did not have a crucial role in Nixon's downfall. As Watergate conspirator and later whistle-blower John Dean later remarked, "If the Nixon White House had had to contend only with the *Washington Post*, the Watergate cover-up would have succeeded." In his estimate it was *New York Times* journalist Seymour Hersh, whose investigative reporting the White House most feared.[18]

Significantly, *All the President's Men* effectively ends in early 1973, several months before the White House cover-up began seriously to unravel. In reality, it was not the press that exposed Watergate, but the agencies of government. The main significance of Bernstein and Woodward was to keep the Watergate pot boiling in the six months after the break-in when the White House cover-up was at its most effective and fewer than 15 of the 430 newspaper reporters in Washington worked exclusively on the issue. In this period, the *Washington Post* published some two hundred articles about Watergate, more than double the number of its nearest rival, the *New York Times*. However, the critical breakthroughs in the investigation came in the summer of 1973, by when the two journalists were fully engaged in writing their book. The damning testimony against Nixon was unearthed by the FBI, District Judge John J. Sirica (who presided over the trial of the Watergate burglars), Special Prosecutors Archibald Cox and Leon Jaworski, and the Senate Select Committee on Presidential Campaign Practices chaired by Sam Ervin (D-NC).[19]

At the time of the film's release, the *Washington Post*'s Gary Arnold remarked that its incompleteness and excessive deference to reporters would limit its political impact. Such caveats did not stop the role of journalism in the downfall of a president becoming part of the press's mythology about its own importance as the guardian of constitutional democracy.[20] On her death in 2001, obituaries lionized *Washington Post* owner Katherine Graham for "having struck a blow for all time against the abuse of power" through her determination to press ahead with the publication of the *Pentagon Papers* in 1971 and the Bernstein-Woodward investigation of Watergate in 1972. Nevertheless, Graham herself had more realistically warned in her memoirs that the post-Watergate press "had to guard against the romantic tendency to picture itself in the role of beleaguered and heroic champion, defending all virtues against overwhelming odds."[21]

The *All the President's Men* movie reinforced the effect of the book in promoting this myth. According to Daniel Schacter, its narrative process aimed "not only to report the past but to make it interesting" through development of a David and Goliath story. The result in essence was a coming-of-age drama whereby the liberal press, "innocent of politics, ever stumbling and learning," was schooled by the Nixon White House about the capacity of those in high places to do wrong. In the case of Bernstein and Woodward, they began their investigation as freshmen but "were seniors ready to graduate" when it ended.[22] After collecting audience data following a screening of the movie, two scholars reported " a substantial attitudinal change" manifesting "a marked increase in political alienation while displaying a more positive attitude toward the press." In their estimate, the film had more influence on attitude to the press than to government.[23] Reaching a similar conclusion, scholar Elizabeth Kraft noted that "in a film about media, everything, including confrontation, is mediated by the newspaper and the television."[24]

Watergate Movies of the 1980s and 1990s: Losing Sight of the Imperial Presidency

In the 20 years that followed *All the President's Men*, there were frequent representations of Nixon in movies, mostly in made-for-television films and miniseries.[25] He also featured in a number of cinematic releases, none of which promoted effective remembrance of Watergate. Robert Altman's one-man movie *Secret Honor*, released in 1984, benefits from a fine performance by Philip Baker Hall as a Nixon engaged in darkly introspective soul-searching in the course of one lonely night in his San Clemente post-resignation exile. In a drunken, rambling, monologue—one littered with obscenities, the ex-president reveals that he himself was Deep Throat. In thrall to organized crime, who put him in power, he had grown disgusted by the mob's use of the Vietnam War to expand its heroin operations; so to stop its game he informed against himself. The movie was a satirical commentary not so much on Nixon but on the renewed acceptance of the old Cold War verities in Ronald Reagan's America. As film scholar Michael Coyne remarks, however, "As a plausible offertory of the truth about Watergate, this was on the far side of weird."[26]

Offering a more comic but equally unrealistic take was *Dick*, the 1999 movie in which two teenage pranksters play the role of Deep Throat. To ensure the silence of the young girls who inadvertently help to foil the Watergate burglars, the president makes them his official dog-walkers. When he fails to respond to the romantic fantasies of one of them, they take revenge by spilling the beans to two *Washington Post* reporters about the cover-up activities they have witnessed in the White House. *Dick* is more than anything else about the baby-boom generation's nostalgia for 1970s America. If it has a serious intent, this focuses primarily on the two female leads turning their disillusion into empowerment in an allegory of the American people's awakening to White House wrongdoing. However, the movie blurs understanding of Watergate through its comedic caricature of the White House. Played by Dan Hedaya, Nixon "appears bumbling, fatherly, a bit paranoid, but never more evil than an ordinary man thrust into the pitfalls of Washington politics." Instead, it is his aides who act like "heavy-handed storm troopers," a construct that does little to explain why Cold War presidents consistently challenged the limits of their constitutional power.[27]

Released in between these movies in 1995 was Oliver Stone's epic *Nixon*, a three-hour exploration of his life. Anthony Hopkins, then at the height of his stardom, played the central character in an Oscar-nominated performance, but some critics felt the casting of such a famous actor distracted attention from the subject he was portraying. Stone had come in for heavy criticism for fantasy in his previous presidential film, *JFK*, which offered his take on a conspiracy behind the assassination of John F. Kennedy. *Nixon* was also slated for historical inaccuracy, but failed to repeat *JFK*'s box office success. Costing $44 million to make, it grossed only $14 million on its U.S. run. If historians criticized its simplifications, its *Citizen Kane*-style framing of Nixon's life in flashbacks was too complex for most filmgoers. Moreover, the narrative of conspiracy that was at its heart lacked the suspenseful invention of that in *JFK* because everyone knew the solution to the mystery. After *JFK*'s release, Norman Mailer had famously remarked that the film had "the power to make new history," but *Nixon* only demonstrated that the truth is less effective than fiction in movies.[28]

As conceived by Stone, *JFK* and *Nixon* "are prologue and epilogue in portraying the perversion of America's founding values in pursuit of Cold War ends." Nevertheless, his depiction of Nixon as a man capable of greatness but undone by his flaws distracts from the representation of an imperial president. The movie focuses mainly on Nixon as the creature and victim of "the Beast," a "metaphor for the darkest organic forces in American Cold War politics," namely the military-industrial complex, the intelligence agencies, the McCarthyite right, and organized crime that were involved in Kennedy's murder in *JFK*. However, this proves an unsatisfactory device for explaining what was at stake in the Watergate crisis. It presents a bleak view of the presidency as powerless to control the antidemocratic elements of the American system rather than as an institutional threat to constitutional democracy in its own right. As Arthur Schlesinger, Jr. commented after seeing *Nixon*, the Beast is "an additive that impairs the whole and could have been deleted without harm to the rest."[29]

Frost/Nixon: Another David and Goliath Story

Based on Peter Morgan's play, the *Frost/Nixon* movie released in 2008 is a dramatization of British broadcaster David Frost's 1977 interviews with

Richard Nixon that attracted massive audiences when they were shown on television.[30] Frank Langella put in another Oscar-nominated performance as Nixon, one not encumbered by a star persona since he was better known as a stage rather than film actor. Michael Sheen, who has thrice appeared as British Prime Minister Tony Blair—most notably in *The Queen* (2006)—in other Morgan ventures, played Frost. Director Ron Howard was best known for his work on films dealing with historical events, *Apollo 13* (1995) about the endangered lunar mission of 1970, and the multiple Academy Award-winning *A Beautiful Mind* (2001) that recounted the life of Nobel laureate scientist John Nash. Drawing on his reputation for depicting real history, Howard looked to imbue his new venture with a sense of authenticity as cinematic truth.

Echoing *All the President's Men*, however, *Frost/Nixon* has a very limited concept of the Watergate truth. It sets up the interviews as a trial by television that substituted for the actual trial that Nixon escaped as a result of being pardoned for unspecified crimes by his presidential successor, Gerald Ford. According to James Reston, Jr., the researcher who assisted Frost prepare for the interviews (and the son of *New York Times* journalist James Reston, who had featured on the Nixon 'enemies list'), at issue in the Frost-Nixon encounter was—"Would the Grand Inquisitor be able to coax from the Master of Deception a sincere confession of crime and an authentic apology to the nation." It was a contest from which "only one winner could emerge." The final outcome in Reston's opinion was clear-cut: "Television had vindicated the decision of the nation."[31]

Whereas *All the President's Men* had celebrated print journalism's role in exposing Nixon's misdeeds, *Frost/Nixon* lauds the role of television in getting him to say sorry. As in the former, however, revelation by the media of wrongdoing becomes more important than understanding the nature of the wrongdoing. As film critic David Edelstein observed, *Frost/Nixon* "elevates the 1977 interviews...into a momentous event in the history of politics and the media."[32] It begins with a blend of fictional documentary, news footage contemporaneous to the period, and audio of Nixon taken from a recording made by the White House taping system. "I don't give a goddamn what the story is," says an irate president in conversation with Attorney General John Mitchell, "he went on television." In reality, the line formed part of a conversation related to the capture of 36 illegal immigrants by the Immigration and Naturalization Service in a raid on a company owned by Nixon appointee Romana Banuelos. In retaliation the president wanted Mitchell to arrange the transfer of the agency's district director, George Rosenberg, who had coordinated the raid. In Howard's film, however, Nixon's words are a manifestation of his mistrust of television's capacity to undermine administration secrecy, thus pointing to his own forthcoming trial on television by Frost.

In its effort to build up the Frost/Nixon encounter, the movie presents the two protagonists in David and Goliath terms. The playboy broadcaster, his career seemingly on the skids, looking for a chance to reestablish himself as a serious journalist is up against the battle-hardened politician and supreme stonewaller looking to rehabilitate himself in the eyes of the nation. As Nixon explained to Frost in a fictional late-night phone call: "Isn't that why we're here now, the two of us, looking for a way back into the sun, into the limelight, back onto the winner's podium, because we could feel it slipping away."

In reality, Frost's career was not in decline in the way suggested. As he later remarked, "That was Peter [the play's author and the movie's script-writer] letting his imagination run riot."[33] What was at stake for Frost was the risk that he would lose the large sum of money he had personally invested in the project, if he could not get Nixon to make the kind of admission that would interest a large television audience.

More seriously, *Frost/Nixon* implicitly exaggerates Nixon's capacity for rehabilitation in order to play up the significance of the interviews in preventing this. As the James Reston character (played by Sam Rockwell) exclaims in the movie, "To say that in this interview that Richard Nixon exonerated himself would be the worst crime of all." In the crucial scene of the film, however, as happened in reality, Frost gets a moist-eyed ex-president to admit that he had let down the nation and the American system of government, a burden he would carry for the rest of his life. This was the nearest that Nixon ever came to an apology in any statement while in office or afterward, and much more than top U.S. news journalists had got out of him. As David Frost put it in his book about the interviews, "The man whose pride would not permit him to say, 'I broke the law; I violated my constitutional duty," had come as close to admitting both as it was within his pathology to do."[34] However, this was not the moment of victory for the Watergate truth that the film implied it to be.

The real Nixon had agreed to be interviewed by Frost for a fee of $600,000 to pay substantial and ongoing legal fees pertaining to the Watergate cover-up. He had not planned this as part of a comeback campaign, and had taken time off from writing the memoirs that he intended to be the first step in the quest for rehabilitation. Though never escaping the obloquy of Watergate, Nixon did achieve a greater degree of reputational recovery than had ever seemed possible on the day of his resignation. Far from continually pinning the former president on the ropes, the Frost interviews allowed him to road test what would become the central theme of his campaign to regain acceptance—namely that he was a geopolitical maestro who had worked to promote peace and security for America in a dangerous world. The admission of sorrow for Watergate was necessary in his first major public appearance since resigning office. Thereafter, however, Nixon's comeback campaign would focus on reminding people of his successes without real admission of his sins.[35]

In 2008, James Reston acknowledged that Nixon's "apology" in the Frost interviews did not fit the mold of classical tragedy as defined by Aristotle that suffering produces enlightenment because "after he delivered it, ... [he] quickly reverted to blaming others for his transgressions."[36] However, the

Frost/Nixon film— in the Hollywood tradition of what Lev described as a "recuperative, happy ending"[37]—contains a final coda that does allow for this Aristotelian construct. In its final scene, Frost revisits Nixon at his home in San Clemente after the interviews have been broadcast. Facing his interlocutor after their battle is over, the former president comes close to recognizing his shortcomings and is left pondering how his quest for greatness ended so badly.

Inevitably, the movie's framing of its subject as a contest results in emphasis on Nixon's personality rather than the presidency as an institution. In a pivotal and entirely fictional scene, he makes a rambling, drink-fuelled, late-night telephone call to Frost that foreshadows his final interview admission of sorrow over Watergate. This builds an image of him as irrational and prone to recklessness, particularly when under the influence of alcohol. Nixon's failure to recollect the call the following day then sews doubts as to both his memory and integrity. The same message of flawed personality is reinforced in other scenes. Nixon's family is kept at a distance—his wife Pat has only one brief and inconsequential appearance—to signify his emotional distance. The silence of his family further privileges Nixon's power, as the few characters who are allowed to speak with him in the film are typically those in his employ, such as the literary agent Swifty Lazar and aide Jack Brennan, or those who oppose him, such as Frost.

This focus on the individual affirms the observation of film scholar George Custon that movie biopics have conventionally served as an accessible version of history that satisfies audience desire for "a loose code of realism."[38] In essence, when recounting historical events, film can make an assertion of truth that has the power to become embedded in popular culture. The simpler the assertion, the more it is elevated and concretized. Conversely, complexity and ambiguity make less impression on the viewer.

The closest that the movie gets to promoting understanding of what Watergate constituted is when Nixon makes his notorious justification for abuse of executive power in the final interview session: "I'm saying that when the President does it, that means that it is not illegal." Broadway theatre audiences seeing the *Frost/Nixon* play in the summer of 2007 generally burst out laughing at that line, but found the follow-up one from Frank Langella's Nixon even funnier, "But I realise that no one else shares that view." According to one analyst, this reflected "wry recognition that yet another president not only believed such sentiments, but had been acting on them as well."[39] In the highly visual imagery of cinema, however, there is no evidence of the line, with its unspoken reference to George W. Bush's renewal of the imperial presidency, having the same effect.

Ultimately, it is the movie Frost's superior understanding of television that allows his David to triumph over the movie Nixon's Goliath. However much Nixon stonewalled on Watergate or boasted of his foreign policy achievements, his inquisitor knew that the former president's "apology" would be what stuck in the popular mind. As the James Reston character observes in the closing scene from the film, [T]he first and greatest sin or deception of television is that it simplifies. It diminishes great complex ideas, tranches of time, whole careers become reduced to a single snapshot." The irony of Howard's movie is that the same could be said of it. For many in the film's audience, the failings of its recollection of historical events have not only been forgotten but have ceased to exist, replaced by a cinematic memory that has at best destabilized history. Rather than consider the larger implications of Nixon's imperial presidency, the film barely engages with them. It boils down his legacy to a simple, easy to understand, but utterly facile final statement from Reston that henceforth all political wrongdoing would attract the suffix 'gate' to its name. The relatively upbeat ending helped to make the movie popular and profitable, but not illuminating in the historical and political sense.

Conclusion

The few films that have attempted to deal with Watergate underline the limitations rather than the possibilities of cinema to assist in remembering and understanding it. The two most popular movies affirm the observation of film scholar Mark Carnes that "Hollywood history sparkles because it is so historically ambiguous, so devoid of tedious complexity." They similarly manifest what Marnie Hughes-Warrington called an "underreading" of history through the use of familiar themes and happy endings that offer "a closed, completed and simple past."[40] This simplification of historical events tend to require the reduction of movies to a singular issue that frames the participation of the main characters.. In celebrating journalism as the champion of constitutional democracy, *All the President's Men* and *Frost/Nixon* propagate a comforting belief that the system works without providing real insight into the threat of the imperial presidency.

Whatever their other merits, *Secret Honor* and *Dick*, reveal the problems of comedic treatment (black humor in the case of the former) that offer the audience an escape into unreality and fantasy, rather than confronting the dangerous reality of Watergate. Conversely, the unpopularity of Oliver Stone's *Nixon* points to the limitations of a more complex and far bleaker take on Watergate that offers an unrelentingly pessimistic assessment of American democracy.

The shortcomings of Watergate movies as history beg the question of whether cinema can ever help remembrance of this episode in America's past and understanding of its implications for the nation's future. There is no doubting the importance of film in making sense of experience. As political scientists Dan Nimmo and James Combs observed, "We build our image of the world by making connections, constructions, and pictures of reality as if they were true. We impute an order and meaning to the world by importing into our images of the world a variety of symbolic structures to which we give reality."[41] This points to the benefits of a Watergate movie that offered a working model of the imperial presidency rather than merely a flawed president. Such a film is more likely to be a fictional rather than a purportedly factual one because of the greater possibility this would offer for developing the appropriate message. As Garrison Keillor remarked, reliance on scholarship and experience ignores the importance of mythic narrative. In his view "a man who has no story is a man with no truth to offer."[42] However, it remains unclear whether the Hollywood equivalent of Arthur Schlesinger, Jr., will ever emerge.

Notes

1. For discussion of cinematic presidents, see: Peter C. Rollins and John E. O'Connor, eds., *Hollywood's White House: The American Presidency in Film and History* (Lexington: University Press of Kentucky, 2003); and Iwan Morgan, ed., *Presidents in the Movies: American History and Politics on Screen* (New York: Palgrave, 2011).

2. A symbolically caricatured Nixon appears in such movies as *Where the Buffalo Roam* (1980), *Black Dynamite* (2009), and *Watchmen* (2009). Nixon masks are also a plot device to represent inauthenticity in films like *Point Break* (1991) and *Ice Storm* (1997).

3. Mark Feeney, *Nixon at the Movies: A Book About Belief* (Chicago: University of Chicago Press, 2004), 249.

4. David Greenberg, *Nixon's Shadow: The History of an Image* (New York: Norton, 2003), xxxii, xxvi.

5. Daniel Frick, *Reinventing Richard Nixon: A Cultural History of an American Obsession* (Lawrence: University Press of Kansas, 2008), 17.

6. Carl Bernstein and Bob Woodward, *All the President's Men* (New York: Simon & Schuster, 1974).

7. Jimmy Carter, *Keeping Faith: Memoirs of a President* (New York: Bantam Books, 1982), 27.

8. Robert Brent Toplin, *History by Hollywood: The Use and Abuse of the Past* (Urbana: University of Illinois Press, 1996), 182–183.

9. David A. Cook, *Lost Illusions: American Cinema in the Shadow of Watergate and Vietnam, 1970–1979* (New York: Scribner, 2000), 201; Deborah Knight and George McKnight, "The Case of the Disappearing Enigma," *Philosophy and Literature*, 21 (April 1997), 123–138; Feeney, *Nixon in the Movies*, 260–261.

10. Seth Cagin and Philip Dray, *Born to be Wild: Hollywood and the Sixties Generation* (Rochester, NY: Coyote Books, 1994), 160; Feeney, *Nixon at the Movies*, 258.

11. Leonard Garment, *In Search of Deep Throat: The Greatest Political Mystery of Our Time* (New York: Basic Books, 2000), 15.

12. David Von Dreble, "FBI's No. 2 Was Deep Throat: Mark Felt Ends 30-Year Mystery of the Post's Watergate Source," *Washington Post*, June 1, 2005. See also Bob Woodward, "How Mark Felt Became 'Deep Throat,'" *Washington Post*, June 2, 2005.

13. Stephen Holden, "Movies That Reflect Our Obsession With Conspiracy," *New York Times*, August 11, 1974.

14. Alan J. Pakula, "Making a Film About Two Reporters," *American Cinematographer* 57 (July 1976); "Cinema: Watergate on Film," *Time*, March 29, 1976. For the director, see Jared Brown, *Alan J. Pakula: His Films and His Life* (New York: Back Stage Books, 2005).

15. For Schlesinger's analysis of the imperial presidency, see Jon Herbert's chapter in this volume.

16. Pakula, "Making a Film About Two Reporters."

17. Peter Lev, *American Films in the 70s: Conflicting Visions* (Austin: University of Texas Press, 2000), 49–50.

18. John W. Dean, *Lost Honor* (Los Angeles: Stratford Press, 1982); Mark Feldstein, "The Myth of the Media's Role in Watergate," August 30, 2004, *History News Network*, http://hnn.us/articles/6813.html.

19. Edward Jay Epstein, *Between Fact and Fiction: The Problem of Journalism* (New York: Vintage, 1975); Louis W. Liebovich, *Richard Nixon, Watergate and the Press: A Historical Retrospective* (Urbana: University of Illinois, 2003); Greenberg, *Nixon's Shadow*, chapter 4. For an excellent summary, see Feldstein, "The Myth of the Media's Role in Watergate."

20. Gary Arnold, "President's Men: Absorbing, Meticulous...and Incomplete," *Washington Post*, April 4, 1976; Michael Schudson, *Watergate in American Memory: How We Remember, Forget, and Reconstruct the Past* (New York: Basic Books, 1992), 103–126.

21. "Katherine Graham 1917–2001—An American Original," *Newsweek*, July 30, 2001; Katherine Graham, *Personal History* (New York: Knopf, 1997), 508.

22. Daniel L. Schacter, *Memory Distortion: How Minds, Brains and Societies Reconstruct the Past* (Cambridge, MA: Harvard University Press, 1995), 355–356.

23. William Elliot and William Schenck-Hamlin, "Film, Politics and the Press: The Influence of *All the President's Men*," *Journalism Quarterly*, 56 (3) (1979), 546. See also, Ernest Giglio, *Here's Looking at You: Hollywood, Film & Politics* (New York: Peter Lang, 2007), 26; and Robert Rosenstone, *Visions of the Past: The Challenge of Films to our Idea of History* (Cambridge, MA: Harvard University Press, 1995), 57.

24. Elizabeth Kraft, "All the President's Men as a Woman's Film," *Journal of Popular Film & Television*, 36 (April 2008), 31.

25. Nixon is the main character in *The Final Days* (1989), *Kissinger and Nixon* (1995), and *Elvis Meets Nixon* (1997). The best of these by far was *The Final Days*, based on Bernstein and Woodward's sequel that explored the meltdown of the Nixon presidency from the inside. It so upset Nixon that he withdrew his custom from AT&T, who had sponsored production. Nixon also appears in productions about Watergate conspirators Charles Colson, John Dean, and Gordon Liddy, respectively *Born Again* (1978), *Blind Ambition* (1979), and *Will: The Autobiography of G. Gordon Liddy* (1982). It is widely agreed, however, that the best representation of Nixon was Jason Robards' performance as the 'fictional' President Richard M. Monckton in the 1977 miniseries, *Washington Behind Closed Doors*, which was loosely based on *The Company*, a novel by another Watergate conspiracy alumnus, John Ehrlichman.

26. Michael Coyne, *Hollywood Goes to Washington: American Politics on Screen* (London: Reaktion, 2008), 81–82.

27. For more detailed discussion, see Charlene Etkind, "Richard Nixon as *Dick* (1999) and the Comedic Treatment of the Presidency," in Rollins and O'Connor, *Hollywood's White House*, 262–274 (quotation p. 272).

28. For discussion, see: Robert Brent Toplin, ed., *Oliver Stone's USA: Film, History and Controversy* (Lawrence: University Press of Kansas, 2000); and Iwan Morgan, "The President Impeached: *Tennessee Johnson* and *Nixon*" in Morgan, *The President in the Movies*, 160–166. Vainly hoping to preempt attacks on the movie's accuracy, Stone published a book explaining his approach in the Nixon movie: Oliver Stone, Stephen Rivele, and Christopher Wilkinson, *Nixon: An Oliver Stone Film* (New York: Hyperion, 1995). For Mailer's comment, see William Grimes, "What Debt Does Hollywood Owe to the Truth?" *New York Times*, March 5, 1992 (A22).

29. Christopher Wilkinson, "The Year of the Beast," in Eric Hamburg, ed., *Nixon: An Oliver Stone Film* (London: Bloomsbury, 1996), 58–59; Arthur Schlesinger, Jr., "On *JFK* and *Nixon*," in Toplin, *Oliver Stone's USA*, 212–216 (quotation p. 215). For a defense of Stone's metaphor, see Donald Whaley, "'Biological Business-as-Usual:' The Beast in Oliver Stone's *Nixon*," in Rollins and O'Connor, *Hollywood's White House*, 275–287.

30. The play opened in London's West End in 2006 and transferred to New York's Broadway in the following year. Broadcast in four programs in May 1977 and a fifth later on, the Frost-Nixon interviews drew what remains at the time of writing the largest worldwide audience for a political interview. In the United States an estimated fifty million watched the first of these. For the story of their making, see David Frost, *I Gave Them a Sword: Behind the Scenes of the Nixon Interviews* (London: Macmillan, 1978).

31. James Reston, Jr., "The Legacy of the Frost/Nixon Interviews," in *Frost/ Nixon* Gielgud Theatre Programme (2006), 10–11.

32. David Edelstein, "Unholy Alliance: Frost/Nixon's iconic TV moment seems quaint after Couric/Palin," *New York Magazine*, November 30, 2008.

33. Jeff Dawson, "Sir David Frost on Frost/Nixon: His duel with Richard Nixon cost him £37 million," (London) *Sunday Times*, January 18, 2009.

34. Frost, "*I Gave Them A Sword*," 273.

35. For Nixon's comeback campaign, see Iwan Morgan's essay in this volume.

36. James Reston, Jr., "Frost, Nixon and Me," *Smithsonian Magazine*, January, 2009.

37. Lev, *American Films in the 70s*, 50.

38. George Custon, "Making History," in Marcia Landy, ed., *The Historical Film: History and Memory in Media* (London: Athlone Press, 2001), 67–97 (quotation p. 69).

39. Frick, *Reinventing Richard Nixon*, 235.

40. Mark Carnes, "Past Imperfect: History According to the Movies," *Cineaste* (March 1997), 33; Marnie Hughes-Warrington, *History Goes to the Movies* (London: Routledge, 2007), 51, 21.

41. Dan Nimmo and James E. Combs, *Subliminal Politics Myths and Mythmakers in America* (Englewood Cliffs, NJ: Prentice Hall, 1980), 5.

42. Garrison Keillor, *We Are Still Married: Stories and Letters* (New York: Viking, 1989), xviii.

Chapter Ten

The Long Legacy of Watergate

Michael A. Genovese

The past is not dead. It is not even past.

William Faulkner, *Requiem for a Nun*

Did the great dismantling really begin with Richard M. Nixon and Watergate? Is it fair to put all or even most of the burden on one man and one scandal? Is it even possible for one man to define and embody his age, impose his personality on an era, infect the body politic? Could one man's hatreds, resentments, and insecurities, strengths and weaknesses, strategic brilliance and petty retributions, really be, or become, those of a nation? The man is Richard Nixon, a "brilliant and tormented man struggling to force a public language that promised mastery of the strange new angers, anxieties, and resentments wracking the nation in the 1960s."[1] Did he create or did he merely represent the fracturing of America? Were we—are we—Nixonland?

Although it occurred nearly two generations ago, the long arm of the Watergate scandal reaches out to us today, strangling the body politic in its infectious grip. We are today still paying a price for the crisis that was Watergate.[2]

Michael Schudson notes that, in spite of Richard Nixon's "campaign against memory," in ways large and small, he remains very much with us. Schudson adds, "The recall of Watergate is surrounded with cries about the dangers (or, much more rarely, the virtues) of forgetting. In talking about Watergate, people frequently express an anxiety that in our society, historical memory is currently fighting a losing battle against the siren song of the present."[3] And yet, we *should* never forget; and we *can* never forget.

Richard Nixon just won't go away. He is in our memory, our consciousness, and our history, and he remains a prominent, if often reviled, part of our political landscape. He continues to be one of the most fascinating characters in modern American history, and has managed to reemerge from oblivion to be once again a figure of note.[4] He is the political equivalent of an automobile accident—we know we should look away, yet our gaze is drawn to visit all the gory details of the disaster.

Plays[5] (Secret Honor, later made into a movie) and an opera (Nixon in China) have been written about him since he left office. He continued to write books and articles about politics, especially foreign policy (e.g., Leaders, The Real War, Real Peace). He continued to advise Republican and Democratic presidents and candidates, visit foreign countries and meet with their leaders, and was admitted to the French Academy of Arts. T-shirts bearing his picture and inscribed with "He's tan, rested, and Ready, Nixon in '88" appeared during the 1988 presidential campaign and also in later contests. His comeback was hailed in a May 19, 1986, Newsweek cover story under the title "He's back."

But he never really left. In a way, even after his death, he is still working, still fighting, struggling against his enemies as well as his demons. But now he is also fighting for his place in history. The efforts at the resurrection and rehabilitation of Richard Nixon have an eye toward how history will view his performance and legacy. The struggle for history has become what historian Stanley Kutler calls Nixon's "final crisis."

Richard Milhous Nixon, he continues to confuse and fascinate. And even today, over 15 years after his death, his shadow hangs over us. Exactly what that shadow represents is contested territory. To some, Nixon was an everyman, one of "us," a symbol of pulling yourself up by your bootstraps and with grit and hard work, making something of yourself. This Nixon symbolized the American Dream, of rising from nothing to the pinnacle; the self made man, constantly reinventing himself, made whole by hard work, determination, and an iron will, he was one of the "common people," who in the end was destroyed by "the elites." As Daniel Frick reminds us "when we fight about Nixon, we are fighting about the meaning of America. And that is a struggle that never ends."[6]

To others, Nixon represents rank hypocrisy, the darker side of the human psyche, political and personal paranoia. This "tricky Dick" was a criminal, a hater, and a collector of resentments. He nearly destroyed the Constitution in pursuit of personal power.

We remain obsessed with Richard Nixon because the answer to the question: "Who is Richard Nixon?" could easily be converted to the question "What is America?" In examining the many meanings of Watergate, Michael Schudson sees a range of possibilities: as a constitutional crisis, a scandal, routine politics, or an aberration[7]. The answers to these puzzles will tell us a great deal about who "we" are. Richard Nixon and the Watergate crisis he spawned are in many ways a Rorschach test, a canvas upon which we paint the portrait of ourselves. He was American, and the many faces of Richard Nixon are our own many faces, and the story we derive from the life and meaning of Richard Nixon and Watergate are, in many ways, is "our story."

At Richard Nixon's funeral, Senator Bob Dole pronounced post–World War II America as the "age of Nixon." Indeed it was—for better and worse. And we are still trying to come to terms with its meanings.

After his death in 1994, several government officials and Nixon friends and family members argued that Richard Nixon should be remembered for the totality of his life and career, not simply on the basis of the Watergate scandal. Sound advice, yet as much as one might wish otherwise, the over-whelming weight of Watergate will always overshadow the successes of the Nixon administration. Opening doors to China, ending the Vietnam War, negotiating détente with the Soviet Union, all add to Nixon's reputation as a skilled foreign policy leader, yet lurking over his reputation hangs the most grievous scandal in presidential history, a scandal that will always taint the reputation of Richard Milhous Nixon, thirty-seventh president of the United States.[8]

Watergate spawned a "politics of scandal" that has even to this day deeply infected the American body politic. Coming as it did in the wake of the contentious war in Vietnam that split the nation apart and planted the seeds of distrust and discontent in the nation, Watergate deeply fractured an already shell-shocked country.

Political scientist Paul Quirk views the "politics of scandal" as:

> American politicians, journalists, and citizens devote extraordinary time and energy to controversies about matters of moral and legal propriety. To some degree, these controversies are the inevitable consequence of maintaining and enforcing strict standards of proper conduct. Nevertheless, the preoccupation with scandal has reacted a point of pathological excess. Scandals destroy or threaten to destroy useful political careers, striking evenhandedly Democrats and Republicans, liberals and conservatives, elected and appointed officials. They distract attention and disrupt government, potentially distorting public policy or undermining the ability to deal with crises. They promote cynicism and alienation among citizens.[9]

This politics of scandal elevates every trivial charge into a crisis, with "gate" added onto the end of any word to raise the scandal stakes to the Watergate level. Be it Travelgate (Clinton), WMDgate (George W. Bush), Pardongate (both Ford and George W. Bush), or Sleazegate (Reagan), one's political adversaries scamper in front of the TV cameras to pronounce and denounce the latest crisis of government. It is the ambiguous "gate" that has become the shortcut accusation against any and all political opponents. And it replaces the accusation with the production of evidence against an adversary. Any politician who can be "gated" is put on the defensive and is in part, presumed guilty.

Post-Watergate, the politics of scandal has inaugurated an age of "politics by other means" in which electoral losers attack opponents on ethics grounds, regardless of the basis of the changes.[10] It has become good, and common, politics, to level charges of ethical violations against ones' opponents and the cable media circus is happy, even anxious to accommodate.[11]

The political culture that nurtures the rot of this dysfunctional brand of political warfare is the culture of mistrust that allows mere charges to become taken as fact. In short, we expect "them" to be venal and corrupt, so they must be. A charge is a conviction. As Suzanne Garment noted, in the first 15 years after Watergate "more than 400 relatively senior federal officials and candidates for federal office...have been publicly accused in the national press of personal wrongdoing."[12]

In short, scandal has become routine.[13]

First Nixon (Watergate), then Reagan (Iran-Contra), then Clinton (Lewinsky), then Bush (WMDs); it seems a presidency under siege. The snowball that was Watergate began rolling down the hill, picking up scandal after scandal in its destructive wake. The scandal siege began with Watergate, then spawned a vicious cycle of recrimination and the development of "gotcha" politics, and the politics of personal destruction. It was not enough to beat an opponent at the polls; one had to utterly destroy the enemy. Politics was morphing into war and in war, victory meant destroying your enemy.

Even the language of politics changed. From Sarah Palin repeatedly using gun and violent references to talk-radio shock-jocks openly spreading hatred, political discourse often became another version of hate speech. And while the United States has had periods of inflated and bombastic, war violent rhetoric, in the modern era such references become an accepted part of political discourse.

While it would be unfair and inaccurate to blame all society's ills on Richard Nixon and Watergate, it seems quite reasonable to trace several political maladies to Watergate.

In the aftermath of Vietnam, the United States sat on a precipice. It could have reunited or split apart. And given the pressures on unity that the rise of several social movements (civil rights, youth counterculture, environmental, and women's movements) that were already threatening to further fracture a divided nation placed upon the system, what we really needed was a leader to, as Richard Nixon promised—"Bring us together."

But Nixon was more interested in exploiting society's cleavages than uniting the nation. He rose by channeling anger, drawing battle lines, dividing the nation. It would be the "silent majority," as represented by Nixon, against "them."[14] In the long run Nixon got his wish in ways he never could have imagined.

Did Richard Nixon do this to us, or did we create the Nixon who would do our bedding for us? Were we his victims or his puppet masters? Did Nixon fight his personal demons or ours? Did Richard Nixon invent dirty politics? No. Did he take dirty politics to a new level? Yes. Are we today paying a price? Yes.

In terms of presidential power, the legacy of Watergate has ironically turned out to be the opposite of what one might have expected. Richard Nixon's outrageous claims of power ("when the president does it, that means that it is not illegal") may have, for a time, been reviled and discredited, yet it was precisely that attitude that animated and sustained the pretensions of the Bush administration in the war against terrorism,[15] as well as his war against the separation of powers and the rule of law regime.

It is Nixon's view of presidential power that became the mantra of the Justice Department's Office of Legal Counsel (OLC) memos that gave the patina of legitimacy to President Bush's actions. Nixon showed the way; Bush, the Nixon disciple, brought the mentor's vision to life.[16]

The Nixon years also served as the model for what would be called "the administrative presidency,"[17] in which the president, as the nation's chief executive, uses an administrative strategy to govern around Congress. The administrative presidency involves a series of extra legislative actions such as using the appointment power, regulatory review, executive orders, signing statements, proclamations, and so on to make policy without or around the Congress. While Nixon failed to fully bring the administrative presidency to life, his strategy served as a template for those who followed. Nixon felt compelled to employ an administrative strategy for governing due to the fact that the Congress was controlled by the Democrats. Later presidents (especially Reagan, Clinton, and George W. Bush) would use administrative approaches to governing even when their party was in control of Congress.[18]

With Nixon's 1972 reelection campaign, the lid burst off the campaign spending jar. The cost of campaigns had been rising since the 1960's, the chief cause being the high cost of television. But Nixon's reelection campaign set new records for fundraising as well as spending. Much of the fundraising was illegal and over one hundred corporate officials were found guilty of illegal campaign donations. While Congress made several efforts to control campaign finances abuses, ways have always been found to get around these laws.

In 1972, the Nixon campaign spent $60 million; McGovern spent a "mere" $27 million. By 2008, over $1.3 billion was spent on the presidential campaign with Obama spending $730 million and McCain spending "only" $333 million.

Table 10.1 Total Spending in Presidential Elections by Democratic and Republican Candidates

Year	Total Spending
1960	$20 million
1972	$91.4 million
1976	$66.9 million
1980	$92.3 million
1984	$103.6 million
1988	$210.7 million
1992	$192.2 million
1996	$239.9 million
2000	$343.1 million
2004	$717.9 million
2008	$1.3 billion

Adapted from: OpenSecrets.org (Center for Responsive Politics); Federal Election Commission (www.FEC.gov)

Watergate has had a profound and largely negative impact on American politics in the 35 years since that scandal was uncovered. It has spawned a corrosive distrust in government among the American people, led to a series of laws enacted to prevent future Watergates that have made it more difficult to govern, unleashed a hostile and highly investigatory press, increased the partisan sniping in the political culture of "gotcha" politics, and led to a more divisive relationship between the president and the Congress. Further, the unintended consequences of the post-Watergate reforms have left presidents more vulnerable, or at least thinking they are so, and less able to function effectively as presidents.

The presidency of Richard Nixon has left a scar on the body politic and undermined the fragile consensus that for decades characterized and animated American politics. The delicate bonds of trust so necessary for a properly functioning democracy have degenerated into a slash-and-burn type of politics in which a "take no prisoners" attitude dominates. It is no wonder that voter apathy is high, voting turnout low, trust in government down, and antigovernment movements such as the Tea Party activists rises. Nixon and Watergate, by themselves, did not cause the degradation of American politics and erosion of public trust, though they contributed mightily to both, but Nixon and Watergate did recast the story of American public life from a narrative of assumed good intentions to one of deep suspicion (see Table10. 2).

Table 10.2   Tracing the Impact of Nixon on Subsequent Presidential Politics

Nixon's Claims/Actions	*Led to...*
Administrative Presidency	Unitary Executive
Corruption	Reagan's Iran-Contra; Clinton's Lewinsky Scandal; Bush's WMD Deceptions
Executive Privilege	Secrecy in Bush Administration
"When the President does it, that means that it is not illegal"	OLC Memos on Presidential Power
Money in Politics	2008: $1.3 billion
Domestic Policy (EPA/HMD Proposal/ Guaranteed Income Proposal)	Big Government Conservatives (Reagan and George W. Bush)
Wage and Price Controls	Bush/Obama Financial Bailout and Regulations
Bring US Together	Compassionate Conservatives
Enemies List	Politics of Personal Destruction (Gingrich)
Illegal Wiretaps	NSA Surveillance
Dirty Tricks Against Democrats	Hyper-Partisan Politics
Media Investigative Journalism	Overly Intrusive/Personal Media
Smallness, hurtfulness	Cable TV/Radio Slash and Burn (Limbaugh)
Cultural Transformation	Celebration of Greed and Selfishness
FP Detente	Improved Relations with Soviet Union/China and end of Cold War
Southern Strategy	Solid Republican South
Post-Watergate Reforms	Cheney Backlash
Immunity	Birth of Special Prosecutor

The Meaning of Watergate

Watergate, that generic word by which we refer to a range of crimes and improprieties, raised a series of legal and moral issues. It spoke to who we are and what we believe. It tested our system and ourselves. Would the United States remain a limited government under the rule of law, or was it to become an imperial nation with an imperial presidency?

Watergate spawned a variety of legislative responses. In the aftermath if Nixon's abuses, Congress went through a period of legislative activism that resulted in the passage of the Budget Control and Impoundment Act (1974), the War Powers Act (1973), the Case Act (1972), the Federal Election Campaign Act (1974), the Ethics in Government Act (1978), the Presidential Records Act (1978), the National Emergencies Act (1976), the Government in Sunshine Act (1976), the Federal Corrupt Practices Act (1977), the Foreign Intelligence Surveillance Act (1978), plus laws relating to privacy in banking and to setting up a vehicle for creating special prosecutors, and the Freedom of Information Act (1974). Many of these efforts were designed to limit and shrink imperial executive claims to republican proportions. Many believe the reaction against presidential power went too far.

One of the more obvious areas where "reform" may have gone too far is the case of the independent counsel laws, which, critics charge, has been overused to the point of creating a potential prosecutorial tyranny (e.g., Kenneth Starr's investigation of President Clinton). After Watergate, the independent counsel law, argue critics, has been used as a part of a partisan game of "gotcha" wherein the party in control of Congress employed this device to harass, and in some cases, needlessly burden officials with investigations. In the Whitewater investigation of President Clinton's real estate dealings in his native Arkansas, independent counsel Kenneth Starr spent over four years and over $40 million, investigating allegations against the president and the first lady, and a half dozen other independent counsels roamed the political landscape in search of official wrongdoings, with mixed results in terms of bringing indictments and getting convictions for crimes.

"Everybody Does It"

One defense of Nixon that says that Watergate is "just politics," or "everybody does it," is both false and dangerous. It is false because even though other presidents did engage in immoral and illegal behavior, not one comes close to Nixon in volume, type, or degree of presidential involvement. Nixon's was a systematic abuse of power and subversion of law. Such an attitude is dangerous because it breeds apathy, disrespect for the government, and contempt for America's political institutions. Aside from that, the "everybody does it" excuse is no justification for misconduct.

What John Mitchell called the "White House horrors" is without precedent in the United States. While the United States is far from perfect, and past presidents are not without sin, historian C. Vann Woodward sums up the difference between Nixon and his predecessors nicely:

> Heretofore, no president has been proved to be the chief coordinator of the crime and misdemeanor charged against his own administration as a deliberate course of conduct or plan. Heretofore, no president has been held to be the chief personal beneficiary of misconduct in his administration or of measures taken to destroy or cover up evidence of it. Heretofore, the malfeasance and misdemeanor have had no confessed ideological purposes, no constitutionally subversive ends. Heretofore, no president has been accused of extensively subverting and secretly using established government agencies to defame or discredit political opponents and critics, to obstruct justice, to conceal misconduct and protect criminals, or to deprive citizens of their rights and liberties. Heretofore, no president had been accused of creating secret investigative units to engage in covert and unlawful activities against private citizens and their rights.[19]

One of the primary differences between Watergate and the scandals of other presidential administrations is that the scandals of the past largely involved greed for private financial gain, and the president was often the unwitting victim. The presidents of scandal ridden administrations (with Ronald Reagan and perhaps Bill Clinton being the exception) were not knowingly a part of the corruption. In Watergate, the greed was for power not money, and the president was a direct participant in the corruption, even the author of some of it.

"The System Worked!" (or Did It?)

After the fall of Nixon, one often heard the refrain: "the system worked!" The existing structures and procedures protected liberty and reestablished the rule of law. After all, Nixon was caught and forced to leave office. But a haunting doubt remains. Did the system work, or did other forces bring about the revelations of abuses of power and criminal conduct by the president and his inner circle?

"The system" is the complex web of interrelated governmental and nongovernmental actors and institutions that serve as a potential check on power. In Watergate, the system included the media, Congress, the courts, the public, the CIA, the FBI, the Justice Department, the special prosecutor's office and the grand jury. How well—or poorly—did the system perform its function?

The media began like a lamb but ended like a lion. While they were manipulated by Nixon during the 1972 campaign and generally gave him very positive coverage, after the election, as the Watergate story got closer to the president, a herd mentality developed and they pounced on the story, as well as the president, pursuing it, and him, relentlessly.

The Congress, especially in the Ervin and the House Judiciary Committees, played a very important role in the Watergate investigation. They moved slowly, methodically, but, as the evidence of abuse and crimes became known, they moved against the president. So too did the House Judiciary Committee, headed by Rep. Peter Rodino (D-NJ).

The courts, especially Judge John Sirica and the Supreme Court at the end, were clearly a key in discovering the facts and pressing for compliance with the law. Again, they acted slowly but effectively.

The public, at first giving Nixon a landslide reelection victory and indifferent to early reports on Watergate, eventually turned on the president. The FBI and CIA were used and manipulated by Nixon, as was the Justice Department. The grand jury was essential in getting to the bottom of Watergate. Finally, the special prosecutor's office played an indispensable part in the process.

In the end, the system had to act in concert to expose the crimes of Watergate. For so many to act in concert is highly unusual. This speaks to the great difficulty of controlling a determined or runaway president. The system is indeed vulnerable when, even with all the institutions and interests working against the president, it was the "luck" of a taping system that finally strengthened the hands of the Congress, the special prosecutor, and the press in their efforts to bring out the truth. This suggests that the system may be a rather weak check on presidential abuses of power. Further, Watergate demonstrates how vulnerable our system can be when in the hands of unprincipled or unscrupulous leaders.

More than anything else, the system worked because of luck, accident, and ineptitude. After all, the first break-in of the Watergate was a botched job, as the bugs weren't properly installed. This necessitated a second break-in, at which time the burglars were caught. And they were caught because a piece of tape, used to keep the doors' lock from catching, was placed across the lock in such a way that it could be seen from the outside. But even this did not alarm security guard Frank Wills who simply removed the tape when doing his rounds. When the burglars returned to the door, they replaced the tape across the lock in such a way that again it could be seen on the outside. When Wills made his second set of rounds of the building and saw the tape across the same door for a second time, only then was he alerted to the break-in and called the police.

If Nixon had not taped himself, there would have been no "smoking gun" and Nixon might have survived politically. Certainly, the dimensions and depth of Nixon's abuses of power and crimes would not have been revealed without the tapes, which continue to suggest patterns of corruption in the Nixon White House as researchers gain greater access to the recordings. If the cover-up had been better managed, it might have held together. If Nixon had destroyed the tapes before their existence had become known, he would not have to defy the subpoena—one of the acts on which an article of impeachment was based.

Nixon and Haldeman recognized the role luck played in the Watergate crisis, as evidence by this March 20, 1973, taped exchange on how Watergate was discovered.

> *Nixon*: ...a lot of bad breaks.
> *Haldeman*: Yeah.
> *Nixon*: We got a bad break with the judge, for example.
> *Haldeman*: Monumental bad breaks and a string of'em—one leading to another.
> *Nixon*: This judge, that...
> *Haldeman*: ...one lousy part time night guard at the Watergate who happened to notice the tape on the, on the locks on the doors. If he hadn't seen them— the thing probably would never have busted, if you hadn't had Watergate—you wouldn't have had Segretti. You wouldn't have had any of that stuff.

In another deeper sense, "the system" refers to the two hundred year old constitutional framework and the assumptions upon which it is based. This Madisonian system, described in *Federalist No.51*, believed that "ambition must be made to counteract ambition," that by separating power, viable checks might protect the liberty of the citizen, and prevent one branch of government from overawing and the trampling on the others, undermining republican government altogether.

The framers of the Constitution saw human nature neither in excessively benign Lockean nor unmercifully harsh Hobbesian terms. Humans were capable of great good but also of great evil. The founders knew man's darker side, his darker impulses, and sought to control this while also empowering government. In a way, it was precisely for the Richard Nixons of the American future that the separation of powers and checks and balances were created.

But one principal instrument the founders thought might check, or at least remedy, executive abuse was the impeachment process. Long before Watergate, impeachment proved a cumbersome and often ineffectual means to prevent or punish abuses of power. Party politics and press scrutiny—nonprescribed checks unanticipated by the framers—had assumed a primary role in identifying abuses. The electoral process was, to the founders, the great "check."

In Watergate, the impeachment process itself was shown to have but limited utility. It can be used only in extraordinary circumstances, and although the United States does have periodic accountability (elections), and ultimate accountability (impeachment), the government and people do not have an effective formal system of daily accountability (routine and continuous). Informal means—public vigilance—must bear the burden of constant oversight of government.

Finally we should not forget that it was "the system" that allowed Richard Nixon to rise to the highest office in the land, in spite of the many clues from his earlier career as to what "the real Nixon" was like. It was the system that Nixon used and manipulated for so long. Thus, the system both nourished and eventually revealed the crimes of Richard Nixon.[20]

Remembering and Misremembering

The battle to shape history's judgment of Richard Nixon began the moment he left office. The former president wrote a number of books on foreign affairs and public policy, consulted widely—if in private—with presidents, leaders, and opinion-makers, and attempted to control and shape his legacy with his presidential library in Yorba Linda, California.

Initially, the library—held by private hands run by Nixon loyalists and not a part of the National Archives and Records Administration (NARA) system of official presidential libraries—presented a highly sanitized and distorted version of the Watergate saga that the *Los Angeles Times* called "a self-serving, oh-really-it-wasn't-so-bad exhibit designed to portray the scandal as a series of presidential misjudgments followed by a 'coup' to run Richard M. Nixon out of office."[21]

Scholars treated the Nixon library as a bad joke. The original Watergate exhibit designed in 1990, was a distorted version of history designed to put the former president in the best possible light. In 2007, after bitter negotiations, the NARA finally assumed control of the library. Then, things changed.

In 2011, a new Watergate exhibition opened. It was a more realistic, less biased exhibit, one that presented both sides of the story, leaving it to the viewer to draw their own conclusion. And for most, the conclusions drawn put the former president in a decidedly negative light.

Conclusion

The abuses of Watergate were the most pervasive and systematic subversion of the political rights of American citizens and sabotage of the democratic electoral process in the history of the United States. Never before had so many done so much to so many at so high a level in violation of so many laws and norms of this nation. Watergate went beyond the presidential corruptions of the past, for while most previous corruption involved isolated crimes or greed for money, Watergate was systematic and comprehensive and aimed at the rights of citizens and the democratic electoral process. And the president himself was right in the middle of the corruption.

Among the casualties of Watergate are a president who was named as an *unindicted coconspirator* by a grand jury and who was eventually forced to resign his office (he was also disbarred), a vice president who pleaded no contest to income tax evasion and was forced to resign (he too was disbarred), an attorney general who went to jail, a former secretary of commerce who went to jail, a chief of staff who went to jail, a president's counsel who went to jail, a president's chief domestic advisor who went to jail, a president's appointments secretary who went to jail, a president's personal attorney who went to jail, and the list goes on. Over two dozen administration figures went to jail because of Watergate.

Thomas Paine once said that in America, the Constitution is king. The downfall of Richard Nixon struck a blow for the concept that no man is above the law, not even a president. Though Nixon attempted to justify his actions in a 1977 interview with David Frost by saying, "When the President does it, that means it is not illegal," this view was rejected by nearly all segments of the American system, only to be revived by the OLC memos during the presidency of George W. Bush. The words of the Supreme Court Justice Louis Brandeis remained operative: "if government becomes the lawbreaker, it breeds the contempt for law." Reverence for the laws, Abraham Lincoln said, should "become the political religion of the nation."

What responsibility do "we, the people" bear for Watergate? If Watergate was due, in large part, to the personality and politics of Nixon, were these who elected him accomplices in the ensuing abuses of power? After all, Nixon the politician had been on the political scene since 1946; his slashing campaign style, his character flaws, his ethical lapses were a part of the public record. All the elements in Nixon that led to the abuses of Watergate were operative and observable in embryonic form in his previous political behavior. There is an old saying, "In a democracy, people tend to get the government they deserve." Did the American people "deserve" Watergate? This sobering possibility was brought home forcefully by historian Henry Steele Commager, who, in 1976, chillingly observed:

> The basic problem posed by Watergate and all its attendant horrors is neither constitutional nor political; it is moral. It is not a problem posed by an administration in Washington; it is one posed by the American people. After all, we can never get away from the most elementary fact: the American people reelected Mr. Nixon by a majority of nearly eighteen million votes. Either they did not know what kind of man he was, in which case they were inexcusably negligent or inexcusably naïve, or they did know what kind of man he was and did not care or perhaps liked him as he was—as some Americans still like him the way he is. The latter explanation is probably nearer to the truth. Did he not—indeed, does he not—represent qualities in the American character that are widespread and even taken for granted? In himself and in the curious collection of associates he gathered around him, he represents the acquisitive society, the exploitive society, and he aggrandizing society. He represents what is artificial, meretricious, and manipulative. He represents the American preference for the synthetic over the real, for advertising over the product, for public relations over character, for spectator sports over active games, and for spectator politics over participatory democracy. He represents, too, the widespread American conviction that anything can be bought: culture, education, happiness, a winning football team or the Presidency.[22]

After Watergate, Congress passed a variety of laws designed to discourage future Watergates and abuses of power. As important as these laws were, they are not sufficient to the task. Laws are not self executing. A nation of laws depends on the people to enliven the law. A dedicated citizenry is the only hope against tyranny. As Judge Learned Hand said, "Liberty lies in the hearts of men and women; when it dies there, no constitution, no law, no court can save it; no constitution, no law, no court can even do much to help it." Of all the checks designed to balance the American political system, none is more powerful than alert and aroused public opinion. A thoughtful, responsible, aware public is our best defense against tyranny. There is no substitute for an aroused citizenry, no hope unless there is a rebirth of what Thomas E. Cronin calls "citizen politics." Richard Nixon exposed one of the vulnerabilities of the American political system. "The system" alone will not protect us; we must be ever vigilant.

The era of cynicism that Watergate spawned, ushered in a period of a deep political combat and public apathy. Democracy cannot long endure the contempt of the people. Rather than recapture their democracy, many people dropped out. Rather than right wrongs, many threw stones (verbal and otherwise) at what was supposed to be "their" government. Swept up in a culture of mistrust, democracy almost became the chief casualty of Nixon's age of cynicism.

After Watergate, scandal moved from the periphery to the center. We became scandal-happy, searching for scandal in every policy or partisan dispute. Our hunt to weed out corruption- or at least to paint our adversaries ("enemies") as excessively corrupt—became a national obsession, endemic and ubiquitous. This preoccupation with scandal-hunting followed an all too predictable pattern; the hint of transgression, followed by media deluge, accusations, and punishment before guilt is even established. The bad truly does drive out the good.

More damaging still, after Watergate we began to stress the character of candidates over their competence as leaders. The search for the pure, replaced the search for the capable. Personal virtue rose as the hunt for competence declined. We are still paying the price for Watergate.

Richard Nixon just won't go away. Try as we might to purge him from our body politic, the toxic sludge of his presidency continues to pollute our politics. He haunts us still. Forty years after leaving office in ignominy, he remains ubiquitous in both American politics and culture. The seeds he planted—some good, some bad—have borne their fruit.

Notes

1. Rick Perlstein, *Nixonland: The Rise of a President and the Fracturing of America* (New York: Schribner, 2008), xii.
2. David Greenberg, *Nixon's Shadow: The History of an Image* (New York: Norton, 2003).

3. Michael Schudson, *Watergate in American Memory: How We Remember, Forget, and Reconstruct the Past* (New York: Basic Books, 1993), 52, 58.

4. Robert Sam Anson, *Exile: The Unquiet Oblivion of Richard M. Nixon* (New York: Simon and Schuster, 1984); and James C. Clark, *Faded Glory: Presidents Out of Power* (New York: Praeger, 1985), Chapter 28.

5. See: Bruce E. Altschuler, *Acting Presidents: 100 Years of Plays about the Presidency* (New York: Palgrave Macmillan, 2010).

6. Daniel Frick, *Reinventing Richard Nixon: The Cultural History of an American Obsession*, Lawrence, (Kansas: University Press of Kansas, 2008), 17.

7. Michael Schudson, *Watergate in American Memory: How We remember, Forget, and Reconstruct the Past* (New York: Basic Books, 1992).

8. Michael A. Genovese, *The Watergate Crisis* (Westport: Greenwood Press, 1999).

9. Paul J. Quirk, "Coping with the Politics of Scandal," *Presidential Studies Quarterly*, 28 (Fall 1998): 898–902.

10. Benjamin Ginsberg and Martin Shefter, *Politics by Other Means* (New York: W. W. Norton, 2002).

11. John B. Thompson, *Political Scandal: Power and Visibility in the Media Age* (Cambridge, UK: Polity, 2000); Larry J. Sabato, Mark Stencel, and S. Robert Lutcher, *Peepshow: Media and Politics in an Age of Scandal* (Lanham, MD: Rowman Littlefield, 2001).

12. Suzanne Garment, *Scandal: The Culture of Mistrust in American Politics* (New York; Anchor, 1992), 3.

13. Michael A. Genovese and Victoria Farrar-Myers, *Corruption in American Politics* (Amherst: Cambria Press, 2010).

14. Rick Perlstein, *Nixonland*.

15. James P. Pfiffner, *Power Play: The Bush Presidency and the Constitution* (Washington, DC: Brookings Institution Press, 2008); Michael A. Genovese, *Presidential Prerogative: Imperial Power in an Age of Terrorism* (Palo Alto, CA: Stanford University Press, 2010).

16. John Dean, "The Nixon Shadow that Hovers Over the Bush White House," *History News Network*, January 6, 2003; and Bruce P. Montgomery, "Nixon's Ghost Haunts the Presidential Records Act: The Reagan and George W. Bush Administration," *Presidential Studies Quarterly*, 32 (Fall 2002): 789–809.

17. Richard P. Nathan, *The Plot That Failed: Nixon and the Administrative Presidency* (New York: John Wiley and Sons, 1975); and Nathan, *The Administrative Presidency* (New York: John Wiley and Sons, 1983).

18. Charlie Savage, *Takeover* (Boston: Book Bay Books, 2008).

19. C. Vann Woodward, *Responses of the President to Charges of Misconduct* (New York: Dell, 1974), xxvi.

20. Rick Perlstein, *Nixonland*.

21. Editorial, *Los Angeles Times*, April 6, 2011.

22. Henry Steel Commanger, "Watergate and the Schools," in David C. Saffell, ed., *American Government: Reform in the Post-Watergate Era* (Cambridge, MA: Winthrop, 1976), 6.

Contributors

David Gray Adler is the James A. McClure Professor at the University of Idaho, where he directs the McClure Center for Public Policy. Professor Adler has specialized in the fields of Public Law, The Supreme Court, Presidency, and American Political Thought. He is a prominent scholar on the subject of presidential war powers. Adler is the author of *The Constitution and the Termination of Treaties* (1986), editor (with Larry George) of *The Constitution and the Conduct of American Foreign Policy* (1996), editor (with Michael A. Genovese) of *The Presidency and the Law: the Clinton Legacy* (University Press of Kansas), and over 40 scholarly articles that have appeared in such journals as *Political Science Quarterly*, *Presidential Studies Quarterly*, *Arizona State Law Review*, as well as *The Encyclopedia of the American Presidency*, and other edited volumes.

Todd Belt is Associate Professor of Political Science at the University of Hawaii at Hilo. He received his BA in Economics and Political Science at the University of California, Irvine, and his MA and PhD at the University of Southern California. His research focuses primarily on mass media and political persuasion. His articles have appeared in the *Journal of Political Communication*, the *Journal of Health and Social Behavior*, the *Columbia Journalism Review*, *Political Linguistics*, *Campaigns & Elections* and the *California Journal of Politics and Policy*. Additionally, he has published several chapters in scholarly books and is co-author of the book *We Interrupt this Newscast: How to Improve Local News and Win Ratings, Too*.

Victoria A. Farrar-Myers is a Professor in Political Science at The University of Texas at Arlington. She is the author of *Scripted Change: The Insitution of the American Presidency* (Texas A&M Press) and the coauthor of *Limits and Loopholes: The Quest for Money, Free Speech and Fair Elections* (with Diana Dwyre, 2007), among many others. Dr. Farrar-Myers served as an American Political Science Association Congressional Fellow from 1997 to 1998. Myers earned her Ph.D. from University at Albany, SUNY in 1997.

Michael A. Genovese received a Ph.D. from the University of Southern California in 1979. He currently holds the Loyola Chair of Leadership Studies, is Professor of Political Science, and Director of the Institute for Leadership Studies at Loyola Marymount University. Professor Genovese has written over thirty books, including *The Paradoxes of the American Presidency*, coauthored by Thomas E. Cronin (3rd Ed. 2009); *The Presidential Dilemma,* (2nd Ed. 2003); *The Encyclopedia of the American*

Presidency, winner of the New York Public Library "Best of Reference" work of 2004 (2004); and *Memo to a New President: The Art and Science of Presidential Leadership* (2007). He has won over a dozen university and national teaching awards, including the Fritz B. Burns Distinguished Teaching Award (1995) and the Rains Award for Excellence in Research (2011). Professor Genovese frequently appears as a commentator on local and national television. He is also Associate Editor of the journal, *White House Studies*, is on the Editorial Board of the journals, *Rhetoric & Public Affairs*, and the *International Leadership Journal*, has lectured for the United States Embassy abroad, and is editor of Palgrave Macmillan Publishing's, "The Evolving American Presidency" book series. Professor Genovese has been The Washington Center's "scholar-in-residence" at three national political conventions and the 2008 presidential inauguration. In 2004–05, Professor Genovese served as President of the Presidency Research Group of the American Political Science Association.

Clodagh Harrington is a lecturer in Politics at De Montfort University in Leicester, UK. She received her MA and Ph.D. in U.S. Politics from London Metropolitan University. Her main area of research is the politics of scandal in the United States. She also works on presidential character and issues relating to public integrity. She recently contributed an essay on George W. Bush's ethical record to Iwan Morgan and Philip J. Davies, eds., *Assessing George W. Bush's Legacy: The Right Man?* (2010). She is a member of the executive committee of the UK American Politics Group.

Jon Herbert is a Lecturer in U.S. Politics and Program Director for Politics in Keele University, UK. He holds a Ph.D. from the University of Cambridge and has studied at University of Pennsylvania. His primary research interest is the presidency, particularly with regard to public policymaking and governing strategies. He coedited *Assessing the George W. Bush Presidency*(2010) and recently contributed a chapter on Bush's domestic policy and the conservative movement to Joel Aberbach and Gillian Peele, eds., *Crisis of Conservatism? The Republican Party, the Conservative Movement, and American Politics after Bush* (2011).

Nancy Kassop is a professor and former chair of the Political Science and International Relations department at State University of New York at New Paltz. She earned her MA and Ph.D. from New York University. She is the Book Review Editor of Presidential Studies Quarterly. Among her many articles and publications is "Expansion and Contraction: Clinton's Impact on the Scope of Presidential Power" in *The Presidency and the Law: The Clinton Legacy*, David G. Adler and Michael A. Genovese, eds., (2002) and "A Political Question By Any Other Name: Government Strategy in the Enemy Combatant Cases of Hamdi and Padilla" from her Lexington Books 2007 publication "The Political Question Doctrine and the Supreme Court of the United States." Kassop studies the Presidency of the United States and Law and Politics.

Kingsley Marshall is a Senior Lecturer in Film and Film program leader at University College Falmouth, UK, where he specialises in journalism, sound design, and philosophical approaches to film. His academic research primarily orientates around the use of sound (including music and effects) in film and other media, and the cinematic representation of the real, including historical figures and events. He has contributed a chapter on George W. Bush to Iwan Morgan, ed., *Presidents in the Movies: American History and Politics on Screen* (2011). A popular culture critic, he has written for over thirty publications, has a weekly newspaper column on film, and in 2010 became editor of Clash magazine's ClashClick section. He is currently engaged on a project concerning the unification of movie sound for which he has interviewed Hollywood and UK filmmakers.

Iwan W. Morgan is Professor of U.S. Studies and Director of the U.S. Presidency Centre at the Institute for the Study of the Americas in the University of London's School of Advanced Study. He holds a Ph.D. from the London School of Economics. He has been a Fulbright exchange scholar at Indiana University-Purdue University, Fort Wayne. He specializes in study of U.S. presidents and contemporary American history. His single-authored publications include *Eisenhower versus 'the Spenders:' The Eisenhower Administration, the Democrats and the Budget, 1953–60* (1990); *Deficit Government: Taxing and Spending in Modern America* (1995); and *Nixon* (2002). His most recent monograph *The Age of Deficits: Presidents and Unbalanced Budgets from Jimmy Carter to George W. Bush* (2009) was awarded the American Politics Group's Richard E. Neustadt book prize. He has also edited/coedited numerous books, including: *The Federal Nation: Perspectives on American Federalism* (2008), *Assessing George W. Bush's Legacy: The Right Man?* (2010), and *The President in the Movies: American History and Politics on Screen* (2011), all of which were Palgrave publications. He is a member of the British Association of American Studies executive committee and is chair of the Historians of the Twentieth Century United States group.

Index